Liturgical Renewal as a Way to Christian Unity

Edited by
James F. Puglisi, S.A., S.T.D.

Contributors
Horace T. Allen, Jr.
Teresa Berger
Thomas F. Best
Ermanno Genre
Donald Gray
David R. Holeton
Gordon W. Lathrop
James F. Puglisi, S.A.
Robert F. Taft, S.J.
Giulio Viviani
Geoffrey Wainwright

A PUEBLO BOOK

Liturgical Press Collegeville, Minnesota
www.litpress.org

Cover design by David Manahan, O.S.B. Illustration by Frank Kacmarcik Obl.S.B.

Quotations from the documents of the Second Vatican Council are taken from *The Documents of Vatican II*, ed. Walter M. Abbott, S.J., © 1966 by The America Press, New York. Used by permission,

1   2   3   4   5   6   7   8   9

Library of Congress Cataloging-in-Publication Data

Liturgical renewal as a way to Christian unity / edited by James F. Puglisi ; contributors, Horace T. Allen, Jr. . . . [et al.].
    p. cm.
    "A Pueblo book."
    Includes bibliographical references and index.
    ISBN 13: 978-8146-6203-8 (pbk. : alk. paper)
    ISBN 10: 0-8146-6203-X (pbk. : alk. paper)
    1. Liturgics and Christian union. 2. Liturgical movement.   I. Puglisi, J. F. II. Allen, Horace T., 1933–

BX9.5.L55L58 2005
264'.001—dc22

2004018617

Contents

Contributors

HORACE T. ALLEN, JR., Professor of Worship, School of Theology, Boston University; Visiting Professor of Liturgical Studies, Yale University; Founding Co-chair of the English Language Liturgical Consultation (USA)

TERESA BERGER, Professor of Ecumenical Theology, Duke University (USA)

REV. DR. THOMAS F. BEST, a pastor of the Christian Church (Disciples of Christ) and a staff member for Faith and Order in the World Council of Churches, Geneva

ERMANNO GENRE, Professor of Practical Theology and former Dean of the Waldensian Faculty, Rome

CANON DONALD GRAY, Canon Emeritus, Westminster Abbey; President, Society for Liturgical Study, England

DAVID R. HOLETON, Professor of Liturgy at the Charles University, Prague

GORDON W. LATHROP, Charles A. Schieren Professor of Liturgy, Lutheran Theological Seminary, Philadelphia (USA)

JAMES F. PUGLISI, S.A., Director, Centro Pro Unione, Rome; Professor of Ecclesiology, Sacraments and Ecumenism at the Pontifical University of St. Thomas Aquinas (Angelicum), Pontifical Athenaeum Antonianum, Pontifical Athenaeum Sant'Anselmo and Ecumenical Institute San Bernardino (Venice).

ARCHIMANDRITE ROBERT F. TAFT, S.J., Professor Emeritus of Oriental Liturgy, Pontifical Oriental Institute, Rome

MSGR. GIULIO VIVIANI, Papal Master of Ceremonies, Office of the Liturgical Celebrations of the Supreme Pontiff, Vatican City

GEOFFREY WAINWRIGHT, Cushman Professor of Christian Theology, Duke University (USA)

James F. Puglisi, S.A.

Introduction

With the publication of *Liturgiam Authenticam* on 28 March 2001, the liturgical movement entered into another stage of its post-Vatican II development. While this book is not about this liturgical document, the impact of this document will be seen in almost all essays contained herein. Moreover, the repercussions after the publication of this document are not only to be felt from within the Catholic church but also from outside it. This fact shows us how much has really taken place since the Second Vatican Council. Prior to the Council, the Christian churches lived in isolation from one another; whatever happened within one church seldom impacted what happened in another church. Furthermore, since Vatican II we have witnessed how much the churches have become involved in the life of one another. This is quite clearly the result of an ecumenical openness and a sign of growing Christian unity.

By now some may be asking why are we talking about a particular document and the relationship between the churches. The reason is fairly simple: no church can any longer do something without affecting another church. Reviewing some recent history will remind us that if the ecumenical movement is a success, it is because of the confluence of renewal in three fundamental and related fields. Vatican II was made possible because of renewed efforts made ecumenically in the fields of biblical, patristic, and liturgical research. These three movements underwent a renewal because of the historical-critical method, which was carried out across ecclesial lines and which had capital importance for the other two.

One of the chief areas renewed was in the field of liturgical and sacramental theology. The work of such scholars as Anton Baumstark, Gregory Dix, Joseph Jungmann, Bernard Botte, and others was fundamental for what would be a profound renewal and rediscovery of Christian worship, its scriptural, patristic, and traditional roots. The place that liturgical and sacramental theology had in the overall schema of "doing theology" changed from being something treated on the periphery of theological reflection to being at the heart of systematic and fundamental theology. The study of the liturgy became a key source for theological reflection, whereby what one believed was seen as being determined and expressed by what one prayed *(lex orandi, lex credendi)*, and not vice versa.[1]

Many books have been written about liturgical renewal in the Catholic church, and some have even been written about renewal in Anglican and Protestant churches. The fact that there is a growing number of liturgical scholars who are engaged in the renewal of worship in their own churches is, I believe, another proof of the ecumenical nature of this discipline. Many of these liturgical scholars have taken their inspiration and even their formation in Catholic institutions of specialization. With the passage of time there has even been an increase and cross-fertilization in the disciplines of liturgical studies, pastoral theology, and sacramental theology.

This book of essays by recognized scholars and experts in their fields of studies arose out of a series of conferences held at the Centro Pro Unione, an ecumenical research center in Rome and a ministry of the Franciscan Friars of the Atonement, with the purpose of showing how spiritual ecumenism growing out of the prayer of Christians is preparing and helping to bring about the unity of Christians. As Jesus prayed on the night before he died for the unity of all those who believe in him for the sake of the mission of the gospel, so all authentic prayer should have this goal that the Savior prayed for at its heart (see John 17).

In a certain number of these essays, the reader will feel the pain that the document *Liturgiam Authenticam* has caused to some of the Catholic church's most faithful dialogue partners, those who greeted Vatican II with great enthusiasm and engaged in a lifetime of study, writing, and teaching the riches of the worship of the Triune God as a result of it. These are the leaders in our brothers' and sisters' churches not only of liturgical renewal but in the search for Christian unity.

Some of the authors, who looked to the Catholic church's rich experience of worship, scholarship, and leadership in liturgical renewal, now feel excluded and not wanted as partners in the search for developing texts that may be used in common to unite the churches in prayer and worship. In spite of their concern and at

---

[1] P. DE CLERCK, "'Lex orandi, lex credendi': The Original Sense and Historical Avatars of an Equivocal Adage," *Studia Liturgica* 24, no. 2 (1994) 178–200.

times hurt at the tone of this document, they remain faithful in their commitment to the renewal of worship within their own traditions and to the possibility of contributing to the betterment of the "work of the people" (the meaning of the word "liturgy") in all churches. Therefore, the reader will discover the riches which other ecclesial traditions carry within their traditions and which caused the Council to affirm that elements of sanctification do indeed exist outside the confines of the Catholic church, because the Spirit of God will blow where it will and leads back to the source, which is Christ.[2]

A recurrent theme that appears in more than one of the essays has to do with the project of a common Lectionary. This project was encouraged by the then Secretariat, now Pontifical Council, for Promoting Christian Unity in the years immediately following the Council. The work done on the revision of the Roman Lectionary led the way to Lectionary revision in other churches, especially in the English-speaking world. Even though the churches continue to be divided at the table of the Eucharist, it is nevertheless a wonderful advance to have the same table of the Word, which unites us, so that in the same city on any given Sunday the readings proclaimed are basically identical in most of the churches that celebrate the Eucharist or Lord's Supper. From this ecumenical advance were born common projects that provided homily or sermon preparations that were truly ecumenical in nature. However, even this project has been called into question by the 2001 document from the Congregation for Divine Worship, as well as projects of joint translation and composition of good texts in the English language.

---

[2] For example: "Moreover, some, and even very many, of the most significant elements or endowments which together go to build up and give life to the Church herself can exist outside the visible boundaries of the Catholic Church: the written word of God; the life of grace; faith, hope and charity, with the other interior gifts of the Holy Spirit and visble elements. All of these, which come from Christ and lead back to Him, belong by right to the one Church of Christ" (*Unitatis Redinitegratio, 3*), and the following citation from *Lumen Gentium,* 8, which is repeated in several other documents: "This Church, constituted and organized in the world as a society, subsists in the Catholic Church, which is governed by the successor of Peter and by the bishops in union with that successor, although many elements of sanctification and of truth can be found outside of her visible structure. These elements, however, as gifts properly belonging to the Church of Christ, possess an inner dynamism toward Catholic unity"; taken up in John Paul II, *Ut Unum Sint,* 12, and the Sacred Congregation for the Doctrine of the Faith, *Mysterium Ecclesiae* (June 24, 1973), section 1.

The ecclesial traditions that are represented in this collection of essays include Anglicanism (Gray and Holeton); Lutheranism (Lathrop); Reformed (Allen and Genre); Methodism (Wainwright); Christian Church-Disciples of Christ (Best); Latin Catholic (Berger and Viviani); and Eastern Catholic (Taft). The book begins with Canon Donald Gray's essay, which gives a good summary of the latest liturgical revisions for the Church of England, called *Common Worship,* while Professor David Holeton introduces us to the liturgical, theological, and eschatological dimensions of the Anglican communion's worship in general and its contribution to the search for Christian unity.

Historically, Methodism grew out of Anglicanism, and therefore Professor Geoffrey Wainwright presents the extensive liturgical renewal that has taken place within the Methodist tradition through the accent placed on the ecumenical significance of hymnology and the theology.

Wainwright's colleague at Duke University, Dr. Teresa Berger, raises the problem that gender plays in the process of liturgical renewal, especially within the Catholic church, and the ecumenical implications of the nonresolution of this issue.

This essay is followed by a very passionate plea for the rethinking of the implications of *Liturgiam Authenticam.* Professor Horace Allen speaks about the project that he has collaborated on since the beginning, the Common Lectionary and texts for hymns especially within, but not exclusively from, the Presbyterian tradition and the projects for common liturgical texts.

Leading off the second series of essays is Dr. Tom Best from the Christian Church-Disciples of Christ but also deeply involved ecumenically as a member of the Faith and Order Commission of the World Council of Churches. Best looks at the tradition of his church, which has a clearly liturgical history and a sense of what it means to be church and serve the unity of the church.

This essay is followed by that of Dr. Gordon Lathrop, liturgical expert from the Lutheran tradition, who presents the principles guiding Lutheran liturgical renewal and how these principles are actually well adapted for the search for Christian unity.

Finally from the Waldensian church, Professor Ermanno Genre, former dean of the Waldensian Theological Faculty in Rome, presents an interesting case study of how even churches that historically were not very liturgical in their worship have begun to explore ways of revitalizing their worship.

The collection of essays draws to a close with two extremely interesting presentations. The first is by Dr. Giulio Viviani, one of the Pope's masters of ceremonies, who has done research on the significance of the ecumenical celebrations that Popes Paul VI and John Paul II have participated in throughout the world. One will be amazed at the breadth and depth of these celebration, which indeed illustrate the Pontiffs' commitment to the search for the unity of Christians, and this in spite of documents that have recently been issued by curial offices.

The collection comes to an end on a note of well-founded hope and a clear challenge for all the churches in their reflection on the principles of worship. Professor Robert Taft walks us through the details and the implications of the historic agreement on the Eucharist between the Catholic church and the Assyrian Church of the East promulgated on 26 October 2001. Taft shows the importance of the task of comparative liturgy, which Anton Baumstark proposed so many years ago, especially for uncovering the weaknesses and strengths of Western theological and liturgical traditions with its almost exclusive emphasis on word. In addition, he exposes the rich theological tradition that is found in one of the oldest churches, the Assyrian Church of the East and its traditional eucharistic anaphora of Addai and Mari. In a certain respect, this closing article puts all of the churches on guard against liturgical reductionism and especially on the necessity to have a balanced Trinitarian theology that derives from the prayer of the church.

It is hoped that this collection of essays will continue to encourage the necessary work of liturgical revision in all our churches so that we find authentic ways of praying and believing, and that this worship and belief will lead eventually to the spirituality necessary for Christian unity.

List of Acronyms and Initialisms

AAS	*Acta Apostolicae Sedis*
ACOL	Australian Consultation on Liturgy
AIL	Association of Irish Liturgists
BAS	*Book of Alternative Services of the Anglican Church of Canada*
BCP	Book of Common Prayer
BEM	Lima text "Baptism, Eucharist and Ministry"
CC	Christian Confessions
CCP	*Celebrating Common Prayer: A Version of the Daily Office*
CLT	Consultation on Liturgical Texts
CEEC	Council of the European Episcopal Conferences
COCU	Consultation on Church Union
DAPNE	*Directory for the Application of Principles and Norms on Ecumenism*
DEM	*Dictionary of the Ecumenical Movement*
EC	Ecumenical Celebrations
ECUSA	Episcopal Church in the United States of America
ELLC	English Language Liturgical Consultation
EŒ	*Enchiridion œcumenicum*
EV	*Enchiridion Vaticanum: Documenti officiali della Santa Sede in Latino e italiano*
IALC	International Anglican Liturgical Consultation
ICEL	International Commission on English in the Liturgy
ICET	International Consultation on English Texts
JLCNZ	Joint Liturgical Consultation within New Zealand

JLG	Joint Liturgical Group
KEK	Conference of European Churches
LC-SACUC	Liturgical Committee of the South African Church Unity Commission
LWF	Lutheran World Federation
MR	*Missale Romanum*
MWB	*Methodist Worship Book*
OLM	*Ordo Lectionum Missae*
OR	*L'Osservatore Romano*
PBA	*A Prayerbook for Australia*
PCPCU	Pontifical Council for Promoting Christian Unity
SC	*Sacrosanctum Concilium*
TMA	*Tertio Millennio Adveniente*
UCEPO	Archive of the Office of the Liturgical Celebrations of the Supreme Pontiff
UMBW	*United Methodist Book of Worship*
UR	*Unitatis Redintegratio*
URC	United Reformed Church
UUS	*Ut Unum Sint*
WA	Weimarer Ausgabe
WARC	World Alliance of Reformed Churches
WCC	World Council of Churches

David R. Holeton

Anglican Liturgical Renewal, Eschatological Hope, and Christian Unity

Planted deep in the heart of Christian experience is the longing that God's will and covenant promises in Jesus Christ will be actualized here on earth. The cry "Maranatha" lies at the core of Christian hope. Again and again Christians have prayed: " your kingdom come, your will be done on earth . . ."

While this eschatological longing for the advent of the fullness of God's reign has always been expressed in the liturgical prayer of the church, there were periods in which it was less evident than in others. The latter half of the twentieth century saw a great reassessment of the eschatological dimension of worship within the *œcumene*— including the churches of the Anglican Communion.

The subject of eschatology and the liturgy is a relatively new interest for Anglican liturgical scholars, *not* because the two matters are unrelated but because our principal inherited liturgical text, the Book of Common Prayer [BCP], came from an age when eschatology was of little theological interest.

In the Tudor worldview, enshrined in the BCP, creation was presumed as a given—and then ignored. The political order was perceived as unchanging (contemporary English political events notwithstanding); those in positions of political power were presumed to be there because of the manifest will of God. Social mobility was a phenomenon that was basically unknown, and each individual was expected to fulfill the duties of state required by his/her own social status. Such a worldview leaves little place for an eschatological vision. The *eschaton* was a very long way off.

The liturgical language used in the BCP reinforced this worldview. Naturally, the language of the text was determined by a culture in which social parameters were neatly drawn, leaving little or no place for God's radical inbreaking. In an established church, eschatologically charged language would have sat uncomfortably alongside this static worldview. As such, the liturgical language studiedly avoided

1

eschatological images and, when compared with the larger biblical and patristic tradition, was extremely hierarchical and patriarchal. The overall effect was to eviscerate the liturgical act of its eschatological power, so that the celebration of the liturgy became an act of social control rather than an act of liberation.

That said, it must be admitted that there were times when various individuals were very aware of the power of the liturgical act (particularly the celebration of the Eucharist) to become an eschatological moment, and in their own work, they managed to transcend the inherent restraints of the received liturgical texts.

In the eighteenth century, many of the eucharistic hymns of the Wesleys were highly eschatological[1] but, of course, were considered suspect by the majority of Anglicans, for at that time Anglicanism was not the singing church as it likes to see itself today, and hymnody was seen as an instrument of the theological vice of the age—enthusiasm.[2]

The ritualists of the late nineteenth century were highly aware of the power of the liturgy to evoke an eschatological vision (hence their appeal to the slums and working-class areas of England and the New World) but had to live with what could only have been the cognitive dissonance between the heavenly splendor they tried to replicate in their ritual and the liturgical texts they were, by law, required to use. But, as Donald Gray has pointed out in his *Earth and Altar*,[3] this was the context out of which English Christian Socialism and the Anglican liturgical movement were born.

Direct relationships were drawn between questions of liturgy and its social and eschatological implications by people like Percy

---

[1] G. WAINWRIGHT, *Eucharist and Eschatology,* 3rd ed. (Akron: OSL, 2002) 70ff.

[2] As hymns were not mentioned in the rubrics—except for the *Veni Creator Spiritus* in the ordination rites—the general assumption was that there was no place for hymnody within Anglican worship. Evangelical clergy in the Church of England, following the model of the Wesleys, first began to introduce hymnody into the services for which they had responsibility. It was not until an 1820 judgment of the Consistory Court of the Archbishop of York that hymnody lost its taint of "enthusiasm" and became commonplace in Anglicanism. See R. A. LEAVER, "British Hymnody in the Nineteenth Century," in R. F. GLOVER, *The Hymnal 1982 Companion* (New York: Church Publishing, 1990) 3A:417ff.; N. TEMPERLEY, *The Music of the English Parish Church* (Cambridge: Cambridge University Press, 1979) 1:204ff.

[3] D. GRAY, *Earth and Altar: The Evolution of the Parish Communion in the Church of England to 1945,* Alcuin Club Collections 68 (Norwich: Canterbury Press, 1986) passim.

Dearmer, who was probably the most widely read of all Anglican practical liturgists of the last century.[4]

Between the two World Wars, Gabriel Herbert, a member of the Society of the Sacred Mission, addressed the question of liturgy and eschatology more extensively in his now classic work *Liturgy and Society*.[5]

At the practical level, the transforming, even revolutionary, power of the liturgical text had occasionally not escaped unnoticed. With the rise of the "quit India" movement, Anglican clergy in the Indian Raj were advised by the civil authorities not to use the *Magnificat* at Evensong with indigenous congregations.[6] Why? The text was potentially dangerous as a source of political unrest:

> He hath shewed strength with his arm:
>> he hath scattered the proud in the imagination of their hearts.
> He hath put down the mighty from their seat:
>> and hath exalted the humble and meek.

When the wholesale reform of Anglican liturgical texts began just before the time of the Second Vatican Council, the gulf between the worldview of inherited Anglican liturgical texts (largely found in the various provincial versions of the BCP) and that of the present age became chillingly clear. The inherited texts, beautiful as many of them were from an aesthetic point of view, had ceased to ring true in the ears of many clergy and laity. At the same time, many of those who were called upon to reform the liturgical texts had themselves been formed by the cumulative effect of the work of the hymnologists, the ritualists, and Christian Socialists, by Dearmer and Herbert, and knew well the potentially transforming power of liturgical texts.

---

[4] Addressing the question of factors in the liturgy that draw or repel certain types of people (ranging from the intellect of music and art), Dearmer remarks: "And there is another class of persons concerned, the largest of all, the working class. For vulgarity in the long-run always means cheapness, and cheapness means the tyranny of the sweater. A modern preacher often stands in a sweated pulpit, wearing a sweated surplice over a cassock that was not produced in fair conditions, and, holding a sweated book in one hand, with the other he points to the machine-made cross at the jerry-built altar, and appeals to the sacred principles of mutual sacrifice and love." P. DEARMER, *The Parson's Handbook* (London: Grant Richards, 1902[4]) 5.

[5] A. G. HERBERT, *Liturgy and Society: The Function of the Church in the Modern World* (London: Faber, 1935).

[6] I owe this information to a former British officer in the Indian army, who, after his return to England, was ordained a priest in the Church of England.

Thus, when they set out on their work of reforming the liturgical texts, liturgical commissions had many members whose sense of the liturgical act (particularly the Eucharist) was that of the antipasto of the reign of God. The results of these reforms of Anglican liturgical texts will be familiar to most contemporary Christians who are members of liturgical churches as the shape of the new texts themselves reflect the so-called "ecumenical consensus" on the "shape," "pattern," or *ordo* of the Eucharist—an *ordo* that is the amalgam of a number of factors of which the liturgical text is but one.

In the course of this *ordo*, there are a number of points which are particularly eschatologically charged and which have become, for many contemporary Anglicans, as well as for Christians in the liturgical churches as a whole, a moment when the radical inbreaking of God's reign is particularly palpable. These would include the gathering of the community, the exchange of the sign of peace, the Eucharistic Prayer, the reception of communion, the sending out, as well as a number of others. A survey of the progression of that *ordo* as it is celebrated in thousands of parish churches every week would make that clear.

THE EUCHARISTIC *ORDO* AS AN ESCHATOLOGICAL ENCOUNTER[7]

a) The Gathering of God's People

The Anglican Communion consists of nearly forty provinces, or member churches, which are to be found on every continent. Today there are far more Anglicans who are African than English. While the importance of British colonialism in the spread of Anglicanism throughout the world cannot be denied, there are many provinces of the Anglican Communion where that colonial past never existed. In the emigrations to the "mother countries" (and, for the British Commonwealth, to the "white dominions") that have characterized the lives of former colonial powers, societies have become pluralistic, but more often than not, not socially integrated, except in the ecclesial assembly. This, however, is not true for questions of race and ethnicity alone, but also for questions of gender, age, social class, and education.

---

[7] In what follows, I am using the divisions recommended by the Working Group on "The Structure of the Eucharist" at IALC-5. See "The Dublin Documents," in D. R. HOLETON, ed., *Our Thanks and Praise: The Eucharist in Anglicanism Today* [*Papers from the Fifth International Anglican Liturgical Consultation*] (Toronto: Anglican Book Centre, 1998) 283–293.

The Sunday liturgical assembly is probably the most socially integrated venue in many of our cities in the course of an entire week. There we find the entire spectrum of our society present: women, men, and children representing a wide variety of ethnic, socioeconomic, and educational backgrounds. Each one of them is there by right and as an equal because of his or her common baptism. In that sense, the gathering of the community is an eschatological moment in which the inbreaking of God's reign is palpable as the divisions that were once "Jew, Greek, male, female"—and extrapolated into the whole range of sorts and conditions that characterize our divided humanity—have been abolished in our baptism into Christ's death and resurrection.

b) Proclaiming and Receiving the Word of God

The Revised Common Lectionary (of which more will be said later) and the calendar on which it is structured, which enjoys widespread use around the Anglican Communion, has an inherent eschatological dimension within its structure. As the liturgical year moves toward its close, the readings become increasingly eschatological in character. Culminating on the final Sunday, kept as the Feast of Christ the King (in some provinces called the Reign of Christ), the year comes to a climax in the proclamation that Christ's rule is over all things and that, in God's time, that will be visible to all. This eschatological theme continues as the leitmotiv for the first days of Advent.

This theme of eschatological hope in which Christians are called to be agents of the transformation of all creation finds itself reflected in the variable liturgical texts:

> Eternal God,
> you exalted Jesus Christ to rule over all things,
> and have made us instruments of your kingdom:
> by your Spirit empower us to love the unloved,
> and to minister to all in need,
> then at the last bring us to your eternal realm
> where we may be welcomed into your everlasting joy
> and may worship and adore you for ever; through . . .[8]
>
> Almighty and everlasting God,
> whose will it is to restore all things
> in your well-beloved Son, our Lord and King,

[8] Collect for the Feast of Christ the King /The Reign of Christ—Year C. *A Prayer Book for Australia* [=PBA] (Wilton: Morehouse Publishing, 1995) 606–607.

5

grant that all peoples of the earth,
now divided and enslaved by sin,
may be freed and brought together
under his gentle and loving rule;
who lives and reigns . . .[9]

It is indeed right, our duty and our joy
that we should always sing your glory . . . .
For you are the hope of the nations,
the builder of the city that is to come.
Your love made visible in Jesus Christ
brings home the lost,
restores the sinner
and gives dignity to the despised.
In his face your light shines out,
flooding lives with goodness and truth,
gathering into one in your kingdom
a divided and broken humanity.
Therefore with all who can give voice in your creation . . .[10]

c) Prayers of the People

The liturgical texts used for the prayers of the people have gone through a remarkable evolution over the recent past. The BCP contained a single, extended prayer, to be prayed by the presiding celebrant. Its phrases invoke divine sanction on both the political and religious status quo, imputing that the existing social and religious order is the manifest will of God and, at best, would be the perfect order should those responsible behave in a "godly" fashion.[11]

The new liturgical books that have appeared throughout the Anglican Communion provide, at the very least, a variety of forms that may be followed or, with increasing frequency, an outline of themes that are to be incorporated into the prayers as the (often lay) person

[9] Collect for the Last Sunday after Pentecost: The Reign of Christ. *The Book of Alternative Services of The Anglican Church of Canada* [=BAS] (Toronto: Anglican Book Centre, 1985) 394.

[10] Preface for use with Eucharistic Prayers A, B, and E. *Common Worship: Services and Prayers for the Church of England* (London: Church House Publishing, 2000) 327.

[11] "We beseech thee also to save and defend all Christian Kings, Princes and Governors; and especially thy servant N. our King; that under him we may be godly and quietly governed; And grant unto his whole Council, and to all that are put in authority under him, that they may truly and indifferently minister justice, to the punishment of wickedness and vice, and to the maintenance of thy true religion, [i.e., the Church of England] and virtue.

6

responsible for the prayers at the celebration sets to work. These are often supplemented with other resources designed to help draw together the themes in the readings and variable prayers. It would be rare to find a celebration of the Eucharist in which these themes do not include those of justice and peace as well as concern for prisoners, captives, the poor, and the marginalized—all themes that implicitly invoke an eschatological view of the world order.

In most contemporary Anglican eucharistic liturgies, the prayers of the people lead to the exchange of a sign of peace. The introduction of the exchange of the sign of peace was, perhaps, the most difficult liturgical reform for many Anglicans, particularly those of Anglo-Saxon background or those schooled in the British system, as the culture is very non-tactile. Being asked to exchange a handshake, let alone an embrace, with others in public was an unnatural act. Being asked to do so in the liturgical assembly was greeted by some with shocked horror. That cultural hurdle transcended, the theological consequence of the act began to be slowly perceived.

Peacemaking is the work of Christians. It is rarely easy. Exchanging a sign of peace in the eucharistic liturgy is an eschatological act. In willing for others the peace of Christ, Christians slowly learn the way of becoming peacemakers and, as such, citizens in that peaceable kingdom of which Isaiah spoke, which is nothing less than the fullness of God's reign. Again, fleetingly, there is a tangible sense of the inbreaking of God's reign.

d) Celebrating at the Lord's Table

Celebrating a common meal with common bread and a common cup at a common table is a radically eschatological sign-act. As the gathering of the community is a sign-act that proclaims that the divisions that mar human society have been overcome through baptism, sharing a common meal is a vivid sign-act of that reality.

The Eucharistic Prayers hold up before the gathered assembly this eschatological vision that is being acted out before them. This can be seen most clearly in the prayers associated with the epiclesis, where a number of themes emerge. First and foremost is the unity of the church. Here the language of the prayers is quite explicit: "gather into one," "grant unity and peace," "grant that . . . all may become one body and one spirit."

The other outstanding theme is that of the renewal and transformation of both the church and the world. The petitions used are strong and evocative: "renew the earth according to your promise," "reconcile all things in Christ and make them new," "gather your Church together from the ends of the earth into your kingdom, where peace and justice are revealed, that we, with all your people, of every language, race, and nation, may share the banquet you have promised."

A few examples drawn from Eucharistic Prayers in current use by Anglicans will illustrate this eschatological tone. The first text is found in the *Apostolic Tradition*, often attributed to Hippolytus and used by many Anglican provinces; the others are modern compositions:

> We ask you to send your Holy Spirit upon
> the offering of your holy church.
> Gather all into one
> all who share in these holy mysteries,
> filling them with the Holy Spirit
> and confirming their faith in the truth,
> that together they may praise you
> and give you glory
> through your Servant Jesus Christ.[12]

> Send the Holy Spirit on your people
> and gather into one kingdom
> all who share in this one bread and one cup,
> so that we, in the company of [N and] all the saints,
> may praise you and glorify you for ever,
> through Jesus Christ our Lord . . .[13]

> We pray you, gracious God,
> to send your Holy Spirit upon these gifts,
> that they may be the sacrament
> of the body of Christ
> and his blood of the new covenant.
> Unite us to your Son in his sacrifice,
> that we, made acceptable to him,
> may be sanctified by the Holy Spirit.
> In the fullness of time,
> reconcile all things in Christ,
> and make them new,
> and bring us to that city of light
> where you dwell with all your sons and daughters;
> through Jesus Christ our Lord,

[12] Eucharistic Prayer 2, BAS 197.
[13] Eucharistic Prayer B, *Common Worship*, 190.

8

the firstborn of all creation,
the head of the Church,
and the author of our salvation . . .[14]

Send your Holy Spirit upon us
and upon this offering of your Church,
that we who eat and drink at this holy table
may share the divine life of Christ our Lord.
Pour out your Spirit upon the whole earth
and make it your new creation.
Gather your Church together
from the ends of the earth into your kingdom,
where peace and justice are revealed,
that we, with all your people,
of every language, race and nation,
may share the banquet you have promised . . .[15]

These Eucharistic Prayers, while praying for unity, assume that all those present who are numbered among the baptized will share in the eucharistic gifts. In so praying, we are reminded that we anticipate a reality that is not yet fully achieved. The Eucharist is the antipasto of the kingdom. In it we play at a proleptic event: the kingdom which is but which is yet to come.

The time during which the baptized receive communion is also an eschatologically charged moment. It is here that Anglican pastoral practice has changed radically over the past three decades. Precipitated by the "confirmation crisis" of the 1950s,[16] Anglicans went through an extensive process of examining their practice of Christian initiation.[17] The conclusion of a number of theological commissions was that it is baptism and not confirmation that admitted one to

[14] Eucharistic Prayer B, *The Book of Common Prayer and Administration of the Sacraments and Other Rites and Ceremonies of the Church, According to the Use of the Episcopal Church* [=BCP-USA] (New York: The Church Hymnal Corporation and the Seabury Press, 1979) 369; Eucharistic Prayer 3, BAS 199–200.

[15] *The Book of Alternative Services*, BAS 203.

[16] During the 1950s several studies of confirmation practice in various parts of the Communion made it clear that there was a vast disparity between the numbers of Anglicans who were baptized and who later returned for confirmation. Even more unsettling was the disparity between those who, in confirmation, made a "mature profession of their faith" and having made such a profession, received the Eucharist with any regularity.

[17] I review this process in a number of provinces in "Christian Initiation in Some Anglican Provinces," *Studia Liturgica* 12, no. 2/3 (1977) 129–150.

9

the Eucharist.[18] Acting on these findings, an increasing number of Anglican provinces are admitting children to the Eucharist from the time of their baptism or at least from a very early age.[19]

The new (for Anglicans) phenomenon of infants and young children receiving communion has become another eschatological moment. The world is turned upside down. What had "traditionally" been a moment for those who were "old enough" and who "understood" has become a moment for all those who are baptized, regardless of age. Thus, with age and understanding no longer the qualifications for communicant status, it becomes clear that the "rational" ordering of things in this world does not hold weight in God's reign. This has led many communities to reflect on the implications of Jesus' holding up a little child and telling those surrounding him that unless they become like a little child, they cannot hope to enter the kingdom of heaven.

What are the qualities of childlikeness that are required of us adults if we are to attain citizenship in God's kingdom? On reflection, I believe that Augustine was right: it is not a question of innocence.[20] Perhaps other qualities that we find in children but un-learn as adults, such as inherent trust, the ability to be an unashamed re-

[18] While it has been demonstrated that the rigorous application of the rubric in the confirmation rite that required Anglicans to be confirmed before receiving communion is of nineteenth-century origin (see C. BUCHANAN, *Anglican Confirmation*, Grove Liturgical Study 48 [Bramcote: Grove, 1986]), the practice was understood as normative, and the thought of communicating while unconfirmed was generally unthinkable in living memory.

[19] Successive meetings of the International Anglican Liturgical Consultation [=IALC] have affirmed that baptism admits to the Eucharist and that all the baptized, regardless of age, are communicants. The first IALC (Boston, 1985) recommended that "the general communion of all the baptized assumes a significant place in all ecumenical dialogues in which Anglicans are engaged." *Children and Communion*, IV, viii (Bramcote: Grove Books, 1985). The Boston Principles and Recommendations were incorporated into "Walk in Newness of Life," the statement of IALC-4 in D. R. HOLETON, ed., *Growing in Newness of Life: Christian Initiation in Anglicanism Today* (Toronto: Anglican Book Centre, 1993) 226–256, which was devoted to Christian initiation. This principle was restated in Principle and Recommendation 1 of IALC-5 (Dublin, 1995), whose principal work was on the Eucharist. D. R. HOLETON, ed., *Our Thanks and Praise :The Eucharist in Anglicanism Today*, papers from the Fifth International Anglican Conference (Toronto: Anglican Book Centre, 1998) 261.

[20] AUGUSTINE, *Confessiones*, I, vii, trans. V. J. Bourke, Fathers of the Church 21 (New York: Fathers of the Church, 1953).

ceiver, and infectious mirth point to qualities that must be found in the citizens of God's kingdom.[21]

e) Going Out as God's People

The prayer after communion and the dismissal bring to a conclusion the series of eschatological moments that have punctuated the progression through the eucharistic *ordo*. The feast over, the community gives thanks to God for the gift of Christ in communion and asks that it might bear the fruits of the Eucharist in the daily lives of its members. They are then dismissed into the world for a life of mission and service. The prayers that form part of this rite are often highly eschatological in tone.

> God of the nations,
> we thank you for nourishing us with this holy sacrament.
> Guide us by your presence,
> that we may bring your light to those who dwell in darkness,
> and establish your justice in the earth.[22]

> May we who share Christ's body live his risen life;
> we who drink his cup bring life to others;
> we whom the Spirit lights give light to the world.
> Keep us firm in the hope that you have set before us,
> so we and all your children shall be free,
> and the whole earth live to praise your name;
> through . . .[23]

> Eternal Giver of love and power,
> your Son Jesus Christ has sent us into all the world
> to preach the gospel of his kingdom.
> Confirm in us this mission,
> and help us to live the good news we proclaim;
> through . . .[24]

All the modern Anglican texts surveyed include the dismissal "Go in peace to love and serve the Lord" among the possible choices to be sung or said by the deacon in sending the community into the world, thus making the connection between the community's actions and

---

[21] I write about this more extensively in "Welcome Children, Welcome Me," *Anglican Theological Review* 82, no. 1 (2000) 93–111.

[22] Prayer after Communion for Epiphany, PBA 150.

[23] Portion of the fixed prayer after communion, *Common Worship* 182; 265.

[24] Prayer after communion for the Ascension of the Lord, BAS 342.

the eschatological hope for the coming of the fullness of God's kingdom. It is significant that it is usually the first choice offered and, as such, the one most often used.

Thus the whole celebration of the Eucharist, from the gathering to the going out, is a series of eschatological moments. Perhaps the most powerful are the sign-acts themselves: the gathering of a polychrome, intergenerational group of people made one by their baptism; the exchange of a sign of peace; the feeding of all from the one bread and the common cup without regard to age, wealth, or status. It is these sign-acts, in the context of the eucharistic *ordo*, that form the consciousness of the community. These sign-acts are then in turn elucidated and reinforced by the liturgical texts themselves.

ESCHATOLOGY OUTSIDE THE EUCHARISTIC CONTEXT

It is not the eucharistic rites alone that are characterized by this new sense of a lively eschatological hope and consciousness. The changes in worldview that have found a place in the eucharistic texts of Anglican churches characterize the reform of the wider corpus of Anglican liturgical texts.

Contemporary liturgical texts draw increasingly on a larger vocabulary than has been used in the liturgical texts of the recent past. This new vocabulary is not per se new, for it is often drawn from biblical and patristic sources but was often ignored by those who composed liturgical texts in the past. The result is often liberating and transformative for those in the liturgical assembly. Like gazing at a ray of light passing through a crystal, they see—or in this case hear—something that has always been there but has never been perceived in quite the same way. This language often evokes images of covenant, grace, justice, partnership, and the feminine among others. This can be seen in the following examples:

> God of the oppressed, we pray for all those who suffer injustice at the hands of indifferent or cruel rulers, especially for the innocent victims of war. Give them strength and patience, and hasten the day when the kingdoms of this world will own the perfect law of love made known in Jesus Christ our Lord. Amen.[25]

> Strength of the weak, Defender of the needy, Rescuer of the poor, deliver us from the power of wickedness that we may rejoice in your justice now and forever, through . . .[26]

[25] Psalm prayer 53, BAS 772.
[26] Psalm prayer 82, BAS 816.

Judge of all the earth,
restrain the ambitions of the proud
and the turmoil of the nations;
establish among us the reign of the Messiah,
who drained for us the cup of judgement
and is alive with you . . .[27]

Each of these examples has been taken from the psalm prayers used after each of the psalms appointed for use at the Daily Office. As such, they would be used on a regular basis following the cursus of psalmody and would routinely call to mind a renewed vision of eschatological hope.

Other texts, such as the variable prayers appointed for a particular feast or commemoration would in a periodic but less frequent manner serve the same end. One of the most pointed examples that focuses the two quite different visions of the world order can be found in comparing the BCP and reformed texts for the Feast of the Holy Innocents. The "traditional" BCP collect is a radical reworking for the 1662 BCP of the original 1549 BCP translation of the Latin text found in the Sarum Missal:[28]

O Almighty God who out of the mouths of babes and sucklings hast ordained strength, and madest infants to glorify thee by their deaths: Mortify and kill all vices in us, and so strengthen us by thy grace, that by the innocency of our lives, and constancy of our faith, even unto death, we may glorify thy holy Name, through . . .[29]

Born in an age in which it was assumed that civilian populations would be the victims of the vagaries of war, the text begins with an assertion that sounds almost blasphemous to the modern ear: "madest infants to glorify thee by their deaths" and then proceeds to spiritualize the event, "mortify and kill within us," then, invoking a clever word-play, "the "innocency of our lives," we ask that we, too, may glorify God. Gone are any images of the horrific reality of the

---

[27] Psalm prayer 75, *Celebrating Common Prayer: A Version of the Daily Office* [=CCP] (London/New York: Mowbray/Cassel, 1996) 584. CCP, a reworking of the Daily Office of the English (Anglican) Province of the Society of Saint Francis, is one of the most popular Office books in many parts of the Anglican Communion.

[28] F. E. BRIGHTMAN, *The English Rites Being a Synopsis of the Sources and Revisions of the Book of Common Prayer, with an Introduction and an Appendix,* 2nd ed. rev. (Westmead: Gregg International, 1970) 1:234–235.

[29] Collect for Holy Innocents, BCP 1662; BCP Canada 1962.

slaughter of infants or an appeal to God's righteous justice. It should not be difficult to understand why Christians living in a world after the Holocaust, the Ethiopian famines, the genocides of the south Slavs, 11 September, or the Taliban would have difficulty praying this prayer. It is no longer possible for the average Christian to imagine God being glorified in innocent death, nor can we allow such events to pass without yearning for an intervention of the God of justice, whom we believe to stand in solidarity with the poor and the marginalized. Thus it should not be surprising to find the new prayers for this feast markedly changed. The following are examples of the new texts for the feast:

> Almighty God, our heavenly Father,
> whose children suffered at the hand of Herod,
> receive, we pray, all innocent victims
> into the arms of your mercy.
> By your great might frustrate all evil designs
> and establish your reign of justice, love and peace,
> through . . .[30]

> Heavenly Father,
> whose children suffered at cruel hands,
> though they had done no wrong:
> give us grace neither to act cruelly
> nor to stand indifferently by,
> but to defend the weak from the tyranny of the strong;
> in the name of Jesus Christ who suffered for us,
> yet is alive and reigns . . .[31]

> Merciful God,
> accept all we offer you this day.
> Preserve your people from cruelty
> and indifference to violence,
> that the weak may always be defended
> from the tyranny of the strong. We ask this . . .[32]

While these texts are used only occasionally, they become part of a larger pattern of liturgical prayer that uses language of a creation that is being transformed and renewed, language, as we have seen earlier, that is encountered regularly in the Eucharistic Prayer.

[30] Collect for Holy Innocents, BAS 398.
[31] Collect for Holy Innocents, PBA 626.
[32] Prayer over the gifts for Holy Innocents, BAS 398.

14

There is nothing unbiblical or unpatristic in these prayers, but the language is unfamiliar in liturgical prayer and can seem quite startling. What is more important, in this instance, is the clear eschatological vision embodied in the prayers. Quite unlike the prayers of the BCP, there is an expectation of and longing for divine intervention in the affairs of the world so that the indifference of cruel rulers is not accepted as a given and that their victims as well as all victims and the socially marginalized are committed not only to God's compassion but also to the care of the Christian community.

The long-term cumulative effect of these prayers is not inconsiderable. While the BCP texts helped form a paradigm in which the social reality was a positive given, the new texts cast serious doubt on the ultimate goodness of any social order, particularly one marked by social injustice or entrenched separation based on gender, race, class, or education, and looks forward to the fulfillment of all things in Christ. It is an eschatological vision that is part of our baptismal vocation to be agents of that kingdom in which the values of this world are overthrown in favor of the values of God's eschatological reign.

ANGLICAN LITURGICAL RENEWAL, ESCHATOLOGICAL HOPE AND CHRISTIAN UNITY?

What does all of this have to do with ecumenism? Much of what I have written to this point will undoubtedly sound familiar and perhaps even old hat to a reader whose own church has experienced the liturgical reforms of the past decades. But that is the very point. The experience of the effects of the modern reform of the liturgical texts and the subsequent renewal of our liturgical life is an experience common to Anglicans and Roman Catholics, as well as to the members of other liturgical churches.

Over the past forty years, ecumenical work in the renewal of liturgy has become normative. Since the time of Vatican II, liturgists have been involved in the task of preparing common liturgical texts. For example, in 1964 an unofficial group of Roman Catholic, Anglican, Lutheran, and Reformed liturgists began to meet in North America. This informal gathering eventually became the Consultation on Liturgical Texts (CCT), which by 2002 included twenty-two churches or agencies among its membership. The CCT has produced a number of ecumenical liturgical texts, such as *A Liturgical Psalter for the Christian Year*,[33] *A*

[33] M. H. SHEPARD JR., *A Liturgical Psalter for the Christian Year* (Minneapolis:Augsburg Publishing/Collegeville: Liturgical Press, 1976).

15

Christian Celebration of Marriage,[34] *A Celebration of Baptism*,[35] and *Ecumenical Services of Prayer*.[36] A number of these texts, particularly the marriage and baptismal rites, have been authorized for use at particular ecumenical occasions by a wide variety of the member churches of the CCT.

At about the same time as the formation of the CCT, a similar group, the Joint Liturgical Group (JLG), was formed in Great Britain and presently contains eight member churches. Like the CCT, the JLG has produced a number of liturgical texts, including a Daily Office,[37] liturgical material for Holy Week,[38] a common Eucharistic Prayer, an ecumenical marriage rite,[39] and a variety of books directed toward the renewal of the liturgical life of the churches.[40] The liturgical texts have found their way into the new liturgical books of a number of the churches of the British Isles and have been important in creating an atmosphere of liturgical convergence.

In more recent years, other national ecumenical working groups have been established including the Australian Consultation on Liturgy (ACOL), the Joint Liturgical Consultation within New Zealand (JLCNZ), the Liturgical Committee of the South African Church Unity Commission (LC-SACUC), and the Association of Irish Liturgists (AIL). Each of these consultations is committed, in a fashion appropriate to the very different ecumenical contexts, to working toward common liturgical texts.

Working together with the Roman Catholic bishops' International Commission on English in the Liturgy (ICEL), the CCT and JLG formed the International Consultation on English Texts (ICET), which was responsible for the creation of modern-language liturgical translations of the Gloria in excelsis, Credo, Sanctus, Pater noster, Gloria Patri, Magnificat, Benedictus, Te Deum, etc., used by the English-

[34] (Philadelphia: Augsburg/Fortress, 1987).

[35] (Nashville: Abingdon, 1988).

[36] (Leominster/New York: Fowler Wright, 1983).

[37] *The Daily Office* (London: SPCK, 1968); *The Daily Office Revised with Other Prayers and Services* (London: SPCK, 1978).

[38] *Holy Week Services* (London: SPCK, 1971); *Holy Week Services—Revised and Expanded Version* (London: SPCK, 1983).

[39] *An Order Marriage: For Christians from Different Traditions* (Norwich: Canterbury Press, 1999).

[40] R.C.D. JASPER, ed., *The Renewal of Worship* (London: Oxford University Press, 1965); N. CLARKE and R.C.D. JASPER, eds., *Initiation and Eucharist* (London: SPCK, 1972); R.C.D. JASPER, *Getting the Liturgy Right* (London: SPCK, 1982).

16

speaking churches. These were published as *Prayers We Have in Common*.[41] The work of ICET is presently carried on by the English Language Liturgical Consultation (ELLC), which also includes ecumenical liturgical consultations from Australia, New Zealand, Canada, and South Africa. In 1989 a revised version of the ELLC texts was published by ELLC as *Praying Together*.[42] Presently ELLC is examining other liturgical possibilities, such as a collection of common Eucharistic Prayers.

In addition to common liturgical texts, English-speaking churches have enjoyed common liturgical lectionaries. The publication of the Roman Catholic *Ordo Lectionum Missae* (OLM) in 1969 attracted widespread ecumenical attention. A variety of North American churches began publishing their own recensions of OLM, and in 1974 the Consultation on Church Union (COCU) produced its own version. A working group of the CCT—the North American Committee on Calendar and Lectionary—produced a common version of OLM, which was published in 1982 as Common Lectionary: The Lectionary Proposed by the Consultation on Common Texts[43]; this was revised and republished in 1992 as the Revised Common Lectionary.[44] This Lectionary quickly found widespread use in the English-speaking churches of North America and overseas, and, in the more recent past, has been incorporated into the liturgical life of many non-English speaking churches around the world.

Anglicans have been instrumental in the foundation and the work of all these ecumenical liturgical groups, and the work of these groups has found its way into the renewed liturgical texts of provinces throughout the Anglican world. A glance at the acknowledgments pages of any contemporary Anglican liturgical book, for example, *Common Worship* (England, 2001); *A Prayer Book for Australia* (1995), *A New Zealand Prayer Book* (1989), *An Anglican Prayer Book* (South Africa, 1989), or *A Book of Alternative Services* (Canada, 1985), will quickly show how the work of these ecumenical groups has been incorporated into the liturgical life of Anglicanism. Thus the *shape* of the liturgy is one example of an emerging liturgical consensus. Most of the basic *texts* (Gloria, Creed, Sanctus, Lord's Prayer, etc.) are common texts produced ecumenically. Some of the *Eucharistic Prayers* are

---

[41] (Philadelphia: Fortress, 1970). Revised and enlarged, 1972.
[42] (Nashville: Abingdon/Norwich: Canterbury Press, 1988).
[43] (New York: Church Publishing, 1976).
[44] (New York / Norwich / Winfield: Abingdon, 1992).

either the work of informal ecumenical working groups (e.g., an ecumenical English translation of the oldest version of the anaphora of Basil the Great) or based on a common ancient text (e.g., the prayer from the *Apostolic Tradition* attributed to Hippolytus). The *readings* are from the Common Lectionary, and commentaries written on the Lectionary have an ecumenical dimension which, in turn, can create a new ecumenical openness in preaching.

Other elements of liturgical celebration also witness to a remarkable convergence. Contemporary hymnbooks, for instance, reflect a sharing of musical resources. Reforms in liturgical space are pursued in common. The alb, once a distinctly "catholic" liturgical garment, has emerged as the quasi-ecumenical garb of liturgical ministers in many Western traditions and has become the standard basic garment worn by Anglicans in eucharistic worship. The overall effect of this on Anglicanism has been of tremendous significance. While modern Anglican liturgical books are unmistakably Anglican in character, they are also unmistakably ecumenical. Anglicans remain bound to one another around the world through their common liturgical heritage of the Book of Common Prayer, but they are also increasingly bound to other churches by the emerging ecumenical liturgical consensus.

In the light of this, the restrictions put on Roman Catholic participation in this enterprise by the instruction *Liturgiam Authenticam* are catastrophic.

THE RENEWAL OF WORSHIP AND AN EMERGING ECUMENICAL CULTURE

Anglicans, like Christians in general, are increasingly exposed to one another's liturgical celebrations through both attendance and the television media. When they visit or watch the liturgical celebrations of other churches (particularly baptism and Eucharist),there is a feeling of "being at home." Parish clergy often report how parishioners, upon returning from travels during which they worshiped with friends in churches of other traditions, express a sense of familiarity with the liturgical shape, texts, and music. Increasingly, Bible study groups meet locally and include members of various churches. As these groups study the Sunday pericopes from the Common Lectionary, they rediscover Scripture as a common inheritance and are often struck by the similarity of interpretation of the pericopes by the previous Sunday's preacher, so that biblical preaching has become a uniting element. Pastors, too, often meet weekly to discuss the Sunday pericopes, and thus a certain ecumenical insight is brought to bear on the biblical text. The overall effect of this is one that has created a sense of ecumenical culture and presses afresh Archbishop Temple's concern that division at the Lord's table is "the greatest of all scandals in the face of the world."[45] But here, too, the reformed liturgical texts offer a particular eschatological vision, particularly in the epicleses of many of the new Eucharistic Prayers.

Even when we celebrate just in our own local community, we know that the sign is marred, for we know only too well the brokenness and division that we bring to the table. And so we pray:

> Grant that all we who share this bread and this cup
> may *become* one body and one spirit,
> a living sacrifice in Christ
> to the praise and glory of your name.[46]

If we are prepared to acknowledge that our own celebrations of the Eucharist bear a marred image of what we ought to be both as individuals and as particular communities, then perhaps our celebrations between ourselves as churches can be seen in a new light. While yet divided and broken, we remain open to the Spirit, who, through the eucharistic gifts, transforms us into what we are called to be. We come to a common table not necessarily seeing in each other everything we would hope to find (just as we know that at our own table we come not finding ourselves as we know we should be) but with the vision of a church transformed and the trust that God, who remains faithful in covenant with us, will work in us that which is promised.

> O God,
> who set before us the great hope
> that your Kingdom shall come on earth
> and taught us to pray for its coming:
> give us grace to discern the signs of its dawning
> and to work for the perfect day
> when the whole world shall reflect your glory;
> through Jesus Christ our Lord . . .[47]

[45] "The Church and Unity," in A. E. BAKER, ed., *Religious Experience and Other Essays and Addresses by William Temple* (London: Lutterworth Press, 1958) 156.

[46] Eucharistic Prayer D, BCP-USA 375; Eucharistic Prayer 6, BAS 210.

[47] Collect for Tuesdays, CCP 98. While liturgical texts usually appear anonymously, this prayer is attributed to Percy Dearmer, a fitting monument to one who did so much to relate liturgy and its social context and eschatology.

Canon Donald Gray

Common Words and *Common Worship*
Praying Together and Apart

My title, as you see, is "Common Words and *Common Worship*." Common prayer has for a few years now been a fashionable issue in the Church of England, because there are, on the one hand, many folk who are concerned with the preservation of ancient and familiar texts that have been prayed in common in the past, while at the same time there are others who have embraced a new vision of commonality, that vision which is the result of ecumenical sharing. We have begun to acknowledge our common liturgical roots, and although ecumenically agreed upon texts "do not necessarily lend to convergence and agreement, yet it is a fact that there is now more "in common" across the denominational boundaries than there ever has been since the divisions of the sixteenth century."[1]

In order to trace the torturous path by which many in England have come to our present (and new) understanding of commonality, I need to give a rapid overview of the process of liturgical revision in the Church of England over the past hundred years. I make no apology for this, because I believe that the latest authorized form of worship (which is indeed called "Common Worship") can only be properly understood by such an examination. Indeed, the title of the new service book *Common Worship* only makes full sense against this background.[2]

However, let me emphasize again that it is the *Church of England* I'm dealing with. Professor Holeton has already contributed to this series of essays by speaking on *Anglican* liturgical renewal, of which, obviously, my subject is part. But notoriously, even the most senior Vatican officials confuse these two categories and sometimes speak as

---

[1] D. GRAY, "An Ecumenical Approach to Common Prayer," in M. PERHAM, ed., *The Renewal of Common Prayer: Uniformity and Diversity in Church of England Worship*, GS Misc 412 (London: SPCK, 1993) 52–53.

[2] *Common Worship: Services and Prayers for the Church of England* (London: Cambridge University Press, 2000).

though they are synonymous. There are, of course, far more Anglicans outside England than there are in the provinces of Canterbury and York, which comprise the Church of England.

Part of the confusion, liturgically, lies in the fact that until the 1950s, the majority of Anglican provinces outside the British Isles used the unexpurgated 1662 prayer book, that same form of liturgy as was then currently authorized in the Church of England. There was one major and increasingly significant deviation from this generalization. The admittedly tiny Episcopal Church of Scotland—never under any circumstances to be mistaken with the (Presbyterian) Church of Scotland—had preserved a eucharistic rite that varied in some major particulars from that contained in the 1662 book. It harked back, behind the 1662 book, to the first English Prayer Book (the work of Cranmer in 1549), which generations of high churchmen in England recalled with considerable nostalgia, believing, in particular, that its prayer of consecration was much superior to that in the later books.[3] Now the remarkable thing is that the Scottish Prayer Book was a crucial influence in the liturgical work of the Protestant Episcopal Church in the United States. It can be clearly seen in the first American Book of Common Prayer authorized "from and after" October 1, 1790.[4]

However, to return to England. The facts of the matter are that serious liturgical revision was not accomplished in the Church of England until late in the twentieth century. That does not mean that the need for revision had not been appreciated earlier. Although there was always easy talk about "our incomparable liturgy," its inadequacies were widely recognized. Ronald Jasper, who might well be celebrated as one of the founding fathers of ecumenical liturgical cooperation, wrote his bachelor of divinity thesis on the various moves to revise the 1662 liturgy, particularly in the eighteenth and nineteenth centuries.[5] All of them came to nothing.

However, in the 1840s the Oxford Movement, a High Church movement, of which John Henry Newman was so much a part at its conception, created a situation in which changes became inevitable. It has to be admitted that the earliest Tractarians (so called because

---

[3] A. CAMPBELL DON, *The Scottish Book of Common Prayer 1929: Notes on Its Origin and Growth* (London: SPCK, 1949) 52.

[4] M. J. HATCHETT, *The Making of the First American Prayer Book, 1776–1789* (New York: The Seabury Press, 1982).

[5] R.C.D. JASPER, *Prayer Book Revision in England 1800–1900* (London: SPCK, 1954).

their propaganda was contained in a series of booklets called *Tracts for the Times*) were what could, not unfairly, be described as "Prayer Book Fundamentalists." They feared state intervention into the church's affairs, which they had seen demonstrated by the plans to disestablish the (Anglican) Church of Ireland. One of their defenses against such aggression, they believed, was the 1662 Prayer Book. They were also conservative in ritual and ceremonial matters. In his Church of England days, Newman never wore eucharistic vestment for instance.

But what has been characterized as the "reserve" of the early adherents of the Oxford Movement became considerably less distinctive by the middle of the century. By 1900, what had previously been a trickle of more ritualistic ceremonial and deviations from the Prayer Book and the introduction of not only words and actions but also vestments, ornaments, and fittings from outside the Church of England had become a flood. It is not unfair to say that liturgical anarchy reigned over vast areas of the Church of England, particularly in the new and crowded areas that had grown up in the industrial towns and cities and other large centers of population. The diocese of London was particularly notorious for many high church, Anglo-Catholic parishes.

Episcopal authority was widely flouted. There were Ritual Riots: mobs who had no interest in the niceties of either liturgy or ecclesiastical politics were "rabble-roused" into causing disturbances at church services. For a recent and readable account of these days, see John Shelton Reed's *Glorious Battle*.[6] There was also a series of high-profile cases in the church courts, and tempers were inflamed when attempts were make to enforce church law by use of secular courts, in particular the powers of the Privy Council. It was all very degrading and quite unnecessary. Amidst it all, five Anglican priests were actually imprisoned for contempt of court, having refused to accept the jurisdiction of civil courts to enforce ecclesiastical discipline.

It was a situation that could not continue, and eventually the government of the day decided that it was its solemn duty to set up, in 1904, a high-powered Royal Commission on Ecclesiastical Discipline, whose task it was

> to inquire into the alleged prevalence of breaches or neglect of the Law relating to the conduct of Divine Service in the Church of England and to the ornaments and fittings of churches; and to consider the existing

[6] J. SHELTON REED, *Glorious Battle: The Cultural Politics of Victorian Anglo-Catholicism* (Nashville: Vanderbilt University Press, 1996).

powers and procedures applicable to such irregularities and to make such recommendations as may be deemed requisite for dealing with the aforesaid matters.[7]

It could only happen in England! Evidence was brought before the Commission by agents of the Church Association, which had been formed in 1865 by several leading Evangelical churchmen to maintain the Protestant ideals of faith and worship in the Church of England. They, together with the Church of England League and National Protestant Union, produced 164 witnesses. The contents of the volume of evidence would be hilarious if it were not so sad. Examples of "lawlessness" varied from the use of the lavabo and mixing the chalice at one end of the scale to the use of the Roman Canon and services of Benediction at the other. The League and Union produced examples from fifteen hundred churches in England and Wales (the disestablishment and disendowment of the Welsh dioceses and the formation of the church in Wales as a separate Anglican province had not yet occurred).

Even the archbishop of Canterbury appeared before the Commission. In what was a masterly, diplomatic, and irenic statement, he explained how, in the nineteenth century, the pattern of worship in the Church of England, in some large part under the influence of the Oxford Movement, had altered. Archbishop Randall Davison had previously been bishop of Winchester, and he gave the Commission examples from that diocese. In 1829, he said, in the 319 parishes in the diocese, divine service took place twice a Sunday in 158 and three times a Sunday in only 11. Seventy years later the Holy Communion was celebrated monthly (or more often) in 557, fortnightly (or more often) in 512, weekly (or more often) in 404.[8]

I will not detail the various items that were reckoned as being "significant of teaching contrary or repugnant to the articles or formularies of the Church of England," but many would surprise you. I have included a catalogue in my book on the history of the way in which the Eucharist returned to the center of worship patterns in the Church of England.[9]

[7] *Report of the Royal Commission on Ecclesiastical Discipline*, Cd 3040 (London, 1906) v.

[8] *Minutes of Evidence taken before the Royal Commission of Ecclesiastical Discipline at Church House Westminster*, Cd 3069 (London, 1906) vol. 1, 11, par. 13265–13257.

[9] D. GRAY, *Earth and Altar: The Evolution of the Parish Communion in the Church of England to 1945*, Alcuin Club Collections 68 (London/Norwich: Canterbury Press, 1986).

The Commission listened to all of this for the better part of two years, having to endure the clear bigotry and intolerances of the "protestant spies." But they themselves were fair and balanced men (no women on a Royal Commission in those days!); they realized that the complaints had come from only a small proportion of churches in the country and that in the large majority of parishes the work of the church was being, as they said, "quietly and diligently performed." Nevertheless, the report does provide what Geoffrey Cuming described in his *History of Anglican Worship* as "an authoritative picture of worship at the turn of the century."[10]

The Commission came to the conclusion that "the law of public worship in the Church of England is too narrow for the religious life of the present generation." They said, "It needlessly condemns much which a great section of her most devoted members value."[11]

In order that there should be an agreed standard of liturgical practice (some commonality), they made this historic recommendation: the Convocations of York and Canterbury should be issued with Letters of Business to provide new rubrics regulating ornaments and vesture, and to frame, with a view to enactment by Parliament, modifications relating to the conduct of divine worship.[12]

Now note the phrase "with a view to enactment by Parliament." In those days there was no other way, nor was there for many years, until the passing (by Parliament) of *The Worship and Doctrine Measure* in 1975. That gave the synodical processes of the church full power over the contents of its services (excluding the power to abolish use of the 1662 Prayer Book, which continues as a legitimate and available form of worship).[13] The 1906 reminder to the Church of England that Parliamentary approval would be necessary to secure liturgical changes was to come back and haunt the church, as you will see.

The immediate outcome of the issuing of the Letters of Business was that the Convocations began to work to produce a Revised Prayer Book. Remember that was only the bishops and representative priests—known as proctors—who were members of these two bodies, one for each province. At first they had the assistance of a

[10] G. J. CUMING, *A History of Anglican Liturgy*, 2nd ed. (London: Macmillan, 1982) 163.

[11] *Report on the Royal Commission*, par. 399.

[12] Ibid., *Recommendations*, 77, 2.

[13] R.C.D. JASPER, *The Development of the Anglican Liturgy 1662–1980* (London: SPCK, 1989) 281–282.

Committee of Experts, whose composition reads like a roll call of some of the great liturgical scholars of the day: W. H. Frere, F. E. Brightman, Percy Dearmer. Sadly, we know the inherent suspicion of the capability of committees to write liturgy, and it was allowed to lapse after a few years. You see, we are talking about a process that lasted over twenty-one years. It was not until 1927 that the book was produced. True, a World War intervened, but, in fact, that did not curtail the meetings. While millions died in war, the Convocations of the Church of England resolutely continued in their liturgical work of producing a book for presentation to Parliament.[14]

However, the Parliamentary hurdle was not to be surmounted! In 1927 the House of Lords gave approval to a Prayer Book that came to them with the overwhelming support of both the clergy and a newly formed House of Laity, but it failed to gain the support of the House of Commons. Once again it was the combination of the forces of conservatism and evangelicalism that united to defeat its adoption. Hasty attempts were made to accommodate some of these low church fears, and the book was resubmitted to Parliament in 1928, but it suffered the same fate.[15]

In the wake of this crisis, the bishops issued an unusual statement in which they stated that in the future they would measure the seriousness of any deviations from the strict letter of the Book of Common Prayer against the provisions of the rejected 1928 book.[16] But although some of the variations, particularly the pastoral offices, were widely used, there was an obvious absurdity in using a book that had been intended to legalize variations, in a way that was itself technically illegal. This, then, was the situation until after the Second World War. The official book of the Church of England was still that issued in 1662—three hundred years earlier.

If the archbishop of Canterbury could explain to the Royal Commission in 1904 the ways in which worship patterns had greatly changed, how even more true was that fifty years later! Consequently, the church gathered up its courage and was emboldened to set up, with the approval of its Convocations and the Church Assembly (an official body comprising both clergy and laity), a Liturgical Commission with a view to revising its services.[17] In preparation for

---

[14] D. GRAY, *Earth and Altar,* 35.
[15] R.C.D. JASPER, *The Development of the Anglican Liturgy,* 122–125.
[16] Ibid., 147–148.
[17] Ibid., 211ff.

this, the canon law of the church had been altered to allow the experimental use of new services. It was believed that in this way, by presenting Parliament with a service that had been widely "road tested" throughout the parishes of the land, that allegations of parochial unacceptability could be challenged and proved inaccurate.[18]

Thus the process of producing such experimental services started. The first ones were, to all intents and purposes, the rejected pastoral offices of 1927/28, which, I have said, had been widely used for the past forty years. This set of services was called Series One and was quickly followed by more original work in Series Two. Prominent in that book was a revision of the Eucharist, intended to furnish the needs of the large proportion of English parishes that had been influenced by the liturgical movement.[19]

The liturgical, or Parish Communion, movement in the Church of England is often called the Parish and People movement because of the influence of an organization set up to foster its principles, but its roots pre-date that organization. It had its origins in the nineteenth-century Christian Socialists, who saw the Eucharist as expressing theologically and liturgically what they were advocating politically. Here the people of God gathered at the Lord's own service on the Lord's own day, empowered at the Eucharist to go out into the world fed by the Corpus Christi to be the Corpus Christi, that is, the hands, feet, and eyes of the Lord in his world.[20] It was, they maintained, the working out in social and political terms of the incarnational principle, indeed being "an extension of the incarnation." It was a phrase, they discovered, that the seventeenth-century Anglican theologian Jeremy Taylor had coined.[21] It is true that the writings of the continental liturgical reformers came to have currency, and indeed influence, on the Parish Communion movement, but its origins do not lie in the exciting developments in Germany, Belgium, and France; it was a bonus to discover that in these places, as in England, there was this seed growing secretly.[22]

One of the agitations in the continental, Roman Catholic liturgical movement was for the use of the vernacular in the liturgy, and we

[18] Ibid., 244–245.

[19] D. GRAY, *Earth and Altar*, 3.

[20] Ibid., 226.

[21] *The Whole Works of the Rt. Revd. Jeremy Taylor DD, With a Life of the Author*, rev. C. P. EDEN, vol. 18, "The Worthy Communicant," 1, 2. 4, Library of Anglo-Catholic Theology (London: J. Moyes, 1854). Originally published 1660.

[22] D. GRAY, *Earth and Altar*, 226.

can recall such attempts to satisfy that need by the introduction of dialogue Masses and the like.[23] In the Church of England there was not the same problem about language, or at least it was a different problem. One of the fruits of the sixteenth/seventeenth-century reforms in England had been the introduction of the "vulgar tongue" into its liturgy, the use of the vocabulary of the sixteenth century. This is one of the essential ingredients of "Common Prayer."

Linguistically, the Series One services reflected the fact that in the 1920s the only real language concerns were the removal of outdated and antiquated words; and, remarkably, the Series Two services published as late as 1965 were still in mock Tudor language.[24] But the common prayer of England was about to change more radically than it had done for four hundred years, and a major, decisive factor in this was the result of ecumenical liturgical cooperation.

When on 4 December 1963 the secretary general of the Vatican Council announced, "Holy Father, the Constitution on the Liturgy is acceptable to two thousand, one hundred and forty-seven Fathers, with four against," it was, as said, "an emotional moment, a historical moment."[25] "The findings and experiences of the last sixty years form the underlying basis of the document and a window is opened onto a future the end of which no man can see," said Monsignor James Crichton.[26] Nevertheless, there was one consideration that lay in the immediate future and required urgent attention: the provision of vernacular liturgical texts, not least material in the English language. There were those who innocently believed that the task needed no more than a discreet adoption of the already available texts of the Book of Common Prayer, but they were swiftly disabused! What was required was liturgical texts in *modern* English.[27]

It was here in Rome, in mid-October 1963, that a meeting was called of what was known at first as the "English Liturgical Commit-

[23] J.R.K. FENWICK and B. D. SPINKS, *Worship in Transition: The Twentieth Century Liturgical Movement* (Edinburgh: T & T Clark, 1995) 28.

[24] THE CHURCH OF ENGLAND LITURGICAL COMMISSION, *Alternative Services: Second Series* (London: SPCK, 1965).

[25] A. BUGNINI, *The Reform of the Liturgy 1948–1975* (Collegeville: The Liturgical Press, 1990) 37.

[26] J. D. CRICHTON, *The Church's Worship: Considerations on the Liturgical Constitution of the Second Vatican Council* (London: Geoffrey Chapman, 1965) 3.

[27] P. BYRNE, "Pastoral Benefits of English in our Liturgy" in P. C. FINN and J. M. SCHELLMAN, eds., *Shaping English Liturgy* (Washington: The Pastoral Press, 1990) 283–284.

tee." It consisted of the appointed bishops and the two English-speaking *periti* of the Conciliar Commission on the Liturgy (Father Fred McManus and Father Godfrey Diekmann, O.S.B.)[28]—"a group born in casual conversation about the need to coordinate translation efforts for inevitable vernacular concessions," says Kathleen Hughes.[29] That was the beginning of the International Commission on English in the Liturgy (ICEL).

In my biography of Ronald Jasper,[30] I have, I trust, justified my earlier description of him as "one of the founding fathers of ecumenical liturgical cooperation." In the same month as the English Liturgical Committee met in Rome, at the invitation of the archbishop of Canterbury (Michael Ramsey, whom Jasper had previously convinced of the possibility of there being ecumenical liturgical cooperation), there was held in London the first meeting of the Joint Liturgical Group. Its members were drawn from the Church of Scotland, Methodists, Baptists, URC as well as the Church of England.[31] This was the first such body in the world.

The North American Consultation on Common Texts (CCT) was not formed until 1964. Jasper had written in a letter to the Archbishop of York: "Time, labor and energy might well be saved if only we would all stop doing our work in splendid isolation. To put it at its very crudest, if we worried a little more about what Scotland is actually doing and a little less about what we think Hippolytus did, we might get somewhere. If needs be, we can study Hippolytus together."[32] There were no Roman Catholic representatives at that first meeting in 1963, but this was quickly remedied as the pace of producing new texts increased.

By the winter of 1964, Jasper had succeeded Archbishop Coggan of York as chairman of the Church of England Liturgical Commission. Arising out of the ecumenical connections he was now building up, Jasper invited two lay Roman Catholics, who were members of the Liturgical Translation Committee for the Roman Catholic Church in England, to attend meetings of the Commission as observers. He, in turn, was invited by Bishop Gordon Wheeler to attend meetings of

[28] F. R. McMANUS, "ICEL: The First Years," in *Shaping English Liturgy*, 435.

[29] K. HUGHES, "Godfrey Diekmann 'Man Fully Alive'" in R. L. TUZIK, ed., *How Firm a Foundation: Leaders of the Liturgical Movement* (Chicago: Liturgy Training Publications, 1990).

[30] D. GRAY *Ronald Jasper: His Life, His Work and the ASB* (London: SPCK, 1997).

[31] Ibid., 77–78.

[32] Ibid., 77.

the Translation Committee. This Committee produced texts that were used in the British Isles until the first work of ICEL was available. The Committee was very proud of the fact that these earliest texts were ecumenical due to Jasper's contributions.[33]

In 1966, as a result of Michael Ramsey's historic visit to Rome, an invitation was issued for two observers from the Anglican Communion to attend the Consilium, which had been charged with the task of working out the practical consequences of the implementation of the Constitution on the Liturgy. The appointed observers were Dr. Jasper and Dr. Massey Shepherd from the ECUSA; also invited were Max Thurian from Taizé, Pastor Künneth of the LWF, and Raymond George (an English Methodist), representing WCC. "They were the first to arrive at the meetings, the last to leave the hall. They were always affable, polite, sparing of words, and ready to engage in a friendly way in any conversation that might be requested" said Archbishop Annibale Bugnini, the secretary of the Consilium.[34]

While in Rome for the Consilium, the English-speaking, non-Roman Catholic observers had been attending the meetings of ICEL. The work was of the greatest interest to all of them, not least Jasper, whose Church of England Commission had just surmounted what he chose to call the "thee/thou hump"; that is, a decision had been made to abandon the attempt to write liturgy for the twentieth-century in a Tudor pastiche.[35] But in this the Church of England realized that it should not go it alone. They were already committed to the work of JLG, were aware of the CCT (in the United States), and now there was this fascinating work being undertaken by ICEL. It was a Roman Catholic priest, Father Gerald Sigler, the secretary of ICEL, who was the main instigator of squaring this particular liturgical circle. He suggested that there should be a meeting of representatives of JLG, CCT, ICEL, and Consilium observers. Out of that came the International Consultation on English Texts (ICET).[36]

This body moved quickly and decisively and produced three editions of a booklet entitled *Prayers We Have in Common*.[37] Its contents

---

[33] Ibid., 80–81.

[34] A. BUGNINI, *The Reform of the Liturgy*, 200.

[35] R.C.D. JASPER, *The Development of the Anglican Liturgy*, 293.

[36] D. GRAY, *Ronald Jasper*, 85–88.

[37] INTERNATIONAL CONSULTATION ON ENGLISH TEXTS, *Prayers We Have in Common, Agreed Liturgical Texts* (Philadelphia: Fortress Press, 1970). Revised, enlarged ed. 1971; 2nd revised ed. 1975.

were immediately and widely adopted, the texts being incorporated into the revised prayer books of all English-speaking churches. The common texts were appropriated and included in the work of ICEL, used throughout the Anglican Communion, and in the Methodist, Presbyterian, and Reformed traditions worldwide. It was, and is, a major success story, one of the most practical and tangible fruits of the modern ecumenical movement.[38]

The production of common texts is a task commended in the 1993 Ecumenical Directory, where it is stated that "Churches and ecclesiastical Communities whose members live within a culturally homogeneous area should draw up together, where possible, a text of the most important Christian Prayers." It goes on to list the Lord's Prayer, the Apostles' and Nicean Creeds, as well as a Trinitarian doxology, and the Glory to God in the highest. These would be both for regular use by all the churches or at least on ecumenical occasions.[39] More recently the Holy Father in his encyclical *Ut Unum Sint* has said:

> Love is the great undercurrent which gives life and adds vigor to the movement towards unity. This love *finds its most complete expression in common prayer* (italics in original). . . .[40] Along the ecumenical path to unity, pride of place certainly belongs to *common prayer* (italics in original), the prayerful union of those who gather together around Christ himself.[41]

In 1980 that process of liturgical revision in the Church of England, which I have described at length, came to an end. Seventy-four years after those Letters of Business had been issued to the Convocations, The Alternative Service Book was authorized for use.[42] Some of us might believe that this long gestation period was providential and that the 1927/28 disasters, traumatic as they were at the time, proved to be a merciful deliverance. It certainly meant that the 1980 book now contained all those ecumenically agreed ICET texts. I would dare to call that infinitely providential. Yet it was never intended that

[38] D. GRAY, *Ronald Jasper*, 87.

[39] PONTIFICIUM CONSILIUM AD CHRISTIANORUM UNITATEM FOVENDAM, *Directory for the Application of Principles and Norms on Ecumenism* (Vatican City: Vatican Press, 1993) 187.

[40] JOHN PAUL II, *Ut Unum Sint: Encyclical Letter of the Holy Father on Commitment to Ecumenism* (Vatican City: Libreria Editrice Vaticana, 1995) 21.

[41] Ibid., 22.

[42] R.C.D. JASPER, *The Development of the Anglican Liturgy*, 360.

The Alternative Service Book remain unchanged for four hundred years, like the Book of Common Prayer, and so liturgical work has continued in the Church of England over the past twenty years. Equally unwilling to remain at a standstill were the ecumenical liturgical partners who had formed ICET. That body was reincarnated in 1983 as ELLC (the English Language Liturgical Consultation, avoiding the confusion between ICEL and ICET). This body was tasked with monitoring and assessing the acceptance of the ICET common texts and furthermore to look at the effect of the second great liturgical and linguistic challenge after the "thee/thou hump"—inclusive language. The result of our work was published as *Praying Together* in 1988.[43] Once again, this work has had wide acceptance. In the Church of England the texts, with only minor amendments, are part and parcel of our new *Common Worship* authorized in 2000. Other parts of the Anglican Communion have followed suit, as have recent Presbyterian and Reformed revisions. And, of course, the drafts of the revised Sacramentary have included the ecumenical texts, as affirmed and described by Mark Francis and Keith Pecklers.[44] Your ecumenical friends and liturgical colleagues hold their breath with you regarding the outcome of that particular saga.

It is also true that we shed tears together over our continuing divisions and long for a swift ending of them. In the meanwhile as we trudge, sometimes wearily, along the road that *must* lead to full communion and eucharistic fellowship—because it is our Lord's will, and nothing can finally thwart that—the existence of texts that we "have in common," that we can "pray together," is of the greatest possible encouragement. Think of two of those texts: we have a common form of the Creed, which means that we can profess our faith in common words, we can affirm our common belief in identical phrases. Secondly, at the very heart of the Eucharist, when we join with the angels and archangels and all the company of heaven; when we blend our voices with the holy doctors, martyrs, and confessors of our churches, the saints known to us and unknown, our loved ones de-

[43] ENGLISH LANGUAGE LITURGICAL CONSULTATION, *Praying Together: A Revision of "Prayers We Have in Common" (ICET 1975)* (Norwich: The Canterbury Press, 1988).

[44] G. W. LATHROP, "The Revised Sacramentary in Ecumenical Affirmation and Admonition," in M. R. FRANCIS and K. F. PECKLERS, eds., *Liturgy for the New Millennium: A Commentary on the Revised Sacramentary* (Collegeville: The Liturgical Press, 2000).

parted, at that timeless moment we sing in *common* words of adoration, humility, awesome praise, and wonder. That has got to be a matter of the greatest possible joy—and a sign of God's blessing upon us in this particular work. For remember, the earliest apostles broke bread together—and—had *all* things in common.[45]

[45] Acts 2:44-47.

Geoffrey Wainwright

The Ecumenical Scope of Methodist Liturgical Revision

In 1976, in the second of its five-yearly reports, the Joint Commission for Dialogue between the World Methodist Council and the Roman Catholic Church made the following observation:

> In recent years . . . there has been a notable recovery of eucharistic faith and practice among Methodists, with a growing sense that the fullness of Christian worship includes both word and sacrament. Similarly among Roman Catholics there has been a renewal in the theology and practice of the ministry of the word. These developments have resulted in a remarkable convergence, so that at no other time has the worshipping life of Methodists and Roman Catholics had so much in common.

Those sentences were written at a high moment in two of the great movements that marked the history of the churches in the twentieth century: the ecumenical movement and the liturgical movement. The ecumenical movement had begun an exciting new phase, with the official entrance of the Roman Catholic Church on the scene at the Second Vatican Council (1962–1965); since 1968 there had been twelve Catholic members in the Faith and Order Commission of the World Council of Churches, which was moving along in the process that would produce the Lima text "Baptism, Eucharist and Ministry" (BEM); and the Roman Catholic Church had started on a series of bilateral dialogues with the various world confessional families, in which the subject of the Eucharist in particular would figure rather prominently.

The liturgical movement was bearing fruit, not only in the major revisions in the Latin-rite service books that followed from the conciliar Constitution on the Sacred Liturgy but also in the composition of new books among the historic Protestant churches. In Methodism, for instance, the British church, after a decade of trial services, in 1975 had published The Methodist Service Book, while the "Alternate Rituals Committee" of the United Methodist Church in the USA in

35

1972 had issued a text for the Lord's Supper that would be the fore-runner of an entire new United Methodist Book of Worship (1992).

The linkage between the ecumenical movement and the liturgical movement finds a personal embodiment in my own mentor and dear friend, the late Raymond George (1912–1998). Raymond George was a member of the WCC's Faith and Order Commission, a WCC observer at the Consilium that revised the Roman books (he was a first-class Latinist), a full participant in the second, third, and fourth rounds of the dialogue between the World Methodist Council and the Roman Catholic Church (1972–1986), and the chief architect of the British *Methodist Service Book* of 1975.

In examining the ecumenical scope of Methodist liturgical revision over the past quarter-century, I will be looking particularly at the convergence that was noted in "the worshiping life of Methodists and Roman Catholics" in 1976, but setting this also within the broader framework of the Lima "convergence text" and especially its "Eucharist" section. By profession I am a dogmatician, and my own involvement in these matters has been more on the ecumenical side than on the directly liturgical. As a member of the Faith and Order Commission, I worked closely for several years on the *BEM* process and chaired the final redaction of the texts at Lima in 1982. Since 1983 I have been a member of the dialogue between the World Methodist Council and the Roman Catholic Church (and co-chairman since 1986).

My plan is as follows. In a first part I will look at the dogmatic underpinning evidenced in the Methodist-Catholic dialogue for the ritual pattern whereby the ministry of the word and the celebration of the sacrament figure as the two foci of a liturgical ellipse, such as *BEM* also favored.[1] In a second part I will look at the Methodist-Catholic dialogue and at Methodist responses to *BEM*, in order to see how Methodists interpret their own tradition of worship as a *terminus a quo* for ecumenical convergence in liturgical practice and in sacramental understanding at the present time—the *terminus ad quem*. Thirdly, I will look at some Methodist service books in order to find some concrete evidence of the theological convergence, although it must be remembered that Methodist Conferences typically "authorize," but do not mandate, the use of service-books. Here I will concentrate on the productions of the Methodist Church of Great Britain and the United Methodist Church based in the USA, since these are

[1] See G. WAINWRIGHT, "Word and Sacrament in the Churches' Responses to the Lima Text," in *One in Christ* 24, no. 4 (1988) 304–327.

historically the flagship churches in the Methodist tradition. Interwoven in this last section will be some observations on actual practice among Methodists on the Lord's Day.

I. WORD AND SACRAMENT

In the Methodist-Catholic dialogue, the dogmatic connection between word and sacrament came strongly to the fore in the Singapore Report of 1991 and the Rio de Janeiro Report of 1996. (The quinquennial reports have popularly been designated—particularly perhaps on the Methodist side—by the place and date at which they were presented to the World Methodist Council, simultaneously of course with their presentation to the Pontifical Council for Promoting Christian Unity.[2]) The Singapore Report of 1991 was entitled "The Apostolic Tradition," and the Rio de Janeiro Report of 1996, "The Word of Life: A Statement on Revelation and Faith."

In a fully Trinitarian, though pneumatologically oriented, paragraph (28), the Singapore Report declared:

> The Holy Spirit prepares the way for the preaching of the Word to those who do not believe, enabling them to respond in faith and to know the saving grace of God. The Spirit thus creates and maintains the oneness of the Church, bringing the many into unity and joining to their Head the members of the Body of Christ. Believers recognize one another as members of the Body, share in one ministry of worship and sacrament, and partake of the eucharistic meal, where, through and with Christ, in the Spirit, they offer a sacrifice of praise and thanksgiving to the Father.

Another paragraph in the same report (55), without omitting the Father and the Spirit, put the matter more in terms of Christ the Word and emphasized the connection between word and deed, not only in Christ's historic activity but also in the liturgical action of his church:

> In the Book of Acts, the apostles are described as "servants of the Word" (Acts 6:4; *cf.* Luke 1:2). This phrase holds a rich meaning, conveying all that is said in Scripture about God's action through his Word in creation and in his saving purpose in history. What he says, he does.

[2] The dialogue reports are officially published in the *Information Service* of the Pontifical Council for Promoting Christian Unity and in the *Proceedings* of the respective meetings of the World Methodist Council. They have been made available in such other places as the periodical *One in Christ* and in the two volumes of *Growth in Agreement*, published by the World Council of Churches (1984 and 2000).

What he does, makes him known to us. There is a solidarity between word and deed. This complete interdependence of word and deed in God's action for us culminates in the coming of the Person who, in his entire being, is the Word of God. "Service of the Word" implies the service of a living Person, whose words are always fruitful and whose deeds make him known. Supremely in Christ, words and actions are one. Through the Spirit these deeds and words culminate in the living presence of Jesus in us. It is in this context that the sermon and the sacrament must be understood. In preaching, the Word of God himself addresses us through the preacher: "Whoever hears you hears me" (Luke 10:16). In the Eucharist, our Lord's words, "This is My Body," "This is My Blood," convey both his meaning and the actual giving of himself.

Later in the same report (paragraph 67), the church is described, in an even more directly liturgical manner, as "the community of worship":

The Christian community continues to flourish by virtue of the common baptism and faith of its members. But it is also sustained and nurtured by the celebration of the memorial of the Lord, the service of thanksgiving in which it experiences, as the Spirit is invoked, the presence of the risen Christ. There the Word of God is heard in the Scriptures and the proclamation of the Gospel. Through the holy meal of the community, the faithful share "a foretaste of the heavenly banquet prepared for all mankind" (British *Methodist Service Book* 1975). As they receive the sacrament of his body and blood offered for them, they become the body through which the risen Lord is present on earth in the Holy Spirit (1 Cor 10:16-17). As they share his body and blood that have brought to the sinful world salvation and reconciliation, they proclaim today the past events of the Lord's death and resurrection, and as they do so they present to the world their confidence and hope that Christ who "has died and is risen" will also "come again."

In grounding its "Statement on Revelation and Faith" in "The Word of Life," the Rio Report of 1996 included "word and sacrament as the intelligible and tangible means of grace" among what could be drawn from its highly—and appropriately—incarnational interpretation of 1 John 1:1-3, the passage that the Commission had taken as its scriptural headline:

This sacred text starts from the particularity of the God of Israel's self-revelation in Christ: the divine Word, who was in the beginning with God and has led the history of the chosen people, has been made flesh in Jesus. That sheer self-gift of God is a word of life to humankind: God so loved the world that he gave his only Son, that whoever believes in him should not perish but have eternal life. In Christ, in his words, his deeds, his entire existence, God has been revealed in audible, visible, palpable form; God has been received by human ears, eyes, and hands. What the first believers have taken in, they then bear witness to and transmit, for the message spreads the offer of a life shared with God. The modes of the announcement will appropriately reflect, echo and hand on what was seen, heard and touched in the embodied manifestation of God in Jesus Christ. Accepted in faith, the words, signs and actions of the Gospel will become the means of communion with the one true God, Father, Son and Holy Spirit. The divine life into which the Spirit introduces believers will be a common life, as each transmits and receives what is always the gift of God.

Again, the more directly liturgical description comes later (paragraphs 117–118):

Communion with God and with one another is lived and experienced by word and sacrament in the worship of the Christian community. In praise and prayer we share the wonderful deeds of God as well as all human joy and the needs which arise among us. Listening to the Word of God brings us together as a community of those who look to God's creative and redemptive Word for all their needs.

The sacramental life of the Church expresses this communion with God and with one another in a profound way. The sacraments are at one and the same time effective signs of God's fellowship with his people and of the fellowship of the people of God with one another. Baptism and eucharist, the sacraments which are common to almost all Christian churches, show this most clearly. Those who are baptized receive a share in the death of the one Lord Jesus Christ and in the power of his resurrection; at the same time they are baptized into the one body, the body of Christ with its many members who suffer and rejoice together. At the table of the Lord's Supper the "cup of blessing" is "a participation in the blood of Christ" and "the bread which we break" is "a participation in the body of Christ," therefore "we who are many are one body, for we all partake of the one bread" (1 Cor 1:16-17). "Discerning the body" (1 Cor 11:29) means both to recognize the reality of our communion with Christ and to be responsible for the fellowship with brothers and sisters in the Lord.

It would hardly seem possible or necessary to find a more solid dogmatic basis than these passages from the Methodist-Catholic dialogue for the simple statements of *BEM*, whether normative or descriptive, concerning the Eucharist, that "its celebration continues as the central act of the Church's worship" (*Eucharist*, 1), and that it "always includes both word and sacrament" (*Eucharist,* 3). Leaving to Roman Catholics the matter of a "renewal in the theology and practice of the ministry of the word" among them, we may still ask: From where are Methodists coming if, for their part, the sense that "the fullness of Christian worship includes both word and sacrament" as an interlocking pair would represent a theological and practical recovery?

FROM THE WESLEYS AND BACK?

It will appear that in the context of ecumenical dialogue, Methodists view their own liturgical history as maintaining a proper emphasis on preaching while having suffered a decline in "eucharistic faith and practice." In the English church of the eighteenth century, early Methodism represented not only an evangelistic and an ethical but also a eucharistic revival. At a time when the typical parish observed the Lord's Supper three or four times a year, John Wesley himself celebrated or received the Holy Communion some seventy or ninety times annually, encouraging Methodists to press the Anglican clergy for more frequent celebrations in their local churches and using the Prayer Book permission for communion of the sick to gather family and neighbors for domestic participation.

Moreover, the collection of *Hymns on the Lord's Supper* published by the Wesley brothers provided a resource for instruction, meditation, and even singing (during the lengthy distribution of the elements at large Methodist gatherings).[3] Eucharistic practice among Methodists fell away in England after John Wesley's death and the gradual separation of Methodism from the Church of England, a tendency that may later have been aggravated by a reaction against the perceived "sacramentalist," and hence Romeward, direction of Anglicanism after the Oxford Movement. It may be doubted whether the eucharistic side of Wesleyanism ever really caught on in the ecclesiastical and cultural conditions of colonial North America and the independent United States.

Here, then, is how Methodists tell their story to the Roman Catholic partners in dialogue. Already in the Denver Report of 1971 it was "agreed" that

[3] First published in Bristol in 1745 under the joint names of JOHN and CHARLES WESLEY, The *Hymns on the Lord's Supper* can be found in *The Poetical Works of John and Charles Wesley*, ed. G. OSBORN, vol. 3 (London: Wesleyan-Methodist Conference Office, 1869) 181–342; in the study by J. E. RATTENBURY, *The Eucharistic Hymns of John and Charles Wesley* (London: Epworth Press, 1948); and in a facsimile edition by the Charles Wesley Society, with an introduction by me (Madison, N.J., 1995).

while traditional Methodist reverence for the preaching of the Gospel finds an echo in recent Roman Catholic theological and liturgical thinking, there are signs that Methodists on their part are re-capturing through the liturgical movement an appreciation of the sacraments such as is enshrined for example in Charles Wesley's eucharistic hymns (19).

Further, in the narrative style of the early reports (9):

> If a Methodist ideal was expressed in the phrase "a theology that can be sung," it was appreciated on the Roman Catholic side that the hymns of Charles Wesley, a rich source of Methodist spirituality, find echoes and recognition in the Catholic soul. This is not less true of the eucharistic hymns, which we saw as giving a basis and hope for discussion of doctrinal differences about the nature of the Real Presence and the sense of the "sacrificial" character of the Eucharist. Methodists on their side were candid in considering Roman Catholic questions on how far the Wesleys remain a decisive influence in contemporary Methodism.

The Denver Report recalled "the emphasis on frequent Communion of the Wesleys, which led to a eucharistic revival in the first part of the Methodist story, and of which the eucharistic hymns of Charles Wesley are a permanent legacy" (79). The conversations "included an appraisal of those hymns from a Catholic view" (79). Yet in "friendly honesty and candor," it "was not disguised . . . that the eucharistic devotion of the Wesleys and the hymns of Charles Wesley are no index at all to the place of Holy Communion in the life, thought and devotion of modern Methodists" (80).

The frankness continued in the Dublin Report of 1976, where it was admitted that "Methodist practice and theology often fall short of those of the Wesleys"; yet "the hymns and sermons of the Wesleys," which supply "the nearest equivalent" to "a comprehensive doctrinal statement on the eucharist," retain "their unique importance for Methodists" (51). There we find stated both the intervening historical lapse, from which recovery is needed, and one internal source, at least, for that "recovery of eucharistic faith and practice among Methodists" (51) that the Dublin Report noted to have begun: "Methodists do not celebrate the eucharist as frequently as Roman Catholics, although in many places the service is now regaining a central place" (71).

Coming from that past history, what is the point that Methodists have now reached in consensus with ecumenical partners with regard to the theological understanding of word and sacrament in worship? Official Methodist responses to *BEM*, especially from the British

church and from the United Methodist Church, display a considerable measure of agreement with the broad lines of eucharistic theology represented in the Lima text, while continuing to stress that the
exaltation of the sacrament must not occur at the expense of the word
read and preached, both as means of grace and as locus and vehicle
of Christ's presence.[4] Alluding to the fact that Methodist societies or
congregations have always far outnumbered the ordained pastors
available, the British response considers that "the history and structure of Methodism make weekly celebration [of the Eucharist] all but
impossible" and asks it to be recognized that "because the Methodist
tradition has always meant frequent services without communion,
Methodists have learnt to nourish themselves on that kind of worship and many would not now wish to see the balance altered in
favor of more frequent communion. They would argue that it is not
now a matter of administrative necessity, but rather that the infrequency of celebration actually heightens the sense of the eucharist's
importance": "A eucharist less frequently celebrated is not necessarily a eucharist less highly valued."

Several Methodist responses question the phrasing of *Eucharist,* 13:
"Christ's mode of presence in the eucharist is unique." Thus the East
Germans: "We see no qualitative difference between celebration of
the Lord's Supper and the proclaimed word"; and the West Germans:
"The Lord is not any more 'present' in the feast of the eucharist than
in prayer or the proclamation of his word." Again, the German responses show themselves uncomfortable with *BEM's* having made
"eucharist," not "the Lord's Supper," the predominant designation of
the sacrament: the emphasis is thereby "shifted from God's action in
Christ to the celebrating congregation and its 'activity' (praising
God)." Nevertheless, the West German response acknowledges that
"thanksgiving and praise are neglected in our eucharistic celebration."

---

[4] See *Churches Respond to BEM,* 6 volumes edited by M. THURIAN (Geneva:
WCC Publications, 1986–1988). Most Methodist responses are found in volume 2
(1986), in particular that of the United Methodist Church on pp. 177–199 and that
of the British Methodist Church on pp. 210–229; the responses of the German central conferences of the UMC are found in volume 4 (1987), pp. 167–172, 173–182. I
analyzed the whole range of responses from Methodist churches and united
churches with an originally Methodist component in "Methodism Through the
Lens of Lima," in K. B. WESTERFIELD TUCKER, ed., *The Sunday Service of the
Methodists: Twentieth-Century Worship in Worldwide Methodism—Studies in Honor of
James F. White* (Nashville: Abingdon/ Kingswood Books, 1996) 305–322.

Issued in the name of the Council of Bishops, the response of the United Methodist Church to *BEM* was one of the most detailed and affirmative responses made by any church to the Lima text. It showed a notable willingness to receive the ecumenical challenge to current practice, judging that Methodism would thereby be brought back to its own better beginnings:

> As we United Methodists regard the Church's practice through the ages, we can recognize now how our own usage has fallen short of the fullness of the holy communion. Like other Protestants, we have allowed the pulpit to obscure the altar. Now, without minimizing at all the preaching of God's word, we more clearly recognize the equivalent place of the sacrament.

For United Methodists, a "vigorous renewal of liturgical theology and practice in the ecumenical movement" has been conjoined with "a remarkable recovery" of the beginnings of their own tradition in the high eucharistic devotion, theology, and practice of the Wesleys; and, say the bishops, "we intend to urge our congregations to a more frequent, regular observance of the sacrament."

In welcoming the "convergence" in *BEM's* witness to Christ's presence, the United Methodist response acknowledges the work of "concentrated liturgical scholarship and ecumenical dialogue." It pinpoints the recovery of the significance of "two traditional Greek words: *anamnesis* and *epiklesis*":

> In terms of the congregation's appropriation of the reality of Christ's presence, the *anamnesis* (memorial, remembrance, representation) means that past, present, and future coincide in the sacramental event. All that Jesus Christ means in his person and his redemptive work is brought forth from history to our present experience, which is also a foretaste of the future fulfillment of God's unobstructed reign. And this presence is made to be a reality for us by the working of God's Spirit, whom we "call down" *(epiklesis)* by invocation, both upon the gifts and on the people.

"All this," the United Methodist response continues, "we find explicitly taught by John and Charles Wesley, who knew and respected the apostolic, patristic, and reformed faith of the Church." The United Methodist bishops make their own densely incarnational confession concerning the full service of word and sacrament: "God's effectual word is there revealed, proclaimed, heard, seen, and tasted."

From the Methodist-Roman Catholic dialogue, the Dublin Report of 1976 lists in paragraph 52 the following five affirmations as expressing "our common mind" about the Eucharist. Their Trinitarian and salvation-historical character bring them very close to the central section in *BEM* on "The Meaning of the Eucharist":

(a) The eucharist as a sacrament of the gospel is the fullest presentation of God's love in Jesus Christ by the power of the Holy Spirit; through it God meets us here and now in his forgiving and self-giving love.

(b) It is the commemoration of the sacrificial death and resurrection of Christ, which is the climax of the whole action of God in creation and salvation.

(c) It expresses our response—both personal and corporate—to God's initiative in a sacrifice not only of praise and thanksgiving, but also of the glad surrender of our lives to God and to his service. Thus we are united with Christ in his joyful and obedient self-offering to the Father and his victory over death.

(d) It is our response of faith and love whereby we receive [Christ's] gift of himself and are renewed as members of his body, that we may be the focus of his presence and the agents of his mission to the world.

(e) It is the pointing to and the anticipation of his final triumph and it is our vision of that hope and our sharing in that victory.

Concerning the historically controversial question of the mode of Christ's eucharistic presence, the Dublin Report of 1976 in paragraph 52 summarizes the points already agreed upon in the Denver Report:

Christ, in the fullness of his being, human and divine, is present in the eucharist; this presence does not depend on the experience of the communicant, but it is only by faith that we become aware of it. This is a distinctive mode of the presence of Christ; it is mediated through the sacred elements of bread and wine, which within the eucharist are efficacious signs of the body and blood of Christ.

The "chief point of difference" appears to lie between the Roman Catholic doctrine of "transubstantiation" and the Methodist view that "the bread and wine acquire an additional significance as effectual signs of the body and blood of Christ" but do not thereby "cease to be bread and wine" (59).[5]

---

[5] A proposal for the reconciling of two such views, made from the Catholic side, is found in T. NICHOLS, "Transubstantiation and Eucharistic Presence," *Pro Eccle-*

Concerning sacrifice, Dublin in paragraph 63 backs away somewhat from Denver's unguarded use (83) of "re-enactment." After a four-point agreement on the senses of sacrifice (65), Dublin details a remaining difference (66):

> When Methodists use sacrificial language it refers first to the sacrifice of Christ once-for-all, second to our pleading of that sacrifice here and now, third to our offering of the sacrifice of praise and thanksgiving, and fourth to our sacrifice of ourselves in union with Christ who offered himself to the Father.
>
> Roman Catholics can happily accept all these senses of the term, but they are also accustomed to speak of the sacrifice of the Mass as something which the church offers in all ages of her history. They see the eucharist not as another sacrifice adding something to Christ's once-for-all sacrifice, nor as a repetition of it, but as making present in a sacramental way the same sacrifice. For some Methodists such language would imply that Christ is still being sacrificed. Methodists prefer to say that Christ has offered one sacrifice for sins and now lives to make intercession for us, so that we in union with him can offer ourselves to the Father, making his sacrificial death our only plea.

That last phrase may in fact point toward a consensus. Elsewhere I have suggested that the unprecedentedly stark expression of the Roman Eucharistic Prayer IV—"offerimus tibi eius corpus et sanguinem"— might be benignly interpreted in terms of a hymn familiar to evangelical Protestants, A. M. Toplady's "Rock of Ages, cleft for me":

> Nothing in my hand I bring,
> Simply to Thy Cross I cling.[6]

After the Dublin Report of 1976, the Methodist-Catholic dialogue has not returned to the contentious issues connected with eucharistic presence and sacrifice. It may be a measure of the consensus already

---

sia 11, no. 1 (2002) 57–75. Sensitive to the ecumenical implications of his argument, the author invokes my presentation of the Eucharist as "an eschatological sign" in my book *Eucharist and Eschatology* (London:Epworth Press, 1971; 3rd ed. Akron, Ohio: OSL Publications, 2002).

[6] See G. WAINWRIGHT, *Doxology: The Praise of God in Worship, Doctrine and Life* (London/New York: Epworth Press/Oxford University Press, 1980) 271–274. The final phrase in the quotation from paragraph 66 of the Dublin Report—"making his sacrificial death our only plea"—echoes a line from another hymn familiar to Methodists: the hymn "Thou didst leave thy throne / And thy kingly crown," by Emily Elizabeth Steele Elliott (1836–1897), contains the line "Thy Cross is my only plea."

achieved—of all that it is both possible and necessary to say—that subsequent reports have spoken rather freely in agreed terms about the Eucharist as both word and sacrament. The clue may reside in the way in which, beginning with the Nairobi Report of 1986, the category of Mystery has been used to join the Incarnate Word himself, his church as his Body, and the various means of grace that sustain the church as it celebrates them.

The Nairobi Report states concisely, if still rather tentatively (10), that

> [t]he Mystery of the Word made flesh and the sacramental mystery of the eucharist point towards a view of the Church based upon the sacramental idea, i.e. the Church takes its shape from the Incarnation from which it originated and the eucharistic action by which its life is constantly being renewed;

and then in paragraph 14:

> The grace which comes through the sacraments is the grace of Christ, the visible image of the unseen God, in whom divine and human natures are united in one Person; the Church proclaims the action of the same Christ at work within us; and the individual sacraments likewise convey the reality of his action into our lives.

The Singapore Report of 1991 called Christ "the primary sacrament" (89). The Rio Report of 1996, structured to take into account the stated aim of the dialogue as "full communion in faith, mission, and sacramental life," made that designation of Christ, with appeal to 1 Timothy 3:16, the starting-point of its two-part exposition of the sacramental life, "the mystery of God in Christ and the Church" and "the sacraments and other means of grace":

> 95. . . . Having taken our humanity into his own person, the Son is both the sign of our salvation and the instrument by which it is achieved.
>
> 96. As the company of those who have been incorporated into Christ and nourished by the life-giving Holy Spirit (1 Cor 12:13), the Church may analogously be thought of in a sacramental way. . . .
>
> 97. In such an approach, the sacraments of the Church may be considered as particular instances of the divine Mystery being revealed and made operative in the lives of the faithful. Instituted by Christ and made effective by the Spirit, sacraments bring the Mystery home to those in whom God pleases to dwell.

98. The particular sacraments flow from the sacramental nature of God's self-communication to us in Christ. They are specific ways in which, by the power of the Holy Spirit, the Risen Jesus makes his saving presence and action effective in our midst. . . .

The Rio Report goes on to give, in paragraphs 102–103, a remarkably agreed upon and ecumenical account of the major sacraments, in which (finally!) a direct quotation from the Wesleys' *Hymns on the Lord's Supper* is made:

102. With the whole Christian tradition Methodists and Catholics find in the New Testament the evidence that baptism is the basic sacrament of the Gospel. They also agree that Jesus Christ instituted the eucharist as a holy meal, the memorial of his sacrifice. As the baptized partake of it, they share the sacrament of his body given for them and his blood shed for them; they present and plead his sacrifice before God the Father, and they receive the fruits of it in faith. Proclaiming, in his risen presence, the death of the Lord until he comes, the eucharistic assembly anticipates the final advent of Christ and enjoys a foretaste of the heavenly banquet prepared for all peoples. In the words of the Wesleys' Hymns on the Lord's Supper:

> He bids us eat and drink
> Imperishable food.
> He gives His flesh to be our meat,
> And bids us drink His blood.
> Whate'er the Almighty can
> To pardoned sinners give,
> The fulness of our God made man
> We here with Christ receive. [Hymn 81]

103. Meanwhile, as believers we seek to enact throughout our lives that which we celebrate in the sacraments. Thus the prayers of the Roman Missal ask that the sacraments received at Easter may "live forever in our minds and hearts," and that "we who have celebrated the Easter ceremonies may hold fast to them in life and conduct."

This entire perspective is substantially—and, in part, even verbally—endorsed in the Brighton Report of 2001, paragraphs 52–55, with an agreed and increased emphasis on "the need for graced, free and active participation in God's saving work" on the part of believers as "God's co-workers" (52).

Before leaving the Methodist-Catholic dialogue, we may notice one more constellation of themes which, like the others so far displayed, presages or reflects the liturgical compositions to which we shall at last come. The cluster brings together ecclesiology, missiology, and eschatology: church, mission, and kingdom. Already the Denver Report of 1971 mentioned "the whole eschatological and forward-looking element in the eucharist, with its implications in the life of the believer, of the whole Body of Christ, and of the Body of Christ in relation to the world" (81): "By partaking of the Body and Blood we become one with Christ, our Savior, and one with one another in a common dedication to the redemption of the world" (83). In a similar vein, the Dublin Report of 1976 concluded (73):

> In the eucharist we proclaim the Lord's death until he comes. We bring closer the day when God will be "all in all" (1 Cor 15:28). The eucharist makes God's kingdom to come in the world, in our churches, in ourselves. It builds up the church as the community of reconciliation dedicated to the service and salvation of mankind.

In describing "the community of worship," the Singapore Report of 1991 followed the already quoted paragraph 67 with these:

> 68. This experience of the presence of the Lord in the setting of worship attunes the hearts and minds of the faithful to all other aspects of his presence. They return to him the love they have received from him, when they serve the poor and when they struggle for social justice. In the sick and suffering they see the sufferings of Christ. In their own pains and sorrows endured for the sake of the gospel they share in the passion of Christ. In all this the faithful experience the wonderful exchange by which, in Christ and the Holy Spirit, all is common to all. And they present to God all that they have and all that they are as their own sacrifice of praise.

> 69. In the worshipping fellowship the community confesses Jesus Christ as Lord, shares the peace which Christ gives, and so anticipates the heavenly kingdom where the risen Christ fills all things to the glory of God the Father. The community of the faithful is thus the proclaiming, celebrating and serving community which gives glory to God in the name of all creatures. By its gatherings on the Lord's Day the community shapes the life of its members, helping them to make their weekly and daily tasks expressions of the royal priesthood of the believers gathered together under the high priesthood of the risen Lord. Thus the community provides for its members a pattern of life consecrated to God and directed towards fulfillment in the final manifestation of Christ.

The book that John Wesley sent across the Atlantic in 1784 was entitled *The Sunday Service of the Methodists in North America, with Other Occasional Services*. It was described by Wesley himself as "a liturgy little differing from that of the Church of England," that is, the 1662 Book of Common Prayer. Karen Westerfield Tucker, in her recent superb analytical history of American Methodist worship,[7] outlines the provisions for Sunday worship thus (pp. 6–7):

> Wesley provided orders of service for morning and evening prayer on the Lord's Day, and for the administration of the Lord's Supper that, following Prayer Book tradition, included the sermon as part of Ante-Communion. . . . A table of proper lessons to be read at Sunday morning and evening prayer, and a listing of proper collects, epistles and gospels to be read on Sundays and other particular days throughout the year were also included. . . . Ideally, morning prayer each Sunday was to be concluded with the service of the Lord's Supper as long as it was presided over by a properly ordained elder (presbyter), but the reality in the new church was that the number of available elders was significantly smaller than the communities in need of one, and, in point of fact, American Methodists were as unaccustomed as Anglicans of the time to weekly Eucharist.

In point of fact, Methodists on both sides of the Atlantic quickly adopted for their regular Sunday worship a much freer form of preaching service, with hymns, Scripture, sermon, and prayers. That Wesley had intended the use of hymns is clear from his sending of *A Collection of Psalms and Hymns for the Lord's Day*, along with the *Sunday Service*, from the *Collection of Hymns for the Use of the People Called Methodists*, which had been published already in 1780 and was to constitute the backbone of official Methodist hymnbooks, particularly in Britain, throughout the nineteenth century. In both Britain and America, the Lord's Supper itself became practically an "occasional service," with a monthly or even quarterly observance of the sacrament. Whereas the "preaching service" abandoned Wesley's pattern for Sundays, the liturgy for the sacrament, when celebrated, remained recognizably close to Wesley's sacramental order in the principal Methodist bodies.

---

[7] K. WESTERFIELD TUCKER, *American Methodist Worship* (New York: Oxford University Press, 2001).

In their liturgical revisions of the final third of the twentieth century, both the Methodist Church of Great Britain and the United Methodist Church returned in broadest structural terms to Wesley's combination of word and sacrament, while almost abandoning the linguistic inheritance of the Cranmerian-Wesleyan Prayer Book.

In its "general directions" to "The Sunday Service," the British Methodist Service Book of 1975 declared that "[t]he worship of the Church is the offering of praise and prayer in which God's Word is read and preached, and in its fullness it includes the Lord's Supper, or Holy Communion." After "The Preparation" (hymn; confession of sins and declaration of forgiveness; collect of the day; hymn or "Glory to God in the highest") comes "The Ministry of the Word": the Old Testament Lesson or the Epistle or both; hymn; the Gospel; the Sermon; the Intercessions; the Lord's Prayer; the first dismissal and blessing ("those who leave do so now"). Then comes "The Lord's Supper": the Peace; the Nicene Creed; the Setting of the Table; the Thanksgiving (invariable); the Breaking of the Bread; the Sharing of the Bread and Wine; the Final Prayers (post-communion; hymn; blessing; dismissal).

The next pages of the book outline an order for "The Sunday Service without the Lord's Supper," with the explanation that "[i]n many churches of the Reformation tradition it has been the custom, once a Sunday, for the shape of the service to reflect that of the Lord's Supper." With hymns to be inserted *ad libitum,* the suggested order goes: "The Preparation" (adoration; confession of sin, and assurance of God's forgiveness); "The Ministry of the Word" (Scriptures; sermon; a historic creed); "The Response" (thanksgiving; intercession; self-dedication; the Lord's Prayer; "blessing and commissioning for the service of God in the world"). This last, non-sacramental outline represents what Raymond George, with a twist on the "missa sicca," used to call a "dry eucharist."

On the grounds of "many requests for the provision of a wider range of services and other worship material," the British Methodist Conference in 1999 authorized the publication of a new Methodist Worship Book, in which the services "are the fruit of a long process of drafting and revision" and "take account of recent liturgical and ecumenical developments throughout the world as well as distinctively Methodist traditions of worship" (p. vii). There is now no explicit attempt to give a eucharistic shape to the principal Sunday service, although it is declared that "Holy Communion, or the Lord's

Supper," without specification of its timing, "is the central act of Christian worship, in which the Church responds to our Lord's command, 'Do this in remembrance of me.'" The 1999 book sets out full eucharistic orders and complete texts—structurally similar, though thematically varied—for Advent, for Christmas and Epiphany, for Ash Wednesday or the First Sunday in Lent, for Lent and Passiontide, for the Easter Season (including Ascensiontide), for the Day of Pentecost (and times of renewal in the life of the church), and for "Ordinary Seasons" (three services).

The 1999 Methodist Worship Book offers of the Eucharist, first (p. 114), a doctrinal account (with many echoes of *BEM*), and then (pp. 114–115), a ritual account (indebted to the classic work of Dom Gregory Dix):

> Many of the themes of John and Charles Wesley's *Hymns on the Lord's Supper* (1745) are reflected in present-day ecumenical understanding of this sacrament. In communion with the people of God in heaven and on earth, we give thanks for God's mighty acts in creation and redemption, represented supremely in the life, death and resurrection of Jesus Christ. In this means of grace, the Church joyfully celebrates the presence of Christ in its midst, calls to mind his sacrifice and, in the power of the Holy Spirit, is united with him as the Body of Christ. At the Lord's table, Christ's disciples share bread and wine, the tokens of his dying love and the food for their earthly pilgrimage, which are also a foretaste of the heavenly banquet, prepared for all people. Those who gather around the table of the Lord are empowered for mission: apostles, sent out in the power of the Spirit, to live and work to God's praise and glory. . . .
>
> The services of *Holy Communion* in this book are set out, after the initial "The Gathering of the People of God," under the two historic headings, "The Ministry of the Word" and "The Lord's Supper." The hinge point between the two is normally the sharing of the Peace. The shape of the Lord's Supper follows the record in scripture of Jesus' characteristic sharing with his disciples, especially after [sic] the final meal on the night before the crucifixion. His seven actions with the bread and wine (four with the bread, three with the wine) were taken up in the Church's tradition as a fourfold shape: Taking, Giving Thanks, Breaking and Sharing. In the Great Thanksgiving, the service of praise offered by God's people on earth is joined with the praises of the heavenly host, praising God, Father, Son and Holy Spirit. This Eucharistic Prayer (the word "Eucharist," derived from a Greek word which means "Thanksgiving," is increasingly accepted by Christians of all

traditions as one of the names for this sacrament) is Trinitarian both in its structure and in its focus.

In the United Methodist Church, the international and ecumenical liturgical movement first showed its influence in the "alternate text" of 1972 for *The Lord's Supper,* which eventually sold two and a half million copies in pamphlet form.[8] The order ran as follows: greeting; hymn of praise; confession and pardon; act of praise (for instance, the Gloria in excelsis); an epicletic prayer for illumination (a feature borrowed from the Reformed tradition); Scripture lessons, interspersed with psalms, canticles, anthems,or hymns; sermon; affirmation of faith; prayer for others; invitation and peace; the offering; the great prayer of thanksgiving; the breaking of the bread and the taking of the cup; the giving; prayer after receiving; hymn or doxological stanza; dismissal and benediction.

The Eucharistic Prayer was marked by several interesting features: first, the Preface focused on the events and themes recorded in the Old Testament (creation, fall, election, exodus, covenant, prophecy), a pattern that continued into later United Methodist anaphoras and seems indebted to the liturgy of *Apostolic Constitutions VIII.* Second, the post-Sanctus commemoration of the earthly ministry of Christ included his practice of table-fellowship with sinners, a feature much emphasized by gospel scholars of the mid-twentieth century and subsequently expanded to "he healed the sick, fed the hungry, and ate with sinners." Third, the words of institution were linked to the ensuing anamnesis-oblation by this sentence: "When we eat this bread and drink this cup, we experience anew the presence of the Lord Jesus Christ and look forward to his coming in final victory." The sentence was later dropped, perhaps because it did not fit into the rhetorical form of a prayer addressed to God, but it made a brave attempt to set, in a characteristically Methodist style, the present experience of believers in relation to the mighty acts of God in Christ and the sacramental gift of their benefits through the liturgical celebration. Subsequently omitted, too, was the neat allusion to the Emmaus story: "Help us know in the breaking of this bread. . . ." The

[8] See TUCKER, *American Methodist Worship,* 139–142. For accounts by the principal author of the 1972 text, see J. F. WHITE, "Making Changes in United Methodist Euchology," *Worship* 57, no. 4 (1983) 333–344; and *idem,* "United Methodist Eucharistic Prayers: 1965–1985," in F. C. SENN, ed., *New Eucharistic Prayers: An Ecumenical Study of Their Development and Structure* (New York: Paulist Press, 1987) 80–95.

"alternate text" went, in fact, through several revisions, while other "supplemental worship resources" included some two dozen and more seasonal and occasional Eucharistic Prayers, in various literary and historic styles, published in *At the Lord's Table* (1981) and *Holy Communion* (1987). The overall rationale for the recommended "basic pattern of Sunday worship" was stated in the significantly entitled *Word and Table* (1976).

The complete United Methodist Book of Worship, authorized by the General Conference in 1992, provides a standard "Service of Word and Table I," while allowing for both a more flexibly arranged service of the word (which may take a quasi-eucharistic shape, even without the Holy Communion) and for "words of the pastor's own composition or selection" at points in the Great Thanksgiving of the Lord's Supper. Fully formulated Great Thanksgivings are supplied for use in Advent; at Christmas; at "New Year, Epiphany, Baptism of the Lord, or Covenant Reaffirmation"; "Early in Lent"; "Later in Lent"; on Holy Thursday Evening; at Easter; at Pentecost; "the Season after Pentecost (Ordinary Time, or Kingdomtide)"; on "World Communion Sunday"; at "All Saints and Memorial Occasions"; on "Thanksgiving Day, or for the Gift of Food"; and "For General Use." The 1992 book also contains, allegedly at the insistence of African-American members of the United Methodist Church, a "Service of Word and Table IV," which retains large portions of the Cranmerian-Wesleyan text, with the units now rearranged to match better the "liturgical-movement" order of Word and Table. (The British Methodist Service Book of 1975 had retained, in second place, the latest previous version of the Cranmerian-Wesleyan service from the 1936 Book of Offices, but this disappeared from the 1999 Methodist Worship Book.)

Concerning current texts and practices at Word and Table in the United Methodist Church and the Methodist Church of Great Britain, further ecumenically important matters have to do with lectionaries, hymnology, the structure of Eucharistic Prayers, the words of distribution, the nature of the elements, the disposal of remains, presidency at the sacrament, and the conditions of admission to it.

Lectionaries. The United Methodist Book of Worship (UMBW) prints a Lectionary "based on the Revised Common Lectionary [1992], with selections made on the basis of United Methodist needs and traditions." The British Methodist Worship Book (MWB) states that "the lectionary for the Principal Service is derived from the ecumenical

Revised Common Lectionary, which has won widespread acceptance in most English-speaking countries." For the British Church, this represented a shift from the Methodist Service Book of 1975, which had employed a two-year Lectionary that itself had been ecumenically generated in the British Isles by the Joint Liturgical Group. The three-year Revised Common Lectionary is an adaptation of the *Ordo Lectionum* for Sundays in the post-Vatican II Roman Missal, displaying particularly a broader understanding of typology in the readings from the Old Testament. It would be an ecumenical move on the part of the Roman authorities to adopt the Revised Common Lectionary; and it would not be the first time in liturgical history that the Roman church had taken back to itself a ritual feature that had undergone improvement in the provinces. Meanwhile, the considerable agreement that already exists in this area allows pastors to work together at the preparation of sermons in their local ecumenical associations. Among Methodists, the use of lectionaries by the preachers has certainly increased over the past couple of generations.

Hymnology. Throughout Methodist history, the successive hymnals used have increased in ecumenical range, though at a proportionate loss of texts from the Wesleys' pens. The British Methodist Hymns and Psalms (1983) contains some 170 Wesleyan hymns out of a total of 823, and the United Methodist Hymnal (1989) around 60 Wesleyan texts out of a total of 678 (some being printed as "poems" rather than set to music). Of the 166 texts in the Wesleyan *Hymns on the Lord's Supper* (many of them admittedly unsuitable for direct liturgical use), the current British book contains sixteen, but the American book a mere two ("O the depth of love divine" and "O thou who this mysterious bread"), to which the supplementary *The Faith We Sing* (2000) added "Victim divine, thy grace we claim." There is clearly a problem when the doctrinally and ecumenically important hymns of the Wesleys have to contend with contemporary literary and cultural tendencies that disfavor rhyme, meter, and complex scriptural allusion.[9]

The structure of Eucharistic Prayers. Liturgical composition among both the British and the United Methodists has broadly favored the Antiochene or West Syrian type of anaphora, which has dominated eucharistic revision in the historic churches of the West in the second

---

[9] See J. R. WATSON, *The English Hymn: A Critical and Historical Study* (Oxford: Oxford University Press, 1999).

half of the twentieth century. The pattern was outlined thus in a classic article by W. J. Grisbrooke: (1) introductory dialogue; (2) preface or (first part of the) thanksgiving; (3) Sanctus; a transition that may either (4) continue the thanksgiving, or (5) take the form of a preliminary epiclesis, if not both; (6) narrative of the institution; (7) anamnesis-oblation; (8) epiclesis; (9) intercessions; (10) concluding doxology and Amen.[10]

Some features of the United Methodist prayers have already been noted, but otherwise the fixed British "Thanksgiving" of 1975, composed in the concise and chaste style of Raymond George, may be taken as rather typical. After the opening dialogue, it runs:

> Father, all-powerful and ever-living God,
> it is indeed right, it is our joy and our salvation,
> always and everywhere to give you thanks and praise
> through Jesus Christ your Son our Lord.
> You created all things and made us in your own image
> When we had fallen into sin, you gave your only Son to be our Saviour.
> He shared our human nature, and died on the cross.
> You raised him from the dead, and exalted him to your right hand in
>   glory,
> where he lives for ever to pray for us.
> Through him you have sent your holy and life-giving Spirit
> and made us your people, a royal priesthood, to stand before you
> to proclaim your glory and celebrate your mighty acts.
> And so with all the company of heaven
> we join in the unending hymn of praise:
> **Holy, holy, holy Lord,**
> **God of power and might,**
> **heaven and earth are full of your glory.**
> **Hosanna in the highest.**
> **Blessed is he who comes in the name of the Lord.**
> **Hosanna in the highest.**
> We praise you, Lord God, King of the universe,
> through our Lord Jesus Christ,
> who, on the night in which he was betrayed,
> took bread, gave thanks, broke it,
> and gave it to his disciples, saying,
> "Take this and eat it. This is my body given for you.
> Do this in remembrance of me."

[10] W. J. GRISBROOKE, "Anaphora," in J. G. Davies, ed., *A Dictionary of Liturgy and Worship* (London/New York: SCM Press/Macmillan, 1972) 10–17.

In the same way, after supper,
he took the cup, gave thanks, and gave it to them, saying,
"Drink from it all of you.
This is my blood of the new covenant,
poured out for you and for many, for the forgiveness of sins.
Do this, whenever you drink it, in remembrance of me."
Christ has died. Christ is risen. Christ will come again.
Therefore, Father, as he has commanded us,
we do this in remembrance of him,
and we ask you to accept our sacrifice of praise and thanksgiving.
Grant that by the power of the Holy Spirit
we who receive your gifts of bread and wine
may share in the body and blood of Christ.
Make us one body with him.
Accept us as we offer ourselves to be a living sacrifice,
and bring us with the whole creation to your heavenly kingdom.
We ask this through your Son, Jesus Christ our Lord.
Through him, with him, in him,
in the unity of the Holy Spirit,
all honour and glory be given to you, almighty Father,
from all who dwell on earth and in heaven
throughout all ages. Amen.

Unlike the Roman Eucharistic Prayers II, III, and IV, Methodist Eucharistic Prayers do not contain a preliminary consecratory epiclesis before the narrative of the institution. Nor do they contain more than a hint of intercession, since that has been taken care of by the prayers of the people toward the end of the ministry of the word. The American prayers, in the manner of the Wesleyan eucharistic hymns, make a closer link than the British between the self-offering of Christ and the self-oblation of the believers; and, in a new development, they include among the fruits of communion an active participation in Christ's redemptive mission and ministry in the world. Thus, from the Thanksgiving in "A Service of Word and Table I," directly after the recounting of the institution:

> . . . And so, in remembrance of these your mighty acts in Jesus Christ,
> we offer ourselves in praise and thanksgiving
> as a holy and living sacrifice,
> in union with Christ's offering for us,
> as we proclaim the mystery of faith.
> **Christ has died; Christ is risen; Christ will come again.**
> Pour out your Holy Spirit on us gathered here,

and on these gifts of bread and wine.
Make them be for us the body and blood of Christ,
that we may be for the world the body of Christ,
redeemed by his blood.
By your Spirit make us one with Christ,
one with each other,
and one in ministry to all the world,
until Christ comes in final victory
and we feast at his heavenly banquet. . . .

For the principal celebration of the Eucharist at the meeting of the
World Methodist Council and Conference at Brighton, England, in
2001, Karen Westerfield Tucker and I composed a classically structured Eucharistic Prayer from phrases and echoes of Wesleyan hymns,
both from the *Hymns on the Lord's Supper* and from other collections,
allowing for congregational sections of the prayer to be sung.[11]

The words of distribution. The British book of 1975 retained as general "words of invitation" a form close to the old words of distribution: "Draw near with faith. Receive the body of our Lord Jesus
Christ, which was given for you, and his blood, which was shed for
you; and feed on him in your hearts by faith with thanksgiving"; and
for the individual communicant, either the Prayer Book words of distribution or simply "The body of Christ given for you," "The blood
of Christ shed for you." The book of 1999 proposes "words such as
the following . . . during distribution": "The body of Christ given for
you / The blood of Christ shed for you," or "The body / blood of
Christ keep you in eternal life." The *United Methodist Book of Worship*
has "these or other words being exchanged": "The body / blood of
Christ, given for you. Amen."

The nature of the elements. The British MWB stipulates "the juice of
the grape," while the UMBW declares:

> Although the historic and ecumenical Christian practice has been to
> use wine, the use of unfermented grape juice by The United Methodist
> Church and its predecessors since the late nineteenth century expresses
> pastoral concern for recovering alcoholics, enables the participation of

[11] See G. WAINWRIGHT and K. WESTERFIELD TUCKER, "A Wesleyan Anaphora," in M. KLÖCKENER and A. JOIN-LAMBERT, eds., *Liturgia et Unitas: In hon-
orem Bruno Bürki* (Freiburg, Switzerland: Universitätsverlag/Geneva: Labor et
Fides, 2001) 145–159.

children and youth, and supports the church's witness of abstinence (p. 28).

The UMBW states that "[t]he bread may be either leavened or unleavened" and contemplates either "a large uncut loaf of bread" or "wafers" or "bread cubes"; and either a "chalice" or "individual cups." In the United Methodist Church in the United States, communion by intinction has become a widespread practice in the past two decades.

Conditions of admission. The British MWB declares:

> One of the keynotes of the Methodist revival was John Wesley's emphasis on "The Duty of Constant Communion" and it is still a duty and privilege of members of the Methodist Church to share in this sacrament. The Methodist Conference has encouraged local churches to admit baptized children to communion. Those who are communicants and belong to other Churches whose discipline so permits are also welcome as communicants in the Methodist Church" (p. 114).

With some foreshortening of historical perspective, the UMBW declares that "we have no tradition of refusing any who present themselves desiring to receive" (p. 29).

Presidency at the Lord's table. In both the British and the United Methodist Church, presidency at the Lord's table is normally assured by ordained presbyters; but, in cases of sacramental deprivation, the Conferences may authorize lay preachers to preside, by name, for a specified period of time, and for specific places. These were the cases envisaged when the United Methodist bishops, in their response to BEM, wrote that "in unique situations we allow unordained pastors to preside at the holy communion, while most churches do not. How can our practice be justified, or can it not?"

The disposal of bread and wine remaining from the sacrament. The British MWB instructs that "[w]hat remains of the elements should be reverently consumed, or otherwise reverently disposed of, at the end of the service" (p. 116). The UMBW waxes more pastoral and indeed poetic:

> What is done with the remaining bread and wine should express our stewardship of God's gifts and our respect for the holy purpose they have served.

1) They may set aside for distribution to the sick and others wishing to commune or unable to attend. . . .

2) They may be reverently consumed by the pastor and others. . . .

3) They may be returned to the earth; that is, the bread may be buried or scattered on the ground, and the wine may be reverently poured out upon the ground—a biblical gesture of worship (2 Samuel 23:16) and an ecological symbol today.

CONCLUSION

While there clearly remain important differences between Methodist and Catholic practice, which may signify differences in understanding and even doctrine, it may fairly be concluded that at the levels of theological dialogue and officially recommended rites, Methodism has been considerably affected by the ecumenical and liturgical movements of the twentieth century, with indeed something of a recovery of the intertwined evaluation of word and sacrament that marked its own early history under Wesleyan auspices. Preaching and the singing of hymns, the components in distinctively Methodist services, are fitted into a ritual structure, and there are signs of a richer eucharistic faith that, in the forms of convergent doctrinal statements and some homegrown anaphoras, matches the *Hymns on the Lord's Supper,* even where those classic texts from the eighteenth-century revival remain underused. In their response to *BEM,* however, the United Methodist bishops issued a salutary warning that might also be heeded by others in the Methodist family: "We United Methodists need to recover the belief that the holy communion is central in our worship and life together before some other Churches will honor our statements of theological accord." In the year 2000, the General Conference of the United Methodist Church commissioned an official study of the Holy Communion that would report on current theology and practice and make recommendations to the General Conference in 2004.

Horace T. Allen, Jr.

Common Lectionary and Protestant Hymnody: Unity at the Table of the Word— Liturgical and Ecumenical Bookends

My gratitude to the Centro Pro Unione for this invitation to me, as a Presbyterian minister, to speak here on the feast of the Ascension. Who would have thought it? Your hospitality has been genuine and generous. Perhaps I might imitate another Calvinist, Professor Karl Barth, late of Basel, in describing this occasion as an *ad limina* visit to this ancient See.

I am subtitling my remarks on Lectionary and hymnody "Ecumenical and Liturgical Bookends." I think that probably most of us have too many books, many of which we have not read and many of which we know we should read. And there they are. The only thing to do with them is to put bookends up to keep them from falling down. And that, in a sense, is my framework for this essay: "Ecumenical and Liturgical Bookends."

There are two of them: (1) *Ordo Lectionum Missae* 1969 and (2) *Ut Unum Sint*, 25 May, the Solemnity of the Ascension, 1995 (then as today). Not bad dates, spanning about twenty-five years. *Ordo Lectionum Missae, Ut Unum Sint*.

Between the bookends, in accordance with Father Jim Puglisi's invitation, I would like to place some other books, namely hymnals, as being in effect Protestant prayer books. That is to say: although the Episcopal Church has its *Book of Common Prayer* and the Lutherans have their *Lutheran Book of Worship*, the rest of us, until now, pretty much have depended on hymnbooks: those poems that we sing, and that we sing so often that we know them by heart. In most services that I attend, I don't even have to open a hymnbook—I know them. And it is much more fun singing them with the book closed than open, because you're not reading something, you're expressing something.

So, the bookends *Ordo Lectionum Missae* 1969 and *Ut Unum Sint*, 1995, and in between the bookends, the hymnals. I remind you that

61

for Protestants, hymnals are simply extended psalters. That is to say, even we Protestants moved beyond the metrical psalter only when Isaac Watts (seventeenth century) and the Wesleys (eighteenth century) appeared on the scene. And even Watts and the Wesleys understood that they were simply carrying forward English-speaking psalmody. Now fast forward to *Ordo Lectionum Missae* 1969.

ORDO LECTIONUM MISSAE

As you know, Vatican II's Constitution on the Sacred Liturgy (paragraph 35) ordered that "[I]n sacred celebrations there is to be a reading of holy Scripture, and it is to be more varied and suitable." In the *Coetus* that followed the Council to work on that project, it was Godfrey Diekmann, O.S.B., of blessed memory, who as early as the conciliar years urged "contact with Protestants, especially in three-year cycle of readings,"[1] and then in the postconciliar *Coetus* he "contributed sensitivity to the ecumenical ramifications of Lectionary preparation."[2]

But, of course, as is always the case with prophets, they knew more than they knew. And, in fact, it became the work of that *Coetus* that produced the *Ordo Lectionum Missae* in 1969 to instruct Protestantism on how to read the Scriptures at public worship! That has been my own enterprise and vocation now for thirty years or so: to instruct Protestantism how to read the Sriptures at the Lord's Day worship according to the Roman Lectionary of 1969.

Thus, as was stated in a rather definitive Roman document issued by the Pontifical Commission on Biblical Studies, "the Lectionary, issued at the direction of the Council's *Sacrosanctum Concilium,* is meant to allow for a reading of sacred scripture that is more abundant, more varied, and more suitable." Further, the Commission stated that "in its present state, it only partially fulfills this goal. Nevertheless, even as it stands, it has had positive ecumenical results."

Quite right!

So the first of my "bookends" is *Ordo Lectionum Missae,* which, in a kind of fascinating way, gave breadth to a whole process of ecumenical connections, liturgically speaking. If I may say, even as a Calvinist, I cannot imagine a more important ecumenical conversation than a liturgical, biblical one.

---

[1] K. HUGHES, *The Monk's Tale: A Biography of Godfrey Diekmann, OSB* (Collegeville: The Liturgical Press, 1991) 232.

[2] Ibid., 252.

The process was as follows. As a result of *Sacrosanctum Concilium*, there was formed a "mixed commission," the International Commission on English in the Liturgy [ICEL], which in turn resulted in a North American ecumenical group, the Consultation on Common Texts [CCT]. At the international level, there was formed the International Consultation on English Texts [ICET], which ICEL also participated in. At a later date, this group was succeeded by the English Language Liturgical Consultation [ELLC], which I co-chaired for eight years. The work of these ecumenical bodies, (including in North America the Bishops' Committee on the Liturgy from both Canada and the United States), as well as ICEL, were able to produce a whole series of agreed upon liturgical texts and finally an ecumenical version of the Roman Lectionary.

All this was largely in place by 1992. In 1994, therefore, I, as co-chair of the Steering Committee of the ELLC came to this city and See, with the Steering Committee, to request that the Sacred Congregation for Divine Worship and the Sacraments provide some faculties for experimental Roman use of the Lectionary system that we had produced, known as the Revised Common Lectionary, which departed from the Roman Lectionary in the Old Testament pericopes for Ordinary Time after Pentecost. Otherwise it followed the Roman pattern quite closely. I said on that occasion:

> We come to you this day of Easter, praying that you might be able, in your wisdom, to provide a way or ways for the experimental use by interested Roman Catholic communities and Conferences of Bishops, of this attempt of ours, to bring Christians of all languages and continents into an *audible* unity around the table of the Word of God, the church's primary catechesis and dogmatic foundation. We long for the continued official participation of the Holy See in this most universal *and* local experience of unity. It is not that we are proposing *revision* of either the Roman *Ordo '69* or of our own *Revised Common Lectionary '92*, but rather that you might make possible faculties for trial use of this parallel and derivative *Ordo* of ours as a means of dialogue (the importance of which His Eminence, your Prefect, has just noted) and convergence concerning this most vital moment in our common liturgies for the Lord's Day, that is, the Ministry of the Word.

I have sadly to report that we have yet to hear anything by way of response from the Congregation. Nevertheless, none of us ever thought that it might be a mere 450 years after the unhappy divisions of the sixteenth century that the Roman Catholic Church would, in fact, be instructing Protestantism how to read the Bible in public worship. Throughout the world, I can testify, priests, pastors, and ministers are meeting every week to develop their Sunday homilies. Just last year when I preached in the First Presbyterian Church in Brookline, Massachusetts, on the text "that they all may be one," I was able to say to my people, "Today, you could go across the street to St. Mary's of the Assumption, and you would hear the same scriptural texts being read as we ourselves have just done." And I could see on the faces of the Calvinist faithful surprise and joy.

I have heard married couples, Protestant and Catholic, say, "Yes, we go to early Mass and receive Eucharist, and then we go to the Protestant service and usually do not receive Eucharist but we do hear the same Word."

That's where we've come via *Ordo Lectionum Missae*.

ICEL was able to encourage the formation of CCT, ICET, and then later ELLC in order to create an international body to enter into dialogue with the Roman Catholic Church. Who knows how much money ICEL poured into CCT and ELLC through the work by people like John Page, Brother Peter Finn, Jim Schellmann, Fred McManus. It hurts even to say these names because of the depths of the commitment and of the achievement of those thirty years—and its present repudiation of all that.

That's one bookend.

UT UNUM SINT

Now let us go to another bookend: *Ut Unum Sint*, authored, we are assured, by His Holiness Pope John Paul II.

> Significant progress in ecumenical cooperation has also been made in another area, that of the Word of God. [*Can you imagine how glad this Calvinist felt at hearing that? And this:*]
>
> I am thinking above all of the importance for the different language groups of ecumenical translations of the Bible. [*Ah . . . translations . . . and what battles have now broken out at this point!*] Following the promulgation by the Second Vatican Council of the Constitution *Dei Verbum*, the Catholic Church could not fail to welcome this development.[3]

---

[3] Cf. SECRETARIAT FOR PROMOTING CHRISTIAN UNITY and the EXECUTIVE COMMITTEE OF THE UNITED BIBLE SOCIETIES, "Guiding Principles for Interconfessional Cooperation in Translating the Bible" (1968). This was revised and then published by the Secretariat for Promoting Christian Unity, "Guidelines

These translations, prepared by experts, generally offer a solid basis for the prayer and pastoral activity of all Christ's followers. Anyone who recalls how heavily debates about Scripture influenced divisions, especially in the West, can appreciate this significant step forward which these common translations represent. (*UUS*, 44)

Corresponding to the liturgical renewal carried out by the Catholic Church, certain other Ecclesial Communities have made efforts to renew their worship. *[Right. And not without pain, I might say.]* Some, on the basis of a recommendation expressed at the ecumenical level,[4] have abandoned the custom *[I can't tell you how unusual that expression sounds to my Calvinist ears!]* of celebrating their liturgy of the Lord's Supper only infrequently. (*UUS*, 45)

["Have abandoned their custom." I have never considered it a custom but an aberration! But this encyclical has reminded me what that looks like from the outside.]

Again, when the cycles of liturgical readings used by the various Christian communities in the West are compared, they appear to be essentially the same. Still, on the ecumenical level, very special prominence has been given to the liturgy and liturgical signs (images, icons, vestments, light, incense, gestures). Moreover, in schools of theology, where future ministers are trained, courses in the history and significance of the liturgy are beginning to be part of the curriculum in response to a newly discovered need.[5] (*UUS*, 45)

(I will retire a year from now, and it is very comforting and interesting to have a pope tell me what I have been doing!)

Ut Unum Sint: the other bookend, which document, as you know, concludes with an appeal by His Holiness for a reconsideration with him of the papal office by Protestants and Orthodox.

Bookends: *Ordo Lectionum Missae* 1969—*Ut Unum Sint* 1995.

---

for Interconfessional Cooperation in Translating the Bible," *Information Service* 65, nos. 3–4 (1987) 140–145.

[4] That's a reference to the World Council's Faith and Order document no. 111, *Baptism, Eucharist, Ministry* [BEM]). See Commission on Faith and Order of the World Council of Churches, *Baptism, Eucharist and Ministry* (January 1982).

[5] For example, at the most recent assemblies of the World Council of Churches in Vancouver (1983) and in Canberra (1991), and of the Commission on Faith and Order in Santiago de Compostela (1993).

HYMNALS

In between the bookends: hymnals. For many of you, it might be a strange idea (we all know the book *Why Catholics Can't Sing?*[6]) that for Protestants, hymns are the prayer book or form the prayer book. So I have brought with me to Rome a few recently published hymnals from North America.

First, The United Methodist Hymnal, 1989. I'm just going to run you very quickly through the Easter hymns to suggest to you the way in which hymnody in the Protestant situation forms piety, and in somewhat ecumenically creative ways. A hymn from 1969:

> We know that Christ is raised and dies no more.
> Embraced by death, he broke its fearful hold;
> and our despair he turned to blazing joy, alleluia, alleluia.

That's not bad poetry.

> We share by water and his saving death.
> Reborn, we share with him an Easter life,
> as living members of a living Christ, alleluia, alleluia.
>
> A new creation comes to life and grows,
> as Christ's new body takes on flesh and blood.
> The universe restored and whole will sing: alleluia, alleluia.

This is a *Methodist* book!

> "Deck Thyself, My Soul, with Gladness." We all know that
>   classic Lutheran chorale.
> "O Thou Who This Mysterious Bread." We know that too—
>   that's Wesley.
> "For the Bread Which You Have Broken." That's by Louis
>   Benson, a Presbyterian.
> *Come, Sinners, To the Gospel Feast*—Wesley

This new hymn by Brian Wren, an English Congregationalist now teaching in a Presbyterian seminary in Decatur, Georgia:

> I come with joy to meet my Lord, forgiven, loved and free,
> in awe and wonder to recall his life laid down for me.
>
> I come with Christians far and near to find, as all are fed,
> the new community of love in Christ's communion bread.

[6] T. DAY, *Why Catholics Can't Sing: The Culture of Catholicism and the Triumph of Bad Taste* (New York: Crossroad, 1991).

As Christ breaks bread and bids us share, each proud division ends.
The Love that made us makes us one and strangers now are friends.

And thus with joy, we meet Our Lord. His presence, always near,
is in such friendship better known; we see and praise him here.

Together met, together bound, we'll go our different ways,
and as his people in the world, we'll live and speak his praise.

I don't think I need to cite more. This is how the Lectionary and the use of the Christian calendar have transformed Protestant worship in the English-speaking world, and a book like this is evidence enough.

But, of course, that's not all. I have also brought with me the book *Hymns for the Gospels*, published by GIA Publications (not a Protestant group), and in the Preface it is pointed out:

> The Second Vatican Council of the Roman Catholic Church led to the development of the three-year lectionary of Sunday readings. The adoption of that lectionary across denominational lines prompted contemporary hymn writers, mostly Protestant, to address the significant increase in the amount of scripture read in Sunday worship. The creative outpouring which occurred has come to be known as the "Hymn Explosion" of the final third of the twentieth century. This creative energy continues to emerge from an ever-growing number of contemporary hymn writers.

Let us turn in this book to hymn no. 109:

> Show me your hands, your feet, your side: I will not be deceived.
> Unless I see, how can I trust the news that I have received?

> Fear not! Let peace be in your soul, reach out and touch and know:
> I died, and yet I am alive with wounds that ever show.

> Not even Easter takes away the marks that Jesus bears:
> The risen Christ still wears the wounds of scourge and nails and spear.

> So blessed are those who have not seen, yet cry, "My Lord and God!"
> Who touched earth's pain in Jesus' name and tell good news to all abroad.

I cite these texts to you to suggest that between the "bookends" something new is happening in Christian corporate piety, namely, the liturgical way in which Christians now worship God on the Lord's Day in song, biblically based.

But now, unhappily, the bad news.

Liturgiam Authenticam, dated May 7, 2001.

When my teaching assistant, a Roman priest, recently sent it to me via the Internet late one night, I fell apart in tears in my apartment, because I suddenly saw all of that—the bookends and everything in between—falling off the shelf. And that's a terrible experience—seeing books falling off a shelf. You have to pick them up. And as I read this document, I realized that something terrible had happened that in my worst imagining I had never anticipated.

That a trusted ecumenical partner would walk away from the table. And, in fact, to walk away so deliberately as to dismiss the others who were at the table, such as "mixed commissions who do not represent their communions" or represent their "communions of insignificant numbers."

I never knew that in the Christian church you needed more than two or three. But that's what it says. I never knew that, I couldn't believe it.

So without reading you further texts from this fearful document, I will simply now report to you from North America and from the English-speaking world that the entire liturgical and ecumenical conversation and dialogue are gone. Finished. Done. That's it.

A week ago I attended, as I have for thirty years, the bi-annual meeting of the Consultation on Common Texts of North America. ICEL, of course, was not there at all. It doesn't exist for us anymore, and apparently something else is coming along. I think it met in Rome or will meet here rather soon: *Vox Clara.* These expressions are too clever for words. Last Monday, in New York City, ICEL was gone. The Canadian Conference of Catholic Bishops was not represented, apparently for economic reasons. And the Bishops' Committee on the Liturgy of the North American Conference of Catholic Bishops was represented by someone who had at a previous meeting distributed a document from the Committee, with the odd instruction, *printed on it,* "Read but do not comment on." To think that thirty years after Vatican II, in North America and in the English-speaking world, Rome is just not there.

I can't think that—and I'm a Calvinist!

No representation in the English Language Liturgical Consultation (ELLC), and silent representation in the Consultation on Common Texts (CCT).

Thus I have to conclude on a very sorry note: bookends have become ends, not books. I don't know what to make of that. I thought that 450 years later we had a partnership again. But at least in matters liturgical, apparently, we don't.

Only two days ago, I went to the sacred Basilica of St. Peter, knelt down, and prayed before the body of Pope John XXIII. And I thought, well, how strange: *His body is in glory and his Council is in ruins.* Human institutions are like that—take it from a Calvinist—but I have to say that, and I regret it, and if that's not gracious of me, forgive me. But I have to tell you the truth.

So, I'd like to conclude with a prayer from a community of which I am a member, the Iona Community of Scotland, a prayer that George MacLeod would never admit to having written, though I know he did:

> O Christ, the master Carpenter,
> who through wood and nails purchased our whole salvation:
> Wield well your tools in the workshop of your world,
> so that we, who come rough hewn to your bench,
> may here be fashioned to a truer beauty of your hand.
> We ask it for your own Name's sake. Amen.

And I would simply say in closing, it was a wonderful moment for me to be at the General Audience yesterday, because I knew that as a Calvinist, dressed all in black, that I had come home to be in the presence of someone all in white, who has done his best. He even sang a little bit, for the Polish delegation, and when he began to sing an old folk song, I turned to my companion and said, "Isn't it beautiful? Even the Pope can sing." Well, I suppose, so can the Church—even in these days.

Again, thank you for this opportunity. I am sorry, as it were, to be the bearer of such sad news, but that's the way it is for now. I am sure we will someday see happier days, whether from above or among.

God bless you, dear sisters and brothers in Christ, however *seiuncti.*

Teresa Berger

Liturgical Renewal, Separated Sisters, and Christian Unity

Of the trinity of terms that make up my title, the middle one, "Separated Sisters," holds what I assume distinguishes my essay from all others in this volume. "Separated sisters" probably is also the term in my title most in need of an explanation. Let me begin, then, with the "separated sisters," and then look to what is at the right hand and at the left hand of these separated sisters (at least title-wise). At the end I will come back to my initial trinity of terms and see whether a *perichoresis,* a mutual indwelling, of these three is at all workable.

"Separated sisters"—this oxymoron was coined during the Second Vatican Council when the absence of *women* auditors at the Council first came to be recognized as a problem.[1] The expression obviously is modeled on the term created by Pope John XXIII and adopted by the Council for its new ecumenical vision: non-Roman Catholic Christians now were designated as "separated brethren" (a definite improvement over the previous terminology, which defined them as either "schismatics" or "heretics"). The two conciliar terms, "separated sisters" and "separated brethren," witnessed to painful ecclesial fragmentations. "Separated brethren" pointed to Christians outside the confines of the Roman Catholic Church; "separated sisters," on the other hand, did not designate non-Roman Catholic Christian women, but Roman Catholic women as "outsiders" within their own church. The dis-unity embodied by the "separated brethren" and the "separated sisters" thus follows different lines: one centers on denominational divisions, while the other highlights asymmetrical gender divisions as a source of dis-unity and fragmentation.

---

[1] See the book by G. HEINZELMANN, *Die getrennten Schwestern: Frauen nach dem Konzil* (Zürich: Interfeminas-Verlag, 1967). For more on the women who did, in the end, attend the Council as auditors, see C. E. McENROY, *Guests in Their Own House: The Women of Vatican II* (New York: Crossroad, 1996).

I take the notion of "separated sisters" as a starting point for my analysis of the conflictual interplay between ecumenical, liturgical, and women-identified visions. As a Roman Catholic woman theologian and liturgical scholar committed to an ecumenical vision, I interpret women-identified concerns as one form of faith-full struggle for the wholeness of the church. That is to say, I claim women-identified concerns as an essential part of the ecumenical vision in the twenty-first century. At the same time, women-identified voices obviously challenge the more traditional ecumenical vision of "unity." A look at the historical development of women-identified voices and the ecumenical vision helps to trace these challenges.

"SEPARATED SISTERS" AND CHRISTIAN UNITY

To put the historical narrative in a nutshell: women are no latecomers or strangers to ecumenism, even if many narratives of the ecumenical movement suggest so. In fact, the history of the ecumenical movement in the twentieth century can be told in such a way that women become visible as integral "movers" right from the start.[2] The beginnings of women's crucial contributions to the ecumenical movement can, in fact, nicely be pinpointed to a *liturgical* initiative, the Women's World Day of Prayer. This first ecumenical liturgical initiative of modern times was initiated well before the Week of Prayer for Christian Unity. The inception of the Women's World Day of Prayer goes back to Mary Allen James, an American Presbyterian, who was president of a women's home mission board. In 1887 James called on other women to join in a day of prayer for "home missions." This day of prayer became an annual event. Three years later, two Baptist women, Helen Barrett Montgomery and Lucy Peabody, called for a similar day of prayer for "foreign missions." The idea of women uniting in prayer around the world and across denominational lines spread rapidly. In 1927 this day of prayer officially became the Women's World Day of Prayer. It is still celebrated to this day, on the first Friday in March, all over the world.

The origins of this World Day of Prayer lie in a field that women had struggled to enter in the nineteenth century, namely, the mission

[2] This story has been told in a variety of ways, e.g., S. HERZEL, *A Voice for Women: The Women's Department of the World Council of Churches* (Geneva: World Council of Churches, 1981); M. A. MAY, *Bonds of Unity: Women, Theology, and the Worldwide Church* (Atlanta: Scholars Press, 1989) 15–58; P. WEBB, *She Flies Beyond: Memories and Hopes of Women in the Ecumenical Movement*, Risk Book 56 (Geneva: WCC Publications, 1993).

field. This, of course, is also the field that birthed the ecumenical movement proper. Not surprisingly, women were present from the earliest inception of the movement—even if their presence was not without constraints. At the first World Conference on Faith and Order in Lausanne in 1927, for example, one of the women delegates, Lucy Gardner, presented a memorandum stating that "it has been laid upon the hearts of the women delegates to ask the Conference to realize the significance of the fact that out of nearly 400 delegates only seven are women"[3]—a very unthreatening way of describing the underrepresentation of women in the ecumenical movement!

When the World Council of Churches began to take shape in the 1930s, women initiated a worldwide questionnaire. This questionnaire, first formulated by the American Presbyterian Twila McCrea Cavert, inquired into the status and participation of women in the different churches. Based on the answers to this questionnaire, Sarah Chakko (1905–1954), a Syrian Orthodox Christian from India, presented a report to the founding assembly of the World Council of Churches in Amsterdam. Chakko was not the only woman who shaped the Amsterdam assembly. Kathleen Bliss from Great Britain drafted a preliminary assembly message including the famous sentence "We intend to stay together." That a woman wrote a first draft of the assembly message led to "prolonged laughter" in Rome, where a Roman Catholic visitor to the assembly had related that fact.[4] It is not surprising that it took twenty years for Roman Catholic women themselves to enter into sustained relations with the World Council of Churches. A Women's Ecumenical Liaison Group was created in 1968, but it was short-lived. There were, of course, Roman Catholic women committed to the vision of Christian unity well before then. Two examples of such women are Mother Lurana White S.A. (d. 1935), co-foundress of the Society of the Atonement at Graymoor, which is dedicated to unity, and the Trappist Maria Gabriella Sagheddu (1914–1939), who chose to offer her life for the unity of the church. Pope John Paul II beatified Sagheddu in 1983; she is also mentioned in the 1995 papal encyclical dedicated to ecumenism, *Ut Unum Sint*, as an exemplary model of the importance of prayer for unity.

---

[3] Quoted in H. N. BATE, ed., *Faith and Order: Proceedings of the World Conference, Lausanne, August 3–21, 1927* (London/New York: Student Christian Movement/ G. H. Doran, 1927) 372.

[4] The story is told by Willem Visser't Hooft, in HERZEL, *A Voice for Women*, 10.

To continue the historical development of women-identified voices and the ecumenical vision: the 1960s were a watershed decade, not only in the Roman Catholic Church and in the ecumenical movement but also in women's lives, which underwent profound changes due to major cultural shifts. In the churches, women began to develop a consciously women-identified ("feminist") theological vision, suspicious of facile band-aid approaches to the ecclesial marginalization of women. With the 1970s, a feminist ecumenical vision increasingly took shape. This feminist ecumenical vision soon became a conflictual presence in the ecumenical movement,[5] ever-strengthening in theological conviction and imaginative expertise, but also calling forth sustained negative reactions and resistance. With the 1980s it was clear, however, that women's voices were there to stay in the ecumenical movement. The most visible recognition of this fact is the Ecumenical Decade of Churches in Solidarity with Women (1988–1998), even if much of the decade was one of women in solidarity with the churches rather than the other way around.

Let me draw this sketch to a close. Obviously, I have only scratched the surface of the historical development of women-identified voices and the ecumenical vision. The point of this historical narrative, nevertheless, should be clear: women have always moved the ecumenical movement, even if not without constraints. In the last four decades, women's visions have developed in distinct ways, challenging the traditional ecumenical paradigm at crucial points. Women force certain subjects on the ecumenical agenda, such as women's ministries in the churches, including ministries of oversight. Women question the established discourse of unity, suspicious that the envisioned unity masks an ecclesial reality that is not fully supportive of women's flourishing. What good is a unity that is also a unity of the marginalization of women? Women engender a new ecumenical vocabulary ("roundtable," "living letters," "mending of creation") and new practices of discourse. Women privilege new conversation partners, especially poor women, and women from different faith traditions.[6]

[5] See, for example, C. F. PARVEY, "The Continuing Significance of the Community of Women and Men in the Church Study: Its Mixed Meanings for the Church," in T. F. BEST, ed., *Beyond Unity-in-Tension: Unity, Renewal and the Community of Women and Men*, Faith and Order Paper 138 (Geneva: WCC Publications, 1988) 34–43.

[6] See M. GREY, "Ist der Dialog eine notwendige epistemologische Voraussetzung für die Findung der Wahrheit? Eine Feministische Perspektive," *Ökumenische Rundschau* 42, no. 2 (1993) 196–208.

One of the responses to these challenges has been to brand-mark women and "women's issues" as ecumenical troublemakers par excellence. Women are accused of rocking the ecumenical boat and of threatening emerging ecumenical convergences. One "water way" that has proved particularly rocky for women in the ecumenical boat (and in the ecclesial boat more generally) is the waters of liturgy. Let me, then, add the third part of the trinity of terms that is my title, "Liturgical Renewal."

SEPARATED SISTERS AND LITURGICAL RENEWAL

If the twentieth century was the century of the ecumenical movement, it certainly also was the century of the liturgical movement. The Second Vatican Council, in fact, acknowledged both these movements as movements of the Holy Spirit through the church (SC 43; UR 1; 4). One of the defining features of this century was the irruption of women into liturgical practice and discourse. The classical liturgical movement had gained official ground in the church particularly since the 1940s (as I have shown elsewhere, women were peculiarly active in this movement from its inception onward[7]). With the Constitution on the Sacred Liturgy, the liturgical movement bore its most highly visible immediate fruit. This Constitution and the liturgical reforms that followed engendered much ecumenical hope,[8] so much so that an ecumenical theologian could claim enthusiastically, "La grande speranza dell'ecumenismo è la liturgia."[9]

The self-description of women as "separated sisters," however, suggests a more complex vision both of ecumenical and of liturgical developments. As women began to develop a self-consciously women-identified ecumenical vision in the 1960s, so they also began to interpret the call to *actuosa participatio* in the liturgy in women-identified ways. They confronted a painful experience: the renewed liturgy did not seem that much more hospitable to women's lives—especially given the now quickly changing nature of those lives—than the Tridentine liturgy had been.

---

[7] See T. BERGER, *Women's Ways of Worship: Gender Analysis and Liturgical History* (Collegeville: The Liturgical Press, 1999) 69–108.

[8] For more, see T. BERGER, "Ecumenism and the Liturgy," in P. E. FINK, ed., *The New Dictionary of Sacramental Worship* (Collegeville: The Liturgical Press, 1990) 385–390.

[9] P. TAMBURRINO, "Lex orandi–Lex credendi. Per un discorso liturgico nell'ecumenismo," *Rivista Liturgica* 68, no. 3 (1981) 313–321, here 321.

Interestingly, this experience of liturgical ambiguity came to be felt by women across denominational lines. A grassroots ecumenical experience of women's shared concerns with the liturgical lives of their churches emerged. Denominational divisions receded into the background as women encountered liturgical marginalization across their various ecclesial communities. Initially, women's questionings were concentrated on individual elements. Women started with the basic acknowledgment that they were all but invisible as authoritative liturgical subjects. Although they would often be the majority of those present at worship, they were not represented as women. Examples of this liturgical invisibility of women were the fact that leadership was almost exclusively in the hands of men and that the language used in and for the liturgical assembly was usually in masculine terms. In the Roman Catholic Church, androcentric language became especially noticeable with the early translations of liturgical books from Latin (generally not understood by women) into the vernacular —a vernacular that was changing in gender-attentive ways precisely at the point at which these translations took place but of which they showed little evidence. And scrutiny of the liturgy grew as feminist tools of analysis grew sharper.

The early problems noted (the absence of women from liturgical leadership and exclusive language) were soon joined by more subtle ones. The limited and stereotypical selection of biblical stories about women in the Lectionary was one of these problems. Added to the absences soon were problematic presences. Women began to resist certain Scripture passages read and then proclaimed unquestioningly from the pulpit. They also found little help in women saints stereotypically honored for their virginity, humility, and self-effacement. On the other side of the spectrum of problematic liturgical presences, many women found various confessions of sins, with their focus on pride, self-determination, and will power, distinctly male-oriented and detrimental to their own beginning discovery of self. These women lost interest in confessing sins that their own subject formation and cultural context did not really allow them to commit in the first place.

Even the argument that worship at heart never was nor is primarily about saints, sermons, or sins but about the Living God, did not help for long. At the heart of worship, women began to confront a God who was imaged and addressed almost exclusively in the masculine. These same women, however, had discovered that the Christian tradition knew feminine images for the Living God, from the early Christian image of the Eucharist as God's breast milk[10] to medieval images of Jesus as mother and as a woman in labor who births new life on the cross.[11] Unfortunately, the liturgy seemed to know nothing about these images nor to be hospitable to their rediscovery.

In short, a growing feminist consciousness had brought recognition of wide-ranging concerns for women at worship. That there was "a problem" for women at worship slowly began to be acknowledged, but depending on how acute and pervasive it was seen to be, the responses differed widely. At the level of liturgical reforms, there has been some openness to acknowledging women-identified concerns, and actual proposals for reform have begun to be affected by women's concerns, be it in relation to liturgical ministries, lectionaries, liturgical language, or the shape and content of rituals as a whole. In what follows, I want to highlight four areas that I see as either indispensable or as fruitful ground for the intersection of ecumenical, liturgical, and women-identified concerns.

LECTIONARY LACUNAE

Much promising ecumenical work has been done on Lectionary readings in and between the churches. Much less work has been done on the occlusion of women-identified readings present in all cycles of readings in the Christian tradition. The Scriptures themselves, after all, have a decidedly androcentric bias; that is to say, the textual representation of women in our scriptural canon is limited. This androcentric bias of the biblical witness is *heightened* by the choice of passages for reading in the liturgy. I take my own tradition, the Roman Catholic Church, as an example. The Lectionary that governs the choice of readings in my church (and that means in more than half of Christianity!) simply has not attended carefully enough to biblical stories about women and their faith.[12] An example is the

[10] See J. BETZ, "Die Eucharistie als Gottes Milch in frühchristlicher Sicht," *Zeitschrift für Katholische Theologie* 106 (1984) 1–26, 167–185.

[11] Balthasar FISCHER is unusual among liturgical scholars in having paid attention to this research; see his "Jesus, unsere Mutter," in A. GERHARDS and A. HEINZ, eds., *Frömmigkeit der Kirche: Gesammelte Studien zur christlichen Spiritualität*, Hereditas 17 (Bonn: Borengässer, 2000) 91–102.

[12] For detailed analyses, see R. A. BOISCLAIR, "Amnesia in the Catholic Sunday Lectionary: Women—Silenced from the Memories of Salvation History," in M. A. HINSDALE and P. H. KAMINSKI, eds., *Women and Theology*, College Theology

following omissions of biblical women's stories from the Lectionary readings (I take as my material the Lectionary for the Roman Catholic dioceses in the United States[13]).

The story of the two Hebrew midwives Shiphrah and Puah, who set the scene for the Exodus by defying Pharaoh, is simply cut out from the liturgical reading of Exodus 1:8-22. The Lectionary reading of this passage jumps from verse 14 to verse 22, thus "disappearing" Shiphrah and Puah from sight. As a result, the liturgical assembly will not hear the stories and names of these women, although in a wonderful irony of history, the biblical witness *does* remember their names while it has forgotten the name of "the pharaoh."

There are other Lectionary omissions of women's stories in the midst of longer narratives. Such omissions have rendered invisible, among others, the Hebrew prophet Hulda (2 Kgs 22:14-20). Hulda's story is that of a temple prophet who is asked to validate a scroll found in the temple during repairs. Feminist scholars have argued that through this validation, Hulda, in fact, authorizes what will become the core of our Scriptures: "Her validation of a text . . . stands as the first recognizable act in the long process of canon formation."[14] Our Lectionary thinks nothing of Hulda's authoritative act. Unfortunately, Hulda, Shiphrah, and Puah are not alone.

There are other women whom the Lectionary renders invisible in its choice of texts, such as Phoebe, the co-worker of the Apostle Paul and "deacon" or "minister" of the church at Cenchreae (Rom 16:1). The prophet Deborah, a judge and military leader of Israel, also is not allowed to speak to a liturgical assembly, although Deborah is a decisive figure in Israel's settling in Canaan. In the book of Judges,

---

Society 40 (Maryknoll, N.Y.: Orbis Books, 1995) 109–135; M. PROCTER-SMITH, "Images of Women in the Lectionary," in E. SCHÜSSLER FIORENZA, ed., *The Power of Naming: A Concilium Reader in Feminist Liberation Theology* (Maryknoll, N.Y.: Orbis Books, 1996) 175–186; R. FOX, "Women in the Bible and the Lectionary," in *Remembering the Women: Women's Stories from the Scripture for Sundays and Festivals,* compiled and annotated J. F. HENDERSON (Chicago: Liturgy Training Publications, 1999) 359–367.

[13] I am using the table of readings of the Lectionary for Mass for Use in the Dioceses of the United States of America, 2nd typical edition. Vol. 1: Sundays, Solemnities, Feasts of the Lord and the Saints. Study Edition (Collegeville: The Liturgical Press, 1998).

[14] C. V. CAMP, "Hulda," in C. MEYERS and others, eds., *Women in Scripture: A Dictionary of Named and Unnamed Women in the Hebrew Bible, the Apocryphal/Deuterocanonical Books, and the New Testament* (Boston: Houghton Mifflin Company, 2000) 96.

Deborah's deeds fill two whole chapters (Judg 4–5). The Lectionary, however, knows nothing of this woman. Similarly, short excerpts from the book of Ruth appear only twice in the Lectionary, and then only in weekday liturgies. This is especially unfortunate since Ruth (re-)appears in the New Testament as a foremother of Jesus (Matt 1:5), making her one of only four women named in the genealogy of the Messiah. Weekdays are also the only times that we hear from Esther, the Jewish exile who becomes queen of the Persian Empire and with her resourcefulness and courage saves her people. Like Esther, Judith, too, is an undocumented alien in the Lectionary. In the Lectionary choice of readings, we simply find no trace of this woman who saved her people (except within the Common of Saints).

The Lectionary furthermore assigns women's stories the status of "optional" in a number of readings, that is to say, these women's stories form part of a longer biblical passage which may be shortened by the presider if he[!] considers the passage too long. The presence of the prophet Anna at the presentation of Jesus in the temple (Luke 2:36-38) thus is rendered "optional," as is the woman with a hemorrhage who is healed by Jesus (Mark 5:25-34). The same applies to the beautiful parable in which Jesus likens the coming of God's reign to a woman baking (Matt 13:33). This passage, too, is optional on the only Sunday when it might be read, although it is one of the few biblical texts which show Jesus drawing on women's everyday lives to image God's reign. There are yet other ways in which women's presence in the Scriptures and the Lectionary readings come to be veiled. Take the reading of Proverbs 31 as just one example. The Lectionary omits precisely those verses that show the woman of Proverbs 31 as a powerful and productive household manager, and focuses instead on her service to her husband.

Let me draw this analysis to a close. It should be clear by now that there are women-identified problems in our Lectionary readings, certainly in those of the Roman Catholic Church. Any ecumenical liturgical work that does not attend to these problems cannot be said to confront the brokenness of the church's life in all necessary depth. Wherever ecumenical liturgical work *does* attend to these problems,[15] all churches do well to listen and learn.

---

[15] Not surprisingly, the Revised Common Lectionary of 1992 does provide a richer fare of women's stories than the Roman Catholic Lectionary for Mass. For more, see F. WEST, *Scripture and Memory: The Ecumenical Hermeneutic of the Three-Year Lectionaries* (Collegeville: The Liturgical Press, 1997) 143, 146–149, 171.

The veneration of saints is a second liturgical area in which issues of gender representation not only are a given but which also have proved fruitful as common ground among women from widely differing ecclesial traditions. The last decades have witnessed a growing interest in holy women, our foremothers in the faith, across denominational lines and beyond.[16] Even in ecclesial traditions without a sustained liturgical practice of the veneration of the saints, women have found the rediscovery of their foremothers in the faith an important element in their women-identified spirituality. As an ecumenical experience, this remembering of holy women among women is not necessarily something that functions on the level of official liturgical reforms (in most calendars, images of holy women in the liturgical calendar continue to follow very traditional constructions of female sanctity anyway[17]). The "current resurgence of women's practices of memory"[18] is more readily visible at the grassroots and in women's lived lives.

Let me give just one example. In the past few years, women in many places and from a variety of different churches and ecclesial communities have begun to gather on the feast day of St. Mary of Magdala (July 22 in the Roman Catholic calendar). This biblical woman until quite recently was known more through the eyes of a tradition that had framed her as a prostitute than through the biblical story itself, which remembers her as the first witness to the resurrection. Today women gather on July 22 to celebrate Mary of Magdala as the woman who stands at the beginning of resurrection faith and rightly bears the title "apostle to the apostles."

One of the promises the liturgical calendar holds for women from all traditions is such invitations to celebrate women of faith who have gone before. As with most of the church's liturgical life in relation to women, however, the sanctoral cycle and its women saints, too, are not without problems. To begin with, the process of canonization throughout history clearly has been male-dominated, one of

[16] An example is the interest in Hildegard of Bingen in ecological circles.

[17] See I. PAHL, "'Eine starke Frau, wer wird sie finden?' Aspekte des Frauenbildes in den Meßformularen der Heiligenfeste," in T. BERGER and A. GERHARDS, eds., *Liturgie und Frauenfrage: Ein Beitrag zur Frauenforschung aus liturgiewissenschaftlicher Sicht*, Pietas Liturgica 7 (St. Ottilien: EOS-Verlag, 1990) 433–452; M. D. WHALEN, "In the Company of Women? The Politics of Memory in the Liturgical Commemoration of Saints—Male and Female," *Worship* 73, no. 6 (1999) 482–504.

[18] E. A. JOHNSON, *Friends of God and Prophets: A Feminist Theological Reading of the Communion of Saints* (New York/London: Continuum/SCM, 1998) 26.

the reasons for the underrepresentation of women in the sanctoral cycle. Furthermore, many of the women who were included in the calendar conform to a certain stereotypical depiction of female sanctity: their piety centers, on the one hand, on obedience and submission to the church and, on the other hand, on stark practices of self-effacement, especially sexual and food renunciations (no wonder, then, that no woman was counted among those saints recognized by the church for their *teaching* authority until St. Teresa of Avila was named such a "teacher of the church" by Pope Paul VI in 1970). The recovery of holy women and the celebration of their memory as an ecumenical liturgical practice of women today thus have to proceed with careful and critical analysis of how the memory of these women has been "traditioned" in the past.

LITURGICAL LANGUAGE, GENDER, AND AMBIGUITY

A third issue readily comes to mind at the intersection of ecumenical, liturgical, and women-identified concerns, namely, that of liturgical language. This issue has garnered a lot of attention ever since the 1970s, with all the contestation that such attention involves. It is worth noting that *Liturgiam Authenticam* devotes a whole section to "gender" in relation to liturgical language, thus proving the importance of the issue, if nothing else. Language, of course, is not an abstract universal (even if *Liturgiam Authenticam* seems to treat it as such), but is time-sensitive, region-specific, and always spoken by human beings who live particular and gendered lives.

A point at which questions of gender and liturgical language have surfaced in ecumenical conversations is the naming of the Holy Trinity at baptism. Feminist theologies had for many years raised questions over exclusively male God-language.[19] In a couple of North American ecclesial communities, these questions led to alternative Trinitarian formulas in baptism, such as baptism simply into the "name of the Holy Trinity" or "the Creator, Redeemer, and Sustainer." Ecumenically, this change is sensitive, since many Christian communities link the validity of baptism to the traditional formula (which is not that traditional, however; until the seventh century, there was a threefold interrogation, affirmation, and dipping or

---

[19] See R. C. DUCK, *Gender and the Name of God: The Trinitarian Baptismal Formula* (New York: Pilgrim Press, 1991). For recent comments on this topic, see G. RAMSHAW, "In the Name: Towards Alternative Baptismal Idioms," J. A. ZIMMERMAN, ed., *Proceedings of the North American Academy of Liturgy Annual Meeting 2002*, 143–154.

effusion rather than the one formula we now consider to be "tradition"[20]). In its statements on baptism, the ecumenical movement has, at most, simply noted such alternative baptismal formulas as a concern.[21]

But what if one wanted to go beyond the purely descriptive statements? As a feminist theologian and liturgical scholar, I begin with the acknowledgment that "the trinitarian tradition, like the Bible, is *both* the source of revelatory truth about the mystery of God *and* a powerful resource for patriarchal culture."[22] This very ambiguity suggests that the Trinitarian formula at baptism does *not* need to be read as inherently patriarchal, that is, as assigning maleness to God.[23] The richness of our tradition tells a different story. What remains unclear is whether the baptismal liturgies of the churches adequately mirror that richness. An insistence on the traditional wording of the Trinitarian name in baptism at minimum would need to be accompanied by an insistence that the baptismal liturgies of the churches signal at other points that male-dominated language falls under the same judgment as any other gender-specific or ungendered language about God—it is limited. Any and every affirmative statement human language can make about God also has to be open to being negated. For the traditional Trinitarian formula, that would most easily be accomplished if our baptismal liturgies at other points included more faithfully the fullness and richness of our tradition, including, for example, the feminine images for God and for Jesus Christ known to earlier centuries. The weight of ambiguity borne by the traditional baptismal formula ("*both* the source of revelatory truth about the mystery of God *and* a powerful resource for patriarchal culture") could thus be lessened.

WOMEN'S LIVED LIVES AND LITURGY

A fourth area of possible ecumenical liturgical ground is the representation (or lack thereof) of women's lived lives in newer liturgies. Some confessional families have begun to include women-identified imagery in their liturgical texts, often drawing on a rich tradition of

[20] See D. HOLETON, "Changing the Baptismal Formula: Feminist Proposals and Liturgical Implications," *Ecumenical Trends* 17, no. 5 (1988) 69–72.

[21] See, for example, a draft of a working group of the Commission on Faith and Order of the World Council of Churches, "One Baptism: Toward Mutual Recognition of Christian Initiation" (Faverges, 2001) 68.

[22] C. M. LaCUGNA, "The Baptismal Formula, Feminist Objections, and Trinitarian Theology," *Journal of Ecumenical Studies* 26, no. 2 (1989) 235–290, here 238.

[23] Ibid., 243.

such imagery, particularly in relationship to baptism. One example is the Thanksgiving over the Water in the United Methodist Hymnal's "Reaffirmation of the Baptismal Covenant." This Thanksgiving over the Water, which celebrates salvation history by retelling it as a water-way, contains the following sentence: "In the fullness of time you sent Jesus, nurtured in the water of a womb."[24] The waters of a pregnant woman's body are here inscribed as a part of God's salvation history. Particularly in the baptism of children, who come to the waters of new birth in temporal proximity to the breaking of waters in their mother's wombs, this is a powerful recognition. The same United Methodist service book also uses birthing imagery in a Eucharistic Prayer. In the anamnesis, God is imaged as birthing the church in the paschal mystery: "By the baptism of his suffering, death, and resurrection, you [God] gave birth to your church."[25]

To mention just one other example of a maternal image for God's redemptive work, this time from a different confessional family, in the Reformed Book of Common Worship, the epiclesis in the Thanksgiving over the Water asks God: "Pour out your holy Spirit upon us and upon this water, that this font may be your womb of new birth."[26] Again, a maternal image is used: God has a womb and gives birth.

Granted, in many ways these are very traditional liturgical images. It is precisely the maternal, and correspondingly natality, that become the key feminine symbols for God and for our entry into new life. No doubt the danger of a stereotypical reduction of women's lived lives lurks just around the corner. And yet, as not only feminist philosophers of religion but also the Pope have recently stressed: natality, being born of a woman, is at the heart of all human existence. Grace Jantzen puts this forcefully: "every person who has ever lived has been born, and born of a woman. Natality is a fundamental human condition. It is even more basic to our existence than the fact that we will die, since death presupposes birth."[27] It would be very odd in-

[24] *The United Methodist Hymnal: Book of United Methodist Worship* (Nashville: The United Methodist Publishing House, 1989) 52.

[25] *The United Methodist Hymnal*, 9.

[26] THEOLOGY AND WORSHIP MINISTRY UNIT FOR THE PRESBYTERIAN CHURCH (USA) & THE CUMBERLAND PRESBYTERIAN CHURCH, *Book of Common Worship* (Louisville: Westminster/John Knox Press, 1993) 412.

[27] G. M. JANTZEN, *Becoming Divine: Towards a Feminist Philosophy of Religion* (Bloomington: Indiana University Press, 1999) 144. Pope John Paul II emphasizes such a symbolic of natality in *Mulieris Dignitatem*, 19: "The history of every human

deed to celebrate liturgy without metaphors of natality, even if women's lives need to be images and represented liturgically with richer metaphors than those of maternity and natality alone.

So much for my four examples at the intersection of ecumenical, liturgical, and women-identified concerns. It will by now be clear that I do not offer an easy vision of how to gather my trinity of terms—liturgical renewal, separated sisters, and Christian unity. There is no elegant *perichoresis* or mutual indwelling and coinherence of all three that is readily available. Rather, their conflictual relationships need to be confronted, if only to create space where all three can flourish in the future. But given that I have to draw to a conclusion in the here and now, I want to close with a non-beatific, clearly chastened vision of my trinity:

ECUMENISM, LITURGY, AND WOMEN: NO EASY EMBRACE

Obviously, all three—the ecumenical vision of unity, women's activism in the churches, and liturgical renewal—share at least one common theological concern. Broadly speaking, they center on ecclesiology, more specifically on ecclesial fragmentations and the corresponding search for the flourishing and the wholeness of the church. For the ecumenical paradigm, fragmentations among confessional bodies are the crucial rupture. The corresponding "good" is couched in the image of "unity." For women-identified concerns, the asymmetry of divisions between gendered bodies are the crucial fragmentations. The corresponding vision is one of well-being and flourishing for every "body," particularly women's bodies. For liturgical renewal, worship that is not clearly God-sustained and communal is a site of brokenness. The corresponding "good" is couched in the image of a liturgy in which "[t]he Spirit and the Church cooperate to manifest Christ and his work of salvation."[28]

All three forms of theological work can also be seen as a similar form of theology: they are self-consciously partisan, and they are prophetic denunciations of an ecclesial status quo. Beyond these shared

---

being passes through the threshold of a woman's motherhood; crossing it conditions 'the revelation of the children of God.'" JOHN PAUL II, *Mulieris Dignitatem: On the Dignity and Vocation of Women,* in *Origins* 18:17 (1988), here 275.

[28] *Catechism of the Catholic Church,* 2nd ed. (Vatican City: Libreria Editrice Vaticana, 1997) 1099; cf. 1108

ecclesiological concerns, however, there is no easy embrace in my trinity of terms—liturgy, ecumenism, and separated sisters. In order to understand the depth of difference between the three, let me glance back at the initial vision embraced by the ecumenical movement. For the early ecumenical movement, the unity of the church was at the heart of its message. Denominational divisions between the churches were recognized as sinful, as something that the ecumenical movement, in accordance with God's desire for the church, was seeking to overcome. The way to overcome these sinful divisions was the struggle for (theological) consensus among the churches. The central motif, unity, simply was accepted as a biblical mandate (*ut unum sint*, "that they may all be one"—John 17:21). With the late 1960s, however, the ecumenical enthusiasm for unity began to undergo changes. Traditional ways of being church and conceptions of ecclesiology were questioned as Black Theology, Feminist Theology, and other Liberation Theologies "irrupted" into theological, and especially ecumenical, discourse. These theologies began to conceive of the core ecumenical vision along new lines.

For women-identified theologies, for example, with their recognition of a deeply gendered asymmetry in the life of the church, confessional differences are not the central threat to the life of the church. There are other, inner threats: the ecclesial marginalization of women, the double oppression of poor and the triple oppression of racialized and poor women, the silencing of women's theological voices, to name just a few. Likewise, the vision of restored well-being for the church no longer centers exclusively on unity between denominationally divided bodies, but on wholeness, on healing, on life in abundance, and on the ecclesial flourishing of all, particularly women. Finally, rather than relegating women's status to the margins, as one of the "non-theological" factors of the fragmentation of the church, women-identified theologians claim the opposite: an asymmetrical fragmentation of the church into women and men is a crucial *theological* problem of the *whole* church and has to be confronted as such.

Where do all these developments leave the original ecumenical vision? Or, to turn to the future, what kind of vision will sustain the ecumenical journey into the twenty-first century? Denominational divisions have lost their defining edge in the lives of many churches, while at the same time deep-seated other fragmentations *within* the churches have become visible. The classical ecumenical vision alone cannot sustain the church's journey into the twenty-first century. Like every other theological vision, the classical ecumenical vision, too, has carried with it its own limitations, its culture-specific constraints, its complicity with wider socio-political shifts, its privileging of some and rendering invisible of others.

One could nevertheless claim that the basic problem the ecumenical movement tried to address since its inception has remained: there are fragmentations among and in the churches that mar and often seem to invalidate their message of the Gospel of Life. The beginnings of the twentieth century gifted the church with a heightened awareness of confessional divisions that mar the Body of Christ. Toward the end of the twentieth century, we were gifted with and challenged by a heightened awareness of manifold other ecclesial fragmentations. If, then, the ecumenical vision is to continue alive among the churches in the twenty-first century, it has to attend to *all* fragmentations that threaten the *oikoumenē*. Such attendance demands the renarrating of the ecumenical vision in consciously contextual terms, a renarrating that validates the very different, always contextually defined fragmentations threatening specific churches or communities within. One of these fragmentations, which any ecumenism worth its name in the twenty-first century must acknowledge, is the ecclesial asymmetry between women and men. The identities of literally all churches have been shaped by a history of the marginalization of women—a historical ecumenism of women's invisibility, so to speak. Any ecumenical vision that does not address this fact perpetuates women's marginalization and cannot ultimately claim truly to struggle for the unity of the church.

If liturgy, indeed, is the "fount and summit" of the churches' life, then here as in no other place ecclesial disunity and fragmentation have to be healed. That healing has only just begun.

Gordon W. Lathrop

Conservation and Critique:
Principles in Lutheran Liturgical Renewal
as Proposals Toward the Unity of the Churches[1]

At first glance, it may seem that a discussion of "Lutheran liturgy" or "Lutheran worship" generally, let alone a discussion of Lutheran liturgical revision, presents significant obstacles. There is no centrally organized Lutheran church, no body that might oversee either liturgical continuity or liturgical reform. There are rather a widespread number of local churches, from Sweden to Sumatra, that are in communion with one another and that have made part or all of the sixteenth-century Lutheran confessions to be their own confession. Furthermore, there is no tradition of a single, model liturgical text, as in the Tridentine Missal and then the *editio typica* of the Roman tradition or in the Book of Common Prayer among the Anglicans. It might seem difficult, then, to consider how current and ongoing Lutheran liturgical reform can be discussed as making any proposal at all to the quest for Christian unity.

But certain central characteristics of Lutheran liturgical life can be discerned. It turns out that these are the very characteristics which now mark ongoing Lutheran liturgical reform and which themselves, at the same time, are two of the most central themes Lutherans propose as important to Christian unity. I will call those characteristics or themes "conservation" and "critique."

The Lutheran approach to worship has regularly involved the willing reception of the great Christian tradition of liturgy, together with a certain conservatism in regard to actual local practices. At the same time, this Lutheran approach has also regularly involved the sharp critique of the tradition and a willingness to rearrange, omit, and reemphasize elements of the tradition when such enacted critique is

---

[1] Parts of this essay have been previously published, in German, in the article "Gottesdienst im lutherischen Kontext," in *Handbuch der Liturgik,* 3rd ed. (Göttingen: Vandenhoeck und Ruprecht, 2002).

seen to serve the clarity of the gospel of Jesus Christ in the celebrations of a participating assembly. Any discussion of worship in the Lutheran churches must note both conservation and critique as central characteristics of that context.

What happens with worship in Lutheran hands thus directly corresponds to several other ways of stating the Lutheran predilections for paradox and for surprising rearrangement: the Lutheran reformation, as some have described it, is "the conservative reformation," marked by "obedient rebellion" and "evangelical catholicity."[2] A central Lutheran concern is with both "catholic substance" and "protestant principle."[3] The Lutheran confessions take one article of traditional catholic faith—justification—and propose to all the churches that this is the "article on which the church stands or falls."[4] Liturgy, in Lutheran use, can be seen as an actualization of each of these statements. Indeed, the Lutheran approach to liturgy sets the doctrine of justification to work as a concrete tool of criticism by constantly asking if a traditional practice supports or hinders the gospel, yet also by constantly resisting the rejection of tradition and the creation of our own new way, as if that were the only righteous thing to do in worship. The Lutheran approach to liturgy tends to embrace and not avoid the paradox of tradition held steadfastly together with a similarly steadfast evangelical critique. For Lutherans, then, the context for worship revision includes this paradox of conservative criticism or critical classicism along with all the other central paradoxes of faith, beloved by those who make the Augsburg Confession their own: law and gospel; two kingdoms; creation and salvation; "at the same time righteous and sinner"; "this man is God"; "this bread is the Body of Christ."

Of course, this two-sided approach can also fail. The reception of the great tradition has sometimes become, in Lutheran hands, merely "the way we have always done it." Respect for the catholic tradition has, then, become simply the Lutherans' own stubborn, local conservatism. And the reform and critique of the tradition, a reform espe-

---

[2] See C. P. KRAUTH, *The Conservative Reformation and Its Theology* (Minneapolis: Augsburg Publishing House, 1913); J. PELIKAN, *Obedient Rebels: Catholic Substance and Protestant Principle in Luther's Reformation* (London: SCM, 1964); and S.-E. BRODD, *Evangelisk katolicitet* (Lund: CWK Gleerup, 1982).

[3] P. TILLICH, *Systematic Theology,* vol. 3 (Chicago: University of Chicago Press, 1963) 245.

[4] E. W. GRITSCH and R. W. JENSEN, *Lutheranism: The Theological Movement and Its Confessional Writings* (Philadelphia: Fortress Press, 1976).

cially accomplished in the early Reformation by a strong reemphasis on the word of God read and preached in the catholic liturgical context, has sometimes become its own new institution: Lutheran liturgies have all too often been turned into long didactic exercises, with the preacher in charge. So, conservation can be directed toward one's own recent practice and criticism reserved for the others.

Nonetheless, tendencies to lively conservation fully joined with lively critique are present in the Lutheran context and sources for worship. These tendencies are not enforced by any central authority. They are simply present throughout the worldwide communion of Lutheran churches, in the settings and presuppositions in which worship takes place—in the earliest Lutheran proposals for worship; in Lutheran catechesis; in Lutheran church buildings and spaces for worship; in hymnody; in the Lutheran confessions; in the "Luther renaissance" in scholarship; and in Lutheran liturgical theology. These tendencies have often given birth to creativity and to movements for renewal in which a new openness toward signal elements of the great tradition has been conjoined with a willingness to criticize one's own practice. Taken together, these two tendencies—conservation and critique—support the recovery of the *ordo* in Christian worship. And these tendencies give rise to a Lutheran proposal about Christian unity.

Let me say this all in a little greater detail.

The Lutheran reception of tradition can be seen in even the most casual encounter with worship in Lutheran context. Lutheran churches generally "retain the Mass" (*non abolere missam, sed religiose retinere ac defendere,* Augsburg Confession, xxiv), frequently surprising other Christians at the extent to which Western catholic forms have continued and still continue to be used in these Protestant communities. "Lutheran liturgy," at its root, has no separate existence. It is simply the historic, pre-Tridentine—and originally diverse—Western catholic liturgy as it has continued to unfold in German, Scandinavian, North American, and then African, Asian, Latin American, and Oceanic contexts. Furthermore, many Lutheran churches know congregational forms of the "Daily Office"— for Matins and Vespers and Compline. They practice baptism as a central congregational event. They ordain liturgical leaders to an office of preaching and sacramental presidency by the laying on of hands and prayer for the Spirit within the assembly. They exercise the absolution of sins in both private and communal rituals. These churches almost always keep the developed Western form of the church year and use a Lectionary that accords with that year. To a very large extent, they retain the Western patterns of church building arrangement, welcome the principal Western traditions of iconography, and utilize the traditions of chant and of historic Latin and vernacular hymnody. Many of them make use of candles, incense, and historic vestments.

Among these conserved traditions, the retention of the Mass may perhaps best stand as a general symbol for the Lutheran use of tradition. So, the eucharistic liturgies that arose at the time of the Reformation had pre-Lutheran sources. These sources included the various local uses of the Western rite as they were known in Mainz, Bamberg, Köln, Uppsala, Lund, Strängnäs, etc., as well as the missals of the orders. But the later Lutheran liturgies were also influenced by a variety of early sixteenth-century attempts at reform of the Mass. We know German-language orders of Mass from Nördlingen (published by Kaspar Kantz) in 1522 and from Worms, Alstedt (published by Thomas Müntzer), and Strassburg in 1524. Both Latin and German were used in reformed orders of Mass in Nuremberg beginning in 1524. A Swedish order for Mass was published in Stockholm in 1531.

All these patterns, in turn, had been influenced by Martin Luther's own discussions of the meanings and the perversions of the Mass in a variety of published essays. While these essays of Luther urged some reformed practices—communion in both kinds for the laity and the audible proclamation of the words of institution, for example— they were not primarily concerned with practical liturgical solutions, but with the central theological distinction between what is given by God's mercy as constitutive of the sacrament and what is added by the church in thankful response. The liturgy that was presumed was the Mass.

There were, after all, alternatives. For example, much of southern Germany and Switzerland—and, at first, parts of Sweden—chose the late medieval prone (the vernacular office of catechizing and preaching, accompanied by vernacular singing, intended to prepare people for penance) as one basic source for reformed liturgy. This ought to be no surprise. Individual penance and not the communal Eucharist functioned as the primary sacrament for many people in the late Middle Ages, the old prerequisite for communion having supplanted the thing for which it was originally intended as preparation. And the notes of catechesis and of preaching for repentance, so basic to the popular vernacular preaching office, continued to be important for many Protestants. In any case, this prone-based service had an ongoing life in Protestant worship, especially in North America in its later reincarnation as the "frontier *ordo.*"

But such was not the decision of most early Lutherans. For them, the *Mass,* the communal assembly for Scripture and preaching, thanksgiving and communion, was established as the Sunday pattern, with penance now made to be an exhortation before communion or a general act of confession and forgiveness or both (as well as the pastoral availability of individual absolution). One could argue that by rearrangement and altered emphasis, "penance" was retained but was made an echo of baptism and a preparation for the table. The church as an assembly around word and sacrament, fully participating in word and sacrament—that is what the Lutherans confessed concerning *ecclesia* (Augsburg Confession, vii). That is what they enacted when they celebrated the renewed Mass. That is what, at their best, they still confess and celebrate.

The most influential books in early Lutheran liturgical formation were Luther's own reluctant contributions: *"Formula missae et communionis pro ecclesia Wittembergensi"* (1523) and *"Deutsche Messe"* (1526). Luther himself, in contrast, for example, to Thomas Müntzer, resisted publishing extensive liturgical materials lest they should become some new, evangelical constraint, some required law. What he did publish, finally, was not a set of liturgical books, not a universal prescription, certainly not a "new liturgy," but two essays on the use of the tradition in a reformed and evangelical way, as that way was being attempted in Wittenberg. Luther did not write a liturgy. He made available two examples of an evangelical way to celebrate the traditional Mass. And, one should note, there were two such examples, differing in details, not just one, supposedly "authoritative" proposal—two proposals, united in the common, great outline of *ordo Missae,* diverging in questions of contextualization and address to culture. But in both of these booklets, the outline of the Mass—the *ordo*—and the counsel about the use of available traditions were exceptionally conservative.

But anyone who knows these essays knows that they were also exceptionally critical. They moved steadily toward the full celebration of the Mass in the vernacular. Against the widespread late-medieval practice, they sought popular participation and encouraged hymnody in the Mass itself. They evaluated classic collects, choir texts, and feast days according to an evangelical understanding of the gospel. They suppressed any mention of "sacrifice" by urging the excision of the silently prayed offertory prayers and the silently prayed Roman Canon. They experimented with a variety of ways to rearrange the traditional materials of eucharistic consecration into a new sort of prayer and proclamation at the altar-table. They encouraged preaching. In fact, their central concern seems to have been to take the old Mass (any participant in these liturgies would have known that it was indeed the Mass in which they were taking part) and make it, newly, forcefully, a place where the word of God is heard in clarity in the midst of a fully participating congregation.

Those two principles—the clarity of the word and the importance of participation—remain two of the most basic of the critical axioms in the Lutheran practice of worship. They have driven the deep Lutheran interest in congregational hymn singing as an essential part of liturgy, an interest in the liturgy as an essentially communal musical act. These principles have been behind the Lutheran accent on preaching, the early and current Lutheran interest in increasing the frequency with which people commune, and the universal Lutheran interest in using a beautiful form of the local vernacular language in worship. Interestingly, when these principles were critically applied to the medieval traditions of worship as these were received in the localities affected by the Lutheran Reformation, the results sometimes approximated very early Christian traditions in liturgy. Large city churches and schools began to sing congregational forms of morning and evening prayer, recalling the origins of the "Daily Office" as what scholars (somewhat anachronistically) call, first of all, a "cathedral" and not only a "monastic" practice. Preachers actually preached on the Scripture readings in the Sunday liturgy of the Holy Communion, just as did Ambrose and Chrysostom. And the people increasingly understood what was going on.

But there was also a third basic axiom of critique. Reform must not be forced. In fact, no liturgical practice benefits from compulsion. Luther's central liturgical essays were reluctantly published, were proposed as temporary examples, and were full of warnings: "ja keyn nöttig gesetz draus machen" (WA 19, 72). Luther's own path toward liturgical reform was full of such counsel. The *Invocavit* sermons he preached in Wittenberg in 1522, after he had returned from the Wartburg to urge the restoration of images, Communion in one kind, and the Latin Mass until changes could be introduced with less authoritarian constraint, called for reform to occur in a way we would call "pastoral"—with teaching and with love. And in the polemical writing directed against Andreas Karlstadt in 1525, *"Wider die himmlischen*

Propheten," Luther argued that among the Wittenbergers, *"ym kloster,"* Mass was celebrated with great simplicity, just as Karlstadt urged, without chasuble or elevation, and *"ynn der pfarr,"* with full ceremony, with alb, chasuble, elevation, incense, and altar. But neither ceremonial practice, neither *"thun"* nor *"lassen,"* was constrained: *"Wyr thun wie die Papisten, on das wyr die lere, gepot und zwang nicht leyden. Wyr lassen auch wie die Carlstadischen, aber das verbot leyden wyr nicht. So sind nu der Bapst und D. Carlstad rechte vettern ym leren, den sie leren beyde, eyner das thun, der ander das lassen, wyr leren aber keynes und thuns beydes"* (WA 18, 113).

Whether or not Luther described the pope and Karlstadt with fairness here, the Lutheran heritage has continued to contain in its best sources a profound criticism of compulsion in matters of worship, especially if that compulsion is supposedly grounded in divine authority, and a call for change to occur by means of teaching and love. This is a heritage newly important to the whole ecumenical church in a multicultural, postmodern time. Still, it needs to be recalled, the shape of the liturgy Luther was discussing, whether done simply or with rich ceremony, was that of the Mass.

The great hesitancy about liturgical constraint, this third axiom of critique, has meant that in Lutheran liturgical history there has never been a generally approved missal, a universal Book of Common Prayer, a set of standard texts. There have indeed been *Kirchenordnungen,* local church documents for the peaceful organization of church life and worship in given areas and countries.[5] Sometimes these *Kirchenordnungen* follow the pattern of Luther's essays: they are prose proposals about the organization of worship in a given area, proceeding by way of personal visitation and persuasion. Sometimes they are legal requirements for worship, though only for a given area church. Sometimes they provide some explicit liturgical materials. And there certainly have been Lutheran liturgical books —agendas, handbooks, hymnals, *cantionales*—that, added to the old missals and antiphonaries which continued in use, could give flesh to the rubrical requirements of the *Kirchenordnungen.*

---

[5] See A. L. RICHTER, ed., *Die evangelischen Kirchenordnungen des sechszehnten Jahrhunderts* (Weimar, 1846; repr. Nieuwkoop: De Graaf, 1967); E. SEHLING, ed., *Die evangelischen Kirchenordnungen des XVI. Jahrhunderts* (Leipzig, 1902–1913; repr. Tübingen: J.C.B. Mohr (Paul Siebeck), 1957–1977); and I. PAHL, ed., *Coena Domini I: Die Abendmahlsliturgie der Reformationskirchen im 16./17. Jahrhundert,* Spicilegium Friburgense 29 (Freiburg: Universitätsverlag, 1983).

A profound history of Lutheran worship would need to inquire from sources other than books—eyewitness accounts, parish registers, letters, the material remains of churches—exactly how the *Kirchenordnungen* and the various liturgical texts and music were enacted in local parishes. But for the purposes of a rough outline, it can be observed that the Mass or Holy Communion or Eucharist continued to be celebrated in Lutheran churches in ways that can be categorized according to their use of Luther's pattern of the *Formula missae* (now put into the vernacular, though sometimes, as in Nuremberg for centuries, still in both Latin and German) or their adoption of the largely hymnic scheme and more radical eucharistic solution of the *Deutsche Messe*. The many church orders influenced by the Brandenburg-Nuremberg *Kirchenordnung* of 1533 and the patterns adopted in Sweden and Finland (and ultimately in North America), for example, followed the former. The church orders written by Johannes Bugenhagen (1485–1558) and the patterns adopted in Denmark, Norway, and Iceland were more inclined to the latter. In many cases, however, considerable continuation of local medieval uses could also be detected. What united this great diversity of practice into a single Lutheran context for worship were the principles of conservation and critique, the retention of the Mass and the great tradition, together with the critical accents upon the word, participation, and an absence of compulsion in ceremony.

These very principles could and did harden into a context for worship marked by considerably less life than the foregoing might suggest. "Conservation" could become local narrow-mindedness or, in certain historic contexts, romantic flights of imagination. The "word" could become didacticism. Or the principles could be forgotten altogether. Lutherans, just as much as other Christians, could force worship practices, especially when ecclesial leadership became allied with the state and allowed liturgical practice to become a legal test of loyalty and obedience or when Lutherans felt threatened and isolated. A profound history of Lutheran worship would also have to explore these occasions of loss.

As with many other churches throughout the Western world, the Lutherans experienced the seventeenth, eighteenth, and early nineteenth centuries as detrimental to a vison of worship marked by communal participation in the sacraments. The devastations of the Thirty Years' War left many Lutheran congregations not only without pastors and buildings but also without those old, frequently medieval, books that were needed for the enactment of the conservative Lutheran liturgy. Then, both Rationalism and Pietism led to infrequency of Communion, and that infrequency inevitably affected the character of Sunday preaching and the understanding of the meaning of the scriptural word. These are losses that have continued to live with European and North American Lutherans into the present and began to be exported into the rest of the world when missions drew their energy from Pietist circles and their patterns of worship from Pietist exercises.

The resultant Sunday liturgy, in both orthodox Lutheran and Pietist hands, frequently became half of the Mass, the word service alone, since there were few or no communicants in the congregation and, by old Lutheran principles, the Eucharist could not be completed if only the priest were to commune. In Rationalist hands, liturgies sometimes became lengthy and word-filled encomiums on the life of virtue. New liturgical texts appeared that were extensively marked by this latter characteristic.

But then, let me say something about the Lutheran movements for liturgical renewal. These centuries of loss were not without moments of renewal, each characterized in its own way with conservation and critique. The seventeenth and eighteenth centuries gave to the Lutherans and to the whole church several great hymnwriters, who sang, often from the midst of great suffering, the depth of the sacramental life in Christ and whose song still deepens Lutheran worship. Whole areas and cities maintained a strong, sacramentally focused life of worship—for instance, Leipzig in the time of J. S. Bach—in the face of widespread decline, while still using the artistic and cultural forms of the times to express the faith. And in North America, the missionary and church founder Henry Melchior Muhlenberg in 1748 presented to the first Lutheran synod in North America a liturgical pattern rooted in the *Formula missae* and the *Kirchenordnungen*. Muhlenberg's work, like Luther's, was an essay about how to do the order for the Holy Communion (including, of course, how to use that order in those times when only the word service was celebrated) and the orders for baptism, confession and forgiveness, and marriage in the new situation of the American colonies. This work was not itself a liturgy but referred to available resources and evaluated them. And it was not even, in this case, a book; it was a handwritten essay, copied by hand and circulated from pastor to pastor. But it stood in the great tradition of conservation and critique.

The nineteenth century among the Lutherans, as among many other Western Christians, brought with it the beginnings of a liturgical renaissance. The first characteristic of this movement involved conservation, the recovery of the classic Lutheran use of catholic tradition. A new accent on the Lutheran Confessions coincided with new attention to the Lutheran conservative attitude toward the sacraments. Depth of scholarship and new pastoral-liturgical materials were provided to this movement by figures like Wilhelm Löhe of Upper Bavaria.

Perhaps the greatest thinker of this nineteenth century movement, however, was Nikolai F. S. Grundtvig of Denmark. In Grundtvig's hands, the conservative character of the Lutheran context for worship came to expression as a call to the centrality of baptism and the Supper for congregational life. And the critical character of that context included, for Grundtvig, a renewed accent on the participating congregation, and because of the sacraments, a resistance to biblicism (*"Kun ved badet og ved bordet, hører vi Guds ord til os,"* he sang in one of his many hymns), a resistance to liturgical coercion, and a resistance to any religiously closed door. One North American Danish congregation summed up the nineteenth-century Grundtvigian version of the Lutheran understanding of liturgy with this inscription on its church bell: *"Til badet og bordet, til bønnen og ordet, jeg kalder hver søgende sjael"* ("To the bath and the table, to the prayer and the word, I call every seeking soul").

In North America, influence from the confessional revival and from the work of Löhe, together with a deep interest in the earliest *Kirchenordnungen,* assisted in the recovery of the *ordo* of the Mass and of daily prayer as the now common inheritance of all the Lutheran bodies of the continent. The Common Service of 1888 served as the source for the liturgical material published in many different worship books and hymnals throughout the twentieth century. In turn, this consensus provided material that was translated for churches in other areas of the world, for example, into Spanish for Lutheran Latin America (*Culto Cristiano,* 1964).

In the second half of the twentieth century, many Lutheran churches throughout the world published new liturgical materials. In doing this they were partly inspired by the Roman Catholic liturgical movement,[6] by its fruit in the Constitution on the Sacred Liturgy of

[6] One influential Lutheran study of that movement was E. B. KOENKER, *The Liturgical Renaissance in the Roman Catholic Church* (Chicago: University of Chicago Press, 1954).

the Second Vatican Council (1963), and by its accent on liturgical *aggiornamento*. But they were also inspired by post-war, mutual inter-Lutheran exchange in the Lutheran World Federation, by new access to Lutheran sources, by the striking growth of the frequency of Communion in all the Lutheran churches, and by the renewed importance of congregational baptismal practice. As a result, new agendas, handbooks, hymnals, rituals or combined worship books appeared for Lutheran churches in Australia, North America, Iceland, Germany, Denmark, Norway, Sweden, Finland, Latvia and Latvian churches in America, Slovakia and parts of Latin America, Africa, and Asia. In several of these places, yet further resources—supplementary hymnals, trial handbooks, official statements on the congregational "use" of word and sacrament[7]—were published in the late twentieth and early twenty-first centuries, witnessing to the continued liveliness and volatility of worship reform in Lutheran context today. Partly as preparation for these new resources and partly as support for them, a large number of pastoral liturgical studies were also published, greatly enriching the Lutheran dialogue on worship. These included introductory manuals, liturgical histories, specific studies of liturgical reform, as well as pastoral-theological reflections on the meaning of worship and its renewal.

The twentieth century also witnessed the specific growth of liturgical theology in Lutheran context. The way was prepared for this growth by the reflective writing of Löhe and Grundtvig, but also by the work of the Swedish scholar-bishop U. L. Ullman and by some strains of resurgent Luther studies. The two towering figures of twentieth-century Lutheran liturgical theology have been Yngve Brilioth of Sweden and Peter Brunner of Germany. But the work of reflecting on the meanings of the liturgical assembly has continued, sometimes with considerable attention to the anthropological context and materials of worship, sometimes as sacramental theology, which is difficult to distinguish from liturgical theology in Lutheran context, sometimes with a focus on liturgical language, sometimes as a central issue in the theology of mission, sometimes with the practice of the assembly itself as the primary data and with a clear agenda for reform. But in all these cases of theological reflection, the classic themes

---

[7] For example, "The Use of the Means of Grace: A Statement on the Practice of Word and Sacrament," Minneapolis, 1997, and "Usages des moyens de grâce," Ngaoundere, Cameroon, 2001.

of the Lutheran approach to worship—conservation and critique—play some role. Often conservation and critique and their continuing interaction establish the central questions: What shall we conserve and why? What are the sources and reasons for liturgical criticism? And—here is the theological question—what does the interaction of conservation and critique actually have to do with God?

These questions have a trajectory into the future. The Lutheran reception of the catholic tradition cannot be seen as a static thing, a continuing "reception" simply of the catholic tradition as it may have been celebrated in late medieval Europe. There is, after all, an ecumenical discussion afoot about what is actually to be regarded as "catholic," about those things that Christians of every time and place have as their heritage, and Lutherans participate in that discussion. Today the catholic conservatism of the Lutheran context for worship needs to include ecumenism and the fruits of ecumenical liturgical study and renewal. This new character of the Lutheran interest in conservation can be seen in such widespread phenomena as the recovery of an Antiochene pattern for praying at the eucharistic table, the interest in the restoration of an adult catechumenate, the interest in encouraging both women and men as leaders of the assembly, and the interest in an *ordo*-based approach to liturgical planning (see the German *Erneuerte Agende* and the American *With One Voice*). None of these things, except the idea of the *ordo*, had any currency in the sixteenth century. All of them are alive in the Lutheran approach to worship because they belong to what is today rightly considered to be "catholic."

The Lutheran approach to worship must also continue to make use of its axioms for critique—the clarity of the gospel-word, the participation of the whole assembly, and the absence of compulsion—applying these axioms also to the new ecumenical consensus. But it may be that precisely the concerns for the clarity of the gospel-word and for participation will push the worldwide Lutheran context for worship toward what may be the most critical of contemporary questions: contextualization or inculturation. This question, of course, matters as much in the changing circumstances of Europe and America as it does in Asia and Africa. And examples of Asian and African integrity in celebrating word and sacrament in new circumstances and with new resonances may give fertile assistance to American and European attempts to do the same.

The use of the ecumenical liturgical consensus and the quest for authentic contextualization—worship and ecumenism and worship and culture—these are creative ways to articulate today the classic characteristics of worship in a Lutheran context: conservation and critique. So, these very characteristics have marked the best Lutheran liturgical life and can be seen as keys to understand ongoing Lutheran liturgical reform. But how do they contribute to the unity of the churches?

That is the very point. In ecumenical liturgical-theological perspective, and not just according to Lutheran ecclesiology, the church is always a communion of local churches. Local assemblies around what the Augsburg Confession calls "the gospel rightly preached and the sacraments celebrated according to the gospel," local assemblies in unity with one another precisely in God's gift of that gospel and those sacraments and not in any coerced pattern of ceremony—these make up and are "the church." But then, from Lutheran perspective, unity between these local churches will be served by sending and receiving mutual encouragement to let the center of each assembly's practice be marked by conservation and critique.

So here is the proposal: Let the churches throughout the world share with one another the best of their liturgical experience and the depth of their current insight into what is catholic. Let us talk together about what is catholic. That catholic reality will necessarily include the ways in which bath and table, prayer and word, are locally being made available to "every seeking soul." Let the churches affirm and admonish each other toward the conservative reception of the catholic liturgical tradition. At the same time, let the churches affirm and admonish each other toward the exercise of critique about their own practice: Is the gospel of Jesus Christ clear? Is participation in these central, catholic matters encouraged and is the door open? Is compulsion avoided? Here is how a Lutheran would say it: Liturgical full-communion will be assisted by such affirmation and admonition, by such conservation and critique. It will not be assisted either by any sort of hierarchical centralism or by a determination to just let each other alone.

One way that both conservation and critique are available to us in current Christian liturgical life is found in the widespread use of the *ordo* of the liturgy as a tool for planning and teaching and as an instrument for communion. It is remarkable to find this tool appearing in the North American Presbyterian Book of Common Worship, in the Lutheran "Renewing Worship" project, in the German *Erneuerte Agende*, in the British *Common Worship*, as also in the Revised Roman

Sacramentary that has been proposed by the International Commission on English in the Liturgy (ICEL). The use of the *ordo* combines both conservation and critique: conservation in the passing on of the great shape of the Mass, for example; critique in using that shape to welcome deeper participation in new cultural contexts, and critique in the sense that such a shared *ordo* is not a matter of ceremonial compulsion.

When Martin Luther—and Henry Melchior Muhlenberg—made use of the *ordo Missae* to teach and contextualize liturgical practice, they were doing a deeply authentic Lutheran thing. But they were not doing a new thing. In fact, the oldest and best church orders of the ancient church—the *Didache*, for example, or the *Apostolic Tradition* or the *Didascalia*—were not primarily liturgical texts, but descriptions and recommendations of an enacted order. Indeed, the oldest tradition of the Roman church comes to expression in just such a described shape—in the pattern of Sunday celebration described by Justin in the remarkable final chapters of his first *Apology*.

Taught by that ancient witness, together making use of conservation and critique, may we be surprised anew by the unity that the Spirit of the Risen Christ is already working among us in the already shared word and sacraments at the heart of our local assemblies.

Thomas F. Best

Christian Unity and Christian Diversity, Lessons from Liturgical Renewal: The Case of the Christian Church (Disciples of Christ)

I wish to thank the Centro Pro Unione for the great privilege of speaking to you on the topic of "Christian Unity and Christian Diversity, Lessons from Liturgical Renewal: The Case of the Christian Church (Disciples of Christ)." Having begun with thanks, I now move, as do many liturgies, to confession: I am not going to deliver precisely what I have promised, but rather something more limited in scope—but thereby sharper in focus—than my original title would indicate. So I ask you to add to my title the words "within a populist sacramental church." The church in question is my own church, the Christian Church (Disciples of Christ), and the memorable description of our church as "populist sacramental" comes from the seminal liturgist we have produced, Keith Watkins.[1] I invite you to see what follows as a case study on how that particular church has come, through the liturgical renewal movement, to a new and more profound understanding of its own identity and mission.[2]

1. THE ORIGIN AND DISTINCTIVE QUALITY OF THE CHRISTIAN CHURCH (DISCIPLES OF CHRIST): FROM THE EARLY NINETEENTH CENTURY ON

To understand this story, it is essential to know something of the distinctive history and beliefs of our church, but also its character and ethos. It began in the first two or three decades of the nineteenth century (1820–1830) on the "frontier" in the United States, the frontier

---

[1] "Breaking the Bread of Life: The Eucharistic Piety of the Christian Church (Disciples of Christ)," *Mid-Stream* 36, no. 3/4 (1997) 293–307 (reference, p. 296, citing *Celebrate with Thanksgiving: Patterns of Prayer at the Communion Table* [St. Louis: Chalice Press, 2001] esp. 11ff.).

[2] The following discussion draws upon my recent articles on Disciples' worship published in P. BRADSHAW, ed., *The New SCM Dictionary of Liturgy and Worship* (London: SCM Press, 2002) 44–45 , 76–77, 110–112, 181–182, 349–350, 483–484.

then being western Virginia and Pennsylvania, Kentucky, and Ohio, from the coalescing of impulses for the "restoration" of the "clear picture," as was thought, of the church as found in the New Testament. Principal founders of the movement were father and son Thomas and Alexander Campbell, who were Presbyterians from Scotland but who had also lived in Ireland, and another Presbyterian, Barton W. Stone. The movement was a remarkable combination of Enlightenment rationalism and evangelistic zeal. It was said that Alexander Campbell would arrive on horseback at frontier camp meetings and revivals with saddle-bags full of books—on one side of the horse, Greek texts and the Bible in various translations, including one that he issued himself,[3] mind you, and on the other side, the writings of Isaac Newton and John Locke.

These founders were driven by the desire to lead the divided churches (Presbyterian, Methodist, Baptist, and others) toward a unity rooted in the weekly celebration of the Lord's Supper. Four things in particular characterized this early unity movement: observance of the Lord's Supper (or communion or Eucharist) on each Lord's Day (or Sunday); baptism by submersion, or full immersion, of not only professing but penitent adult believers; a decidedly congregational polity, with elders providing leadership; and a hunger for the unity of Christians. I have been told, upon describing this constellation of core beliefs, that we are a "cafeteria church," formed by taking the eucharistic frequency of the Anglicans, the baptismal practice of the Baptists, and the polity of the Congregationalists; but we would say that the reality is just the reverse: we have taken each and every one of these practices, as well as the imperative for unity, from a single source—the New Testament—while other churches have devolved from this coherent pattern, specializing in one aspect of the New Testament picture, sometimes to the extent, as with the Baptists, that the church has taken its very name from that one aspect of Christian faith and practice.

The early Disciples were also shaped and characterized by two negative factors. The first was a positive dislike, born of personal experience, of the divisions and rivalries among Christians. One of the Disciples' foundational myths tells how one of the Campbells, still in

[3] G. CAMPBELL, J. MacKNIGHT, and P. DODDRIGE *The Sacred Writings of the Apostles and Evangelists of Jesus Christ: Common Styled the New Testament. Translated from the original Greek, with Prefaces, Various Emendations, and an Appendix by Alexander Campbell,* Bethany, Virginia, 1833, compiled by Alexander Campbell).

the Old Country, had been excluded from the Lord's Supper in a Presbyterian church, not because he was not a Presbyterian (he was), but because he was the wrong *kind* of Presbyterian. The will to unity in this early period had a radical, almost visceral side to it, and the cause of unity was something, ecclesially speaking at least, to die for: in the "Last Will and Testament of the Springfield Presbytery," one of the more remarkable documents of church history, an ecclesial body publicly declared the following: "We will that this body die, be dissolved, and sink into union with the Body of Christ at large." It was not for nothing that the early leaders called Christian unity the Disciples' "polar star," for us the fixed point around which all else revolves.[4]

A second negative factor in these formational days was a healthy suspicion of creeds, not so much in themselves as positive statements of faith, but in their negative use. As Campbell said—and remember he was thinking of divisions among Protestant bodies at least as much as between Protestants and Roman Catholics—wherever he saw divided churches, he saw their respective creeds justifying, and maintaining, them in their division. But the situation was nuanced: the Apostles' Creed was considered "catholic" (of value for *all* the churches) "because it is a recital of the facts of the gospel."[5] And I myself grew up in a Disciples church that recited the Apostles' Creed every week.

But let us now look in more detail at the worship practice of the churches in the early Disciples movement. Since no definitive, detailed rite is described, much less prescribed, in the New Testament, it was incumbent upon congregations and particularly their elders, in the maturity of their faith and exercising reason, to order the community's worship (which, remember, included the Lord's Supper each Sunday). Typically the service included prayers, hymns, Scripture readings, the celebration of the Supper itself, preaching (if, and only if, a person of suitable gifts was available!), and a concluding collection. Leadership was provided, at each point in the service, by those best suited according to the gifts they had received from the Lord.

A clear and colorful sense of these early days comes from Alexander Campbell's account, taken from his "memorandum-book," of Lord's Day worship in one church that he had visited:

[4] The image continues to fascinate Disciples. See, for example, P. A. CROW, JR., "Three Dichotomies and a Polar Star," *Mid-Stream* 21, no. 1 (1982) 21–30.

[5] W. J. RICHARDSON, "Alexander Campbell as an Advocate of Christian Union," in *Lectures in Honor of the Alexander Campbell Bicentennial, 1788–1988* (Nashville: Disciples of Christ Historical Society, 1988) 104.

Not having any person whom they regarded as filling Paul's outlines of a bishop [meaning a local overseer or pastor], they had appointed two senior members, of a very grave deportment, to preside in their meetings. These persons were not competent to labor in the word and teaching; but they were qualified to rule well, and to preside with Christian dignity. One of them presided at each meeting.[6]

At a certain point in the service,

he [the presiding officer] then called upon a brother, who was a very distinct and emphatic reader, to read a section of the evangelical history. He arose and read, in a very audible voice, the history of the crucifixion of the Messiah.[7]

Later on Campbell records, with satisfaction, that following one of the prayers "the whole congregation, brethren and sisters, pronounced aloud the final *Amen*."[8]

Note in particular the early eucharistic practice of the Disciples of Christ, this being the most distinctive aspect, the heart of their identity as a church, and, as we shall see later on, perhaps the area of our greatest interaction—and learning—from the liturgical movement. As Campbell's account continues, then, we have his description of the Lord's Supper as conducted in a Disciples' congregation in a frontier town, perhaps in western Virginia and perhaps about 1830:

The president [usually a lay elder, duly appointed by the congregation] arose and said that our Lord had a table for his friends, and that he invited his disciples to sup with him. [Following a brief meditation, focusing on Christ's giving of himself for the world's salvation:] He [the president] took a small loaf from the table, and in one or two periods gave thanks for it. After thanksgiving he raised it in his hand, and significantly brake it, and handed it to the disciples on each side of him, who passed the broken loaf from one to another, until they all partook of it. There was no stiffness, no formality, no pageantry; all was easy, familiar, solemn, cheerful. He then took the cup in a similar manner, and returned thanks for it, and handed it to the disciple sitting next to him, who passed it round; each one waiting upon his brother, until all were served. The thanksgiving before the breaking of the loaf, and the distributing of the cup, were as brief and pertinent to the occasion, as

[6] A. CAMPBELL, *The Christian System*, 2nd ed. (Cincinnati: Standard Publishing Company, 1839) 290.

[7] Ibid., 291.

[8] Ibid.

the thanks usually presented at a common table for the ordinary blessings of God's bounty.[9]

Significantly, the Supper was followed by prayers of supplication on behalf of the afflicted, the poor and the destitute, and on behalf of the conversion of the world.[10]

As the account of the service continues, no sermon is mentioned, and indeed the practice was to dispense with the sermon when no one considered suitable to preach was at hand; but Scripture readings and some sort of reaction to them were always included, and after the collection, a number of persons rose to read biblical passages and to propose, and inquire on, matters "tending to the edification of the body." Following several spiritual songs, "on the motion of a brother who signified that the hour of adjournment had arrived," the president pronounced the apostolic benediction.[11] Characteristically, Campbell offers this whole account, not as a fixed prescription for Disciples' worship, but as an example that included the essential elements, conducted in a way that he found to be commendable in practice, of the Lord's Day service, that is, the Lord's Supper service.

If gathering at the Lord's Table was "the one essential act of Sunday worship," repeated again and again, then it was balanced by baptism as a decisive single moment in the believer's lifelong journey in faith. Disciples' baptismal theology and practice were, I think, less distinctive than their understanding and conduct of the Eucharist, and here we need only outline it briefly. Their baptismal position was, of course, explained with the usual vigor and clarity of thought. Again, the determining factor was what was understood to be New Testament practice, and so baptism for Disciples was characterized by the profession of faith offered by a penitent believer, the use of the Trinitarian formula, and full immersion in water. In excluding "indiscriminate" (including but not limited to infant) baptism, the Disciples' founders also sought to distinguish the church from the surrounding culture and from the state, and to expunge the memory of baptismal practice in the established churches of the Old World. This was one area where the early Disciples' leadership had significant differences of opinion among themselves, notably over whether immersion was the only valid "mode" of baptism. Barton Stone did

[9] Ibid., 291–292.
[10] Ibid., 292.
[11] Ibid.

105

not insist absolutely on it, but Alexander Campbell did, and partly to make the point, in his own translation of the New Testament he famously rendered every occurrence of *baptizein* as "immerse."

Let us conclude this initial exposition by looking more closely at the *sacramental* dimension of this frontier unity movement. Early Disciples found the term "sacrament" uncongenial, mainly, I think, for historic reasons and preferred to speak of "ordinances," that is, practices "ordained" (or commanded) by Christ as a means of making God's saving action present and visible in the world. They understood the Lord's Supper and baptism to be the chief ordinances; each uses material substances (bread, the fruit of the vine, water), and each is a visible sign and seal of God's grace. Each ordinance, moreover, has its own particular grace, or special role in the plan of salvation: for baptism, it is the remission of sin unto newness of life in Christ; for the Supper, nourishing the faith and unity of believers. I have spoken elsewhere about the "starkly realistic nature"[12] of early Disciples' sacramental thought and life, which was indeed rationalist (though never reductionist). Thus for Alexander Campbell, "the Holy Spirit works upon *the understanding and affections* of saints and sinners,"[13] so that Christians "must perceive, realize, appropriate, and feel the *blood* of Christ *applied* to our reason, our conscience, our will, and to our affections."[14]

The Table is Christ's; he is our host, and the whole church is invited to his Table. He is present; he enters into head and heart alike in a way that is tangible and has visible effects in our lives. If that's not "presence," and if it isn't "real," then I don't know what is.

2. DEVELOPMENTS WITHIN THE CHRISTIAN CHURCH (DISCIPLES OF CHRIST): THROUGH THE MID-TWENTIETH CENTURY

Thus by about 1840 or so the main outlines of this "populist sacramental" church were established, its most distinctive feature being the observance each Lord's Day of the Lord's Supper, presided over by elders, who used extemporaneous prayers at the Table.[15] But my

[12] T. F. BEST, "Disciples Identity and the Ecumenical Future," *Disciples Theological Digest* 8, no. 1 (1993) 5–20.

[13] *Millennial Harbinger* (May 1855) 258; emphasis mine.

[14] *Millennial Harbinger*, Extra, no. 8 (October 1935) 508; see *Millennial Harbinger* (December 1855) 662.

[15] "Breaking the Bread of Life," 293–307.

topic is finally the encounter of the Disciples with the movement for liturgical renewal, and the early nineteenth-century Disciples of Christ church I have just described is not, of course, the same as that which encountered the liturgical movement in the mid-twentieth century. To understand *that* church, and thus the significance of that encounter, we must see how the Disciples developed over the hundred years or so from about 1840 to 1940 or 1950.

In some areas of the church's faith and life, there was growth and development; in other areas, there was growth. The "Restorationist" movement stemming from the Campbells, Barton Stone, Walter Scott, and others had brought together diverse persons and viewpoints; as these leaders died and the movement moved into its second and third generations, a fault line became apparent between more "progressive" and more "conservative" wings.

One fundamental problem was the interpretation of Scripture, particularly on the question of how to order the life of the church on matters not resolved by the first generation of leaders, and about which the New Testament was inconveniently silent. This came to a head on the question of how far musical instruments could be used in worship, since such use was not recorded in the New Testament. A second problem was the relation of local congregations to church structures beyond the local level, with some refusing to join cooperative institutions—even for reasons of mission—which were seen as threatening local autonomy. A third problem was the relation of the church to the state, with some pastors or congregations refusing to take actions that might be interpreted as seeking "recognition" by the state. By the early twentieth century, the most conservative forces had left, coalescing to form separate churches carrying a different (and from a Disciples of Christ perspective, more limited) form of the Campbell-Stone "Restoration" vision. Meanwhile the Disciples of Christ, through a series of specific decisions (all tending in a "progressive" direction) about the issues named above, had defined itself as a recognizably "mainline" denomination.

But the pattern was different in different areas of the church's life, and we need to consider a number of factors in more detail, beginning, inevitably, with the Lord's Supper. The conviction remained that since the Table was Christ's, the church had no authority to exclude anyone from the Table who had been claimed by Christ, that is, who had been baptized. The practice of elders offering prayers—usually one elder praying over the bread and one over the wine—

continued. I say "wine," but in fact (reflecting the founders' aversion to alcohol, based on their experience on the frontier) the use of unfermented grape juice continued as the norm.

What did change, and for the worse, was the relation of the Table to the Word, that is, of the Supper to the sermon. Originally the sermon was dispensed with if no suitable elder or traveling evangelist was on hand. In any case, the sermon was placed at the conclusion of the service, partly because there it could be more easily dispensed with if necessary. But with the gradual development of an ordained, professional, paid clergy, the sermon became the prerogative of the local pastor, and a fixed and necessary part of the Lord's Day service. It remained at the conclusion of the service, but increasingly for a different reason: as a divine rhetoric, an evangelistic message reinforcing or calling out belief, the sermon increasingly replaced the Supper as the climax of the service.

Furthermore, the ordained minister came to have a prominent role in the service of the Table itself. It became the norm for elders and deacons to be joined at the Table by the ordained minister, who would recite the words of institution from the Gospels or 1 Corinthians 11, and perhaps give a brief meditation, before the elders' prayers for the loaf and the cup. The deacons would then distribute the elements to the congregation, who remained seated and passed the elements to one another. At best, this sharing of leadership by laity and ordained clergy modeled the ministry of the whole people of God; and some elders' prayers reflected, in simple and beautiful language, a lifetime of growth into Christ. But often enough the elders' prayers showed neither theological understanding nor spiritual depth, thus only reinforcing the dominance of the sermon that followed. Meanwhile, the liberal theology of the first half of the twentieth century and a general resistance to representational thought diminished the sense of the sacred in worship and encouraged a commemorative understanding of the Supper as an event that evoked the lively memory, but not the actual presence (however understood), of Christ.

In the case of baptism, there is a twofold story to be told. We noted earlier that Barton Stone and Alexander Campbell differed on the necessity for immersion, and in this case it was the stricter position of Campbell that prevailed generally in the church, at least until about 1900. This meant that persons joining a Disciples' congregation who had been baptized, but in other ways, were normally expected to "complete their obedience to Christ" by undergoing full immersion. I hesitate to call this "re-baptism," since the language of "completing" obedience implied at least the partial efficacy of the baptism that had already been received elsewhere. It was striking that the logic of Disciples' eucharistic theology led to the practice of an open Table, so that many congregations that required full immersion baptism for membership would nevertheless receive at the Lord's Table persons who had been baptized in other ways.

While full immersion remained, and indeed remains, the practice in Disciples' churches for persons first entering the body of Christ, the attitude to a "re"- or "completing" baptism began to change from about 1900, with some congregations beginning to accept earlier the baptism of persons transferring membership from "non-immersion" churches. I am not sure of the reasons for this, but I like to regard it as representing a rebirth or reawakening of the early Disciples' ecumenical conviction and zeal, which had faded somewhat as the Disciples consolidated their position as a denomination in the latter half of the nineteenth century. Perhaps this renewed sense of their vocation to unity came from the increasing ecumenical experience of Disciples as they engaged with others in associations for practical Christian work (such as the Sunday School Movement around the turn of the century). Perhaps it came from the awareness of figures such as Peter Ainslie, who became a well-known proponent of the nascent Faith and Order movement worldwide. Perhaps it reflected the emergence of the Disciples as one of the principal actors in the formation of councils of churches at all levels from local to national. It would be a mistake to say that the "mind" of the church had fully changed on this issue by 1950, but there was certainly a growing reluctance to call into question baptisms duly performed in other churches.

Other points in our profile can be noted more briefly. As mentioned before, this period saw the emergence of a professional, salaried clergy understood as the, or a, leader of the local congregation. But that was precisely the question: was it "the" or was it "a" leader? The role of the elder was so deeply ingrained in Disciples' ethos that there was no question of the professional ministry supplanting it. Yet the functions of the elder, who was ordained locally to oversee the life of a local congregation, including administering the Lord's Supper and baptism and, if suited for it, to preach as well, were precisely those for which the professional clergy was being trained. It should be stressed that the pattern described earlier, with both elders and the minister active at the Lord's Table, was understood as an enrichment of the church's life, drawing on the gifts of both lay and clerical leadership. But the fundamental questions remained: what is the relation of pastor and elders, and what is the role of lay leadership in an age of increasing specialization and professionalization, in the church as everywhere else?

A special word is in order about our use of liturgical books and resources. We produced our first authorized liturgical book, for voluntary use, in 1953. That is, through the whole period that we are presently considering, there was no official, standard worship text. This followed from the fact that local congregations had, from our earliest days, been entrusted with the responsibility of ordering of their own worship, and from a reluctance to introduce anything other than the New Testament as authoritative in matters of faith and practice, including worship practice.

Yet there was, in fact, a discernible, distinctive "Disciples'" worship practice, based primarily on two factors. The first factor was, inevitably, the widely followed pattern of the Lord's Supper observance (with minister and elders, as described above). The second was the hymnals published by Disciples, which, through widespread use rather than official prescription, gave a considerable measure of common worship experience throughout the whole church. The tradition began with Alexander Campbell's own widely used hymnal;[16] perhaps most prominent later on was *Hymns of the United Church* (1924, co-edited by C. C. Morrison and Herbert L. Willett),[17] whose title reflects the growing appeal of things ecumenical for many Disciples of that day. In this, and not only in this, the hymnals were prophetic forces in the life of the church: the next widely used hymnal, *Christian Worship: A Hymnal* (1941),[18] was published by the Disciples denominational press together with the American Baptist Convention.

---

[16] In one form in use as early as 1834: see *Psalms, Hymns, and Spiritual Songs, Original and Selected* (Bethany, Va.: printed by A. Campbell, 1834), and *Psalms, Hymns, and Spiritual Songs, Original and Selected: Adapted to the Christian Religion* (Carthage, Ohio: printed by W. Scott, 1835); later versions include *The Christian Hymn Book: A Compilation of Psalms, Hymns, and Spiritual Songs, Original and Selected, by A. Campbell and Others* (Cincinnati: H. Bosworth, 1968 [1865]).

[17] Chicago: Christian Century Press, 1924.

[18] Christian Board of Publication, St. Louis: Bethany Press.

A final point should be noted; it is implicit in my description of the Lord's Day service as normative for Disciples but may have escaped your notice. Simply put, Disciples, as they had developed through the mid-twentieth century and in contrast to the Reformed aspects of their heritage, had little idea of a service of the Word in the classical Reformed sense, that is, a Sunday service including entrance, Scripture reading, proclamation of the gospel and response, statement of faith, and prayers of intercession, but stopping short of the sharing of Christ's body and blood at the Lord's Table.

There were, of course, frequent and fervent small-scale occasions for prayer and meditation upon Scripture, such as personal devotions or the prayers held by staff in church offices. These were understood to be sufficient unto themselves. But there were also occasions on which a more elaborate, but non-eucharistic service was called for, especially in interchurch and special ministry contexts, for example installation services for officers of councils of churches, services in institutional settings such as church camps or hospitals, or services in observance of special occasions in the life of the local community. Such services would normally include the reading of Scripture and some form of response to it, but other elements, and their overall order, followed no fixed or classical pattern. And I think it is fair to say that most Disciples, attending a non-eucharistic service beyond the level of personal devotions or of any complexity, would have felt that "something was missing" when the service did not include the Lord's Supper.

This was, then, in broad outline, the personality of the Disciples of Christ in the United States around the middle of the twentieth century: centered on the Scriptures as the basis of faith and the life of the church; populist, that is, solidly middle class and with a preference for direct, simple symbols; sacramental, with the center of the church's life found, in each Lord's Day worship, at the Lord's Table service led by elders and (often) the minister, but less sacramental, perhaps, than earlier in our history as the sermon tended to overshadow the Supper; firmly committed to the baptism of professing believers by submersion, but increasingly ready to respect the practice of other churches; recovering its original ecumenical vocation; searching for the right relationship between professional pastoral leadership and the witness of elders; evincing a fervent piety, especially in personal prayer and congregational hymn singing; with a firm sense of order in worship, maintained not through prescribed worship texts but through widely used hymnals and other worship resources. Worship had settled into nurturing, comfortable patterns and, I suppose, seemed likely to continue that way.

3. THE CHRISTIAN CHURCH (DISCIPLES OF CHRIST) AND LITURGICAL RENEWAL — DEVELOPMENTS SINCE 1950

Fifty years later, at the beginning of the twenty-first century, we find ourselves as Disciples in the midst of a transformation in our self-understanding as a church. My own understanding is that this has been caused by, and expressed through, our engagement in two of the central movements of the Holy Spirit within the whole church in our times. Through interaction with these movements, we have clarified our own identity as a church, have come to a new appreciation of our strengths, and have learned to see where, perhaps, our own history has left us lacking in some things we need to be church fully and faithfully today.

The first of these movements is the ecumenical movement. We came early to it or, indeed, were born of it, as mentioned above; but particularly over the past fifty years, ecumenical engagement has become a central part of the life of our church. Here I will simply mention a few examples of this. There is our engagement, almost from its beginning, in the Consultation on Church Union (now Churches Uniting in Christ) in the United States (indeed, two of the general secretaries of the Consultation have come from our church). There is our seconding, since the 1970s, of an executive staff position in the Faith and Order secretariat of the World Council of Churches. There is our serious engagement with the Faith and Order convergence text *Baptism, Eucharist and Ministry.*[19] There is our close partnership with the United Church of Christ in the U.S., to the extent that these two major denominations share one and the same common board for overseas mission. There is our international bilateral dialogue with the Roman Catholic Church, which has been of deep importance to our own self-understanding.[20] And there is the striking fact that we

[19] For an early example in the liturgical context, see Keith WATKINS, "The Lima Liturgy: When Theology Becomes Liturgy," *Mid-Stream* 23, no. 3 (1984) 285–289.

[20] For the first series of discussions (1977–1982), see *Apostolicity and Catholicity* (Indianapolis: Council on Christian Unity, 1982); for the second (1983–1992), "The Church as Communion in Christ," *Mid-Stream* 33, no. 2 (1994) 219–239; for the third (1993–2002), "Receiving and Handing on the Faith: The Mission and Responsibility of the Church (1993–2002)," *Mid-Stream* 41, no. 4 (2002) 51–79; the reports

have encouraged Disciples-related churches around the world not to continue relating primarily to us as their missioning, or "parent," church but rather to enter church unions, so that Disciples in the Republic of Congo, Thailand, Japan, Jamaica, the United Kingdom, and elsewhere would now be found not as a separate church body but as part of a united church.

Perhaps it was this ecumenical contact with the larger church that made us more aware of the need for responsible ecclesial structures beyond the congregational level. In any case, one of the most profound developments in our life was a process of "Restructure" in the 1960s, which established much clearer patterns of oversight at regional and national levels. A robust sense of local responsibility and initiative remains, but we are much more aware now that local congregations belong to the whole of our church—and to the whole of the whole church. Certainly the encounter with ecumenical theology has had serious consequences for our understanding of both the Lord's Supper and baptism, as we will see in a moment.

The second movement that is transforming our church is, of course, the movement for liturgical renewal. We should note at the beginning that our encounter with this movement was a very particular one, and perhaps quite different from that of other churches. To understand this, we need to recall the intention of the liturgical reform movement, as stated well by Ellsworth Chandlee:

> [The liturgical movement] seeks a recovery of those norms of liturgical worship of the Bible and the early church which lie behind Reformation divisions and medieval distortions, and which are fundamental to Christian liturgy in every time and place. It aims, however, not at an attempt to resuscitate the liturgy of the early Church in the twentieth century, but at the restatement of the fundamentals in forms and expressions which can enable the liturgy to be the living prayer and work of the church today.[21]

Thus the liturgical movement presented Disciples with an understanding of the sources of Christian worship that was broader than that of our own tradition and ethos. In particular, it not only called us

---

from the first and second series are also printed in *Mid-Stream* 41, no. 4 (2002) 80–95 and 96–114 respectively.

[21] J. C. DAVIS, ed., *A New Dictionary of Liturgy and Worship*, 2nd ed. (London: SCM Press, 1986) 314.

to an encounter with the worship of the earliest Christian communities as described in the New Testament but required us to engage seriously with the worship traditions of the early Christian centuries, and indeed beyond. Thus it called us to an engagement with liturgical scholarship in the strict sense of the development of liturgies historically, but also with research on the psychological, sociological, and cultural factors at play in the experience of worship.

Let me sketch the course of our encounter with the liturgical movement, indicating the main personalities involved and some results as reflected in worship materials produced in and for our church. Three persons have been central to the process. G. Edwin Osborn produced the church's first "semi-official" worship book in 1953 (mentioned above). Osborn was a student of the psychology of worship and favored "relevant worship" focused on themes of direct concern to the community, but he stressed the importance of a sound biblical and ecumenical basis for worship. William Robinson was in the forefront of our recovery of the centrality of the Lord's Supper, to which we come in a moment. Both Osborn and Robinson died in the 1960s, and since then it has been Keith Watkins who has led both in recovering our own distinctive worship heritage and in our engagement with the liturgical movement.

Watkins' approach was through a series of liturgical studies aimed at renewing Disciples' worship practice. The book *Thankful Praise: A Resource for Christian Worship* (1987)[22] sought "to strengthen Christian public worship and especially the celebration of the Lord's Supper." Its goals can serve as a summary of Disciples' aspirations for their worship today: to connect our worship with the great tradition of Christian worship through the ages; to reflect liturgically the results of ecumenical convergence; to be faithful to the crucial features of traditional Disciples' worship; to be sensitive to social injustice, especially in its anti-Jewish and sexist expressions; to enhance the beauty and diversity of worship through vivid, biblical, and felicitous language; and to encourage a healthy variety within our worship life.[23] In 1991 Watkins followed this book with *Baptism and Belonging: A Resource for Christian Worship,*[24] which sought a parallel renewal in Disciples' understanding and practice of baptism.

[22] St. Louis: Christian Board of Publication.
[23] See T. F. BEST, "Christian Church (Disciples of Christ) Worship," in P. BRADSHAW, ed., *The New SCM Dictionary,* 181.
[24] St. Louis: Christian Board of Publication.

This liturgical process has proceeded alongside a theological one, namely, a study on our church's ecclesiological self-understanding begun by its Commission on Theology in 1978. Three of the texts from this study touch directly on worship: that on ministry (1985), on baptism (1987), and on the Lord's Supper (1993). The overall report, issued in 1997, affirms that in worship the church makes "defining signs of its true identity" as it listens to Scripture, proclaims the word, confesses sin and receives God's forgiving grace, celebrates the sacramental acts of baptism and holy communion, and communicates in prayer with God.[25] This is unfamiliar language for some Disciples, who still expect divine worship to be described more subjectively and in terms of pious emotions warmly felt. Yet it *is* where Disciples find themselves today in their worship. Further, we realize that the theology study could not have come to its conclusions without the study on worship that ran parallel to, and in interaction with, it. One of the true gifts of the Spirit to our church in this process was that we have not only visionary liturgists but also theologians, such as Paul Crow and James O. Duke, who understand that theologians need to listen to liturgists. Many of you will understand how precious that is.

Now let me illustrate our encounter with the liturgical renewal movement and the ecumenical movement by looking in more detail at a number of specific issues.

A. The Lord's Supper

We have experienced, I think, a dramatic renewal of Disciples' eucharistic practice and theology in the past thirty years. Today we would understand the Eucharist as

> a public act in which the church, having heard the proclamation of the word, partakes of Christ's body and blood, thereby remembering God's reconciling initiative in Jesus Christ, celebrating the gift of the Spirit upon the Church, and anticipating the coming reign of God. The Lord's Supper is a sacrament, an expression of Christ's body and blood in the visible signs of bread and wine. The host is the Lord, and the whole church is invited to his Table. The Supper has immediate social consequences; sharing at Christ's table compels the church to work in order that all may have "bread and enough" to eat. The Lord's Supper

---

[25] P. A. CROW, JR., and J. O. DUKE, eds., *The Church for Disciples of Christ: Seeking to Be Truly Church Today* (St. Louis: Christian Board of Publication, 1998) 56.

115

is central to the faith and piety of Disciples, who refer to themselves as "people of the chalice."[26]

The service suggested in *Thankful Praise* includes the classic dimensions of gathering, proclamation of the word, response to the word, coming together around the Lord's Table, and sending forth. The Lord's Table service includes an invitation extended "upon Christ's behalf for all baptized believers," an offering, the classic Disciples' feature of elders' prayers over the loaf and cup, responsive prayers, the institution narrative from Scripture, the breaking of bread, the Lord's Prayer, an expression of peace, the sharing of the elements (normally by passing the loaf and cup through the congregation, who remain seated), and a final prayer.

We noted above the Disciples' drift, through the first half of the twentieth century, toward a restricted "memorial" view of the Supper, in which Christ was more a memory than an actual presence at the Table. Thus one of the central challenges posed to us by the liturgical and ecumenical movements was the recovery of the biblical notion of *anamnesis*, of an *active remembering* that brings into the present the power and effective action of a past event. But as we tackled this question, we remembered that we had resources from our own tradition: thus our great early evangelist and theologian Walter Scott had spoken of baptism and the Lord's Supper as "the crucifixion, or death, burial and resurrection of Christ, repeating themselves in the life and profession of the disciples"[27] and, he might have said, of those who down the ages have followed. The liturgical and ecumenical movements, then, helped us to recover something which had been central to our own identity as a church, but which we had lost through a forgetting of our past, and an accommodation to the surrounding culture. We have recovered the true meaning of the words traditionally carved across the front of the Lord's Table in most Disciples' churches: "Do this in remembrance of me."

Another challenge posed to us was the recovery in the liturgical movement of the *social sense* and significance of worship, a recovery of the awareness that the liturgy led to, demanded, and was the source of, the "liturgy after the liturgy," namely, our Christian service

---

[26] T. F. BEST, "Eucharist. Christian Church," in P. BRADSHAW, ed., *The New SCM Dictionary*, 181.

[27] W. SCOTT, *The Messiahship; or Great Demonstration* (Cincinnati: H. S. Bosworth, 1859) 284.

in the world. Recall from the ecumenical movement the famous statement in *Baptism, Eucharist and Ministry:*

> The eucharist embraces all aspects of life . . . The eucharistic celebration demands reconciliation and sharing among all those regarded as brothers and sisters in the one family of God and is a constant challenge in the search for appropriate relationships in social, economic and political life . . . All kinds of injustice, racism, separation and lack of freedom are radically challenged when we share in the body and blood of Christ. . . .[28]

Some claimed that if we took this liturgical and ecumenical insight too seriously, it would introduce "the world" into worship, threatening to divide congregations on social issues. But then we recalled words of Alexander Campbell himself, who wrote the following:

> The Lord says to each disciple, when he receives the symbols into his hand . . . "For *you* my body was wounded; for *you* my life was taken."[29]

and then continued:

> Each disciple in handing the symbols to his fellow-disciples, says in effect, "You, my brother, once an alien, are now a citizen of heaven: once a stranger, are now brought home to the family of god. You have owned my Lord as your Lord, my people as your people. Under Jesus the Messiah we are one. Mutually embraced in the Everlasting arms, I embrace you in mind: thy sorrows shall be my sorrows, and thy joys my joys." Joint debtors to the favor of God and the love of Jesus, we shall jointly suffer with him, that we may jointly reign with him. Let us, then, renew our strength, remember our King and hold fast our boasted hope unshaken to the end.[30]

Thus for Campbell, in contrast to the "rugged individualism" of his culture, the Supper was both profoundly personal *and* profoundly social. The Supper,

> [i]n relating us each to God, links us to our brothers and sisters in Christ; through the Supper we are made one family and given that eschatological hope which sustains us in suffering, and which enables us mutually to sustain one another. The *koinonia* which we share and

---

[28] *Baptism, Eucharist and Ministry,* "Eucharist," par. 20, Faith and Order Paper 111 (Geneva: World Council of Churches, 1982).
[29] A. CAMPBELL, *The Christian System,* 273.
[30] Ibid.

express at the Lord's Table compels—and empowers—our *diakonia* in all of life.[31]

Such texts have brought a new awareness within our church of the social dimension of the Lord's Supper and encouraged us to see our witness in the world as coherent with, and faithful to, the central role of the Supper in our worship and our self-understanding. Thus again, challenged through the liturgical movement, we rediscovered in our own heritage an aspect that had fallen fallow: the integration of the whole of life, both personal and social, in and through the meal offered by Christ at his Table.

But we did not draw *all* the elements of our eucharistic renewal from our own tradition. Perhaps the most striking development has been in our understanding of the proper *structure* of the Lord's Day service. We noted above that by 1950 the norm was that the service concluded with a powerful sermon as its high point. But through the liturgical movement we gradually learned another pattern, and today it is the norm in our churches that the Supper comes at its conclusion and as its climax, with the sermon seen increasingly as a preparation for the Supper.

Through this shifting of the Supper within the structure of the Lord's Day service, we restored the coherence between our liturgical expression of the meal and the role that it plays in our life and thought. And in so doing we have *aligned our liturgy with the great tradition of eucharistic worship through the ages.* Some of our members, to be sure, would be very surprised to hear our change in practice described in these terms, but that is indeed what we have done. Along with this structural change, we find an increasing desire to symbolize the unity of the church in our liturgical practice: if the communion is given in small, individual cups (as is still usual), then the congregation will hold these and then partake all together. On special, more intimate occasions, a common cup may be used. In all these areas the liturgical renewal movement has been our main inspiration and challenge.

Our understanding and practice of the Lord's Supper is still developing and, I hope, deepening.[32] Some important issues remain to be

[31] I have treated this text also in T. F. BEST, "Koinonia and Diakonia: The Ecumenical Implications of Two Biblical Perspectives on the Church," in D. FIENSY and W. D. HOWDEN, *Faith in Practice: Studies in the Book of Acts* (Atlanta: European Evangelistic Society, 1995) 365–366.

[32] See further "A Word to the Church on the Lord's Supper (1991), A Report of the Committee on Theology," in P. A. CROW, JR., and J. O. DUKE, eds., *The*

resolved. While at the Table the combination of ordained and lay leadership is the norm, in some congregations the line between lay *presence* and lay *presidency* is blurred.[33] In many congregations the prayers offered by elders at the Table are an area where growth is needed, in both liturgical sensitivity and theological content. There is a cultural pressure for children to be admitted to the Table before baptism, and a corresponding pressure for baptism to be performed at younger ages. We want to explore the meaning of Christ's presence at the meal more fully and are suggesting, with our Catholic colleagues, that the next, fourth round of the Disciples–Roman Catholic dialogue should focus on "the presence of Christ in the church, with special reference to the eucharist,"[34] this being "important, given the emphasis that both Disciples and Roman Catholics put on the weekly celebration of the Lord's Supper and its link with the visible unity of Christians."[35]

B. Baptism

The past fifty years have seen significant developments in our appreciation of baptism as well. Our current understanding can be stated in this way, parallel to our grasp of the Lord's Supper:

> [B]aptism is a public act of the church in which a believer, responding by personal profession of faith to God's saving initiative in Jesus Christ, is immersed in water in the name of the Father, Son and Holy Spirit and thereby incorporated into the church and set on a path of lifelong growth into Christ. Baptism is a sacrament, an expression of God's grace in the visible sign of water. It has immediate social consequences,

---

Church for Disciples of Christ, 139–152; and "A Word to the Church on Ministry (1985), in *The Church for Disciples of Christ,* 109–120; and J. O. DUKE and R. HARRISON, JR., *The Lord's Supper* (St. Louis: published for the Council on Christian Unity by Christian Board of Publication, 1993).

[33]On the historical background and present extent and significance of lay presidency in some Disciples' congregations, see K. WATKINS, "Worship as Understood and Practiced by the Christian Church (Disciples of Christ)," in T. F. BEST and D. HELLER, eds., *Worship Today: Understanding, Practice, Ecumenical Implications* (Geneva: WCC Publications, 2004).

[34] "Receiving and Handing on the Faith: The Mission and Responsibility of the Church (1993–2002)," par. 6.2.

[35] "The Church as Communion in Christ," para. 53a, quoted in "Receiving and Handing on the Faith: The Mission and Responsibility of the Church (1993–2002)," par. 6.2.

for the life entered into is one of love of neighbor and sacrificial service in the world.[36]

Our baptismal practice[37] is a process that continues several characteristically Disciples' traditions: the personal profession of faith often comes in response to a "hymn of invitation" sung at the end of a Sunday service; the candidate affirms Jesus as the Christ, the Son of the living God, and his or her own personal Lord and Savior; the period of instruction is meant to explore the depth of this profession and to set it within the faith of the church as a whole, as well as to prepare the candidate to embark on a lifetime's journey with and toward Christ. Baptism is normally performed within a Lord's Day service and in a baptistery visible to the whole congregation.

A number of developments in our practice of baptism are due to the influence and challenge of the liturgical movement and the ecumenical movement. Increasingly, Disciples agree that the rite itself should include the following elements: proclamation of Scripture; repentance and renunciation of evil; profession of faith in Jesus Christ; invocation of the Holy Spirit; full immersion; administration "in the name of the Trinity," normally following the formula in Matthew 28:19; and welcome into the life of the church. *Baptism, Eucharist and Ministry* has been influential, especially in its insistence on the social as well as personal dimensions of baptism, and on the fact that baptism, as a sacrament of unity, is unrepeatable. Since 1950 more and more congregations have refused the practice of "re"-baptism, and the Disciples' official response to *Baptism, Eucharist and Ministry* may be taken as having consolidated the church's official rejection of that practice. At the same time, we have stressed increasingly the fact that baptism is into the *whole* church, not just "our" particular part of it.

Open questions remain, perhaps more so than with the Lord's Supper. For example: what is the proper age for baptism, and what is its relation to church membership? Should there be a blessing or dedication of children, anticipating their later personal commitment, or perhaps a dedication of parents, solemnizing their intention to raise the child in the faith? Thoughtful and honest questions have been raised

---

[36] T. F. BEST, "Baptism. Christian Church," in P. BRADSHAW, ed., *The New SCM Dictionary*, 44.

[37] For a current example of Disciples' baptismal practice and commentary thereon, see K. WATKINS, "Christian Baptism: The Christian Church . . . ," 124–128.

about the masculine imagery of the traditional baptismal formula, but the traditional formula remains for us very much the norm, not least in view of our extensive ecumenical commitments. How can the service of baptism be enriched liturgically—perhaps by a blessing of the water—to emphasize God's initiative in the event? How to renew the awareness of one's own baptismal commitment—perhaps by incorporating a renewal of baptism vows into other worship events? How to convey the broader dimensions of the baptismal commitment? Here, strikingly, the church's Theology Commission has proposed a new form of the profession of faith, stressing the ecclesial and social as well as the personal dimensions of baptism: "Do you, with Christians of every time and place, believe that 'Jesus is the Christ, the Son of the Living God' (Mt 16:16)?"[38]

C. The "Service of the Word"

Let us look briefly at another area of growth that has come largely due to our encounter with the liturgical movement. This is the increased awareness of the service of the Word as a liturgical event with its own proper structure and process, normally including the elements of entrance, Scripture reading, proclamation of the gospel, response, prayer and intercession, the Lord's Prayer, and dismissal/sending forth, with a blessing. The discovery that this basic structure or pattern of worship (the notion of *ordo*, which has been central to current Faith and Order work on worship[39] and which Gordon Lathrop has taken up elsewhere in this series; see pp. 87–100) is one shared by Christians of many times and places has done much

---

[38] See "A Word to the Church on Baptism (1987), A Report of the Committee on Theology," in P. A. CROW, JR., and J. O. DUKE, eds., *The Church for Disciples of Christ*, 121–137, citation p. 133. See also C. M. WILLIAMSON, *Baptism, Embodiment of the Gospel: Disciples Baptismal Theology, The Nature of the Church*, Study Series 4 (St. Louis: published for the Council on Christian Unity by Christian Board of Publication, 1987).

[39] See T. F. BEST and D. HELLER, eds., *So We Believe, So We Pray: Towards Koinonia in Worship*, Faith and Order Paper 171 (Geneva: WCC Publications, 1995); T. F. BEST and D. HELLER, eds., *Eucharistic Worship in Ecumenical Contexts: The Lima Liturgy—and Beyond* (Geneva: WCC Publications, 1988); T. F. BEST and D. HELLER, eds., *Becoming a Christian.: The Ecumenical Implications of Our Common Baptism*, Faith and Order Paper 184 (Geneva: WCC Publications, 1999); "One Baptism: Towards Mutual Recognition of Christian Initiation," FO/2001:24, text under development, publication forthcoming; and the forthcoming publications given in notes 30 and 34, above.

to increase the vitality of our own non-eucharistic worship. Here, too, we have learned from the liturgical renewal movement that we stand within the long tradition of the church, even as we bear witness to our distinctive worship traditions.

D. Worship Materials

None of these developments would have had an impact liturgically without worship materials to bring them into the lives of local congregations. And thus we need to conclude this review of developments in the second half the twentieth century with a brief look at Disciples' hymnals, worship books, and other materials. Already the *Hymnbook for Christian Worship,* published in 1970[40] (done jointly with the American Baptist Convention, as was *Christian Worship: A Hymnal* of 1941) included many modern hymns, including some from other continents and from the ecumenical movement, while discreetly "'retiring' hymns considered overly sentimental or theologically simplistic."[41] The principal worship book at this point was still *Christian Worship: A Service Book* (1953),[42] the work of G. Edwin Osborn. Its stress on "relevant" worship on specific themes is not perhaps in accord with much of the liturgical movement, yet it was advanced for Disciples in including a Lectionary, and it did encourage a more positive attitude toward practices in worship common to the whole of our church.

These materials are now superseded by fully modern resources, including both a strong hymnal and a service book produced in the 1990s. The *Chalice Hymnal* of 1995[43] combines classic hymns from the long Christian tradition with a generous collection of songs from churches around the world and from the ecumenical movement, as well as from African American and Hispanic contexts. It is sensitive to issues of language. Reflecting Disciples' piety and tradition, it "includes probably more communion hymns than any other currently available hymnal."[44] A partial psalter, a Lectionary for years A, B, and C, quotations from a wide variety of sources, some ancient, and some service materials are also included. Happily, it has been warmly re-

[40] St. Louis: Bethany Press. See also A. N. WAKE, *Companion to Hymnbook for Christian Worship* (St. Louis: Bethany Press, 1970).

[41] T. F. BEST, "Books, Liturgical. Christian Church," in P. BRADSHAW, ed., *The New SCM Dictionary,* 76.

[42] St. Louis: Christian Board of Publication.

[43] St. Louis: Chalice Press.

[44] T. F. BEST, "Books, Liturgical, 76.

ceived within the church. A companion to the hymnal for worship leaders was published in 1998.[45]

The hymnal is beautifully complemented by *Chalice Worship* of 1997, the service book edited by Colbert Cartwright and Cricket Harrison.[46] With this the church has, finally, a rich collection of services and material that honor both its own tradition and that of the wider church, and is thoroughly modern in its engagement with the liturgical and ecumenical movements, as well as its attention to contemporary worship needs. Thus, in addition to Lord's Day services (one including a clear epiclesis in the Eucharistic Prayer) and baptismal rites, there are services for the installation of elders, an Easter Vigil service, material for use during the Week of Prayer for Christian Unity, three examples of worship in ecumenical contexts (including one for use on Martin Luther King Jr. day), a prayer service for healing, and prayers for special and difficult pastoral situations (for example, for "one who has been molested" or for those "in a coma or unable to communicate"), as well as, of course, the more familiar special occasions of weddings and funerals. The worship book has a "message," namely, that worship is important and worth doing well. And that is a message of hope for our church as a whole.

Finally, I want to mention the wealth of worship materials being produced by individuals within the church; these are un- or semi-official but bear witness to important trends in our life as a church. Especially important is the first Disciples' set of Lectionary-based communion and post-communion prayers, *Fed by God's Grace: Communion Prayers for Year A* (2001), *Year B* (1999), and *Year C* (2000).[47] These are broadening the appreciation for the Lectionary within the church, as well as improving the quality, both theological and liturgical, of the elders' prayers offered during the service of the Supper.

A normative liturgy or body of hymns would be inimical to Disciples' ecclesiology and ethos alike, yet all these materials are clear evidence of our new liturgical vitality and our engagement with our tradition, the tradition of the whole church, and the modern world.

---

[45] S. L. ADAMS, C. S. CARTWRIGHT, and D. B. MERRICK, eds., *Chalice Hymnal: A Worship Leader's Companion* (St. Louis: Chalice Press).

[46] St. Louis: Chalice Press.

[47] M.E. DIXON and S. DIXON (St. Louis: Chalice Press).

And now let us return to our title as amended: "Christian Unity and Christian Diversity, Lessons from Liturgical Renewal in a Populist Sacramental Church: The Case of the Disciples of Christ." For Disciples, the fundamental questions raised by the liturgical movement have been how to hold unity and diversity together within our own church and how we, as a church, fit within the diversity of churches that make up the church as a whole.

From this perspective, I see three central lessons that we have learned in the course of our engagement with the movement for liturgical reform. The *first* is that the liturgical and ecumenical movements are part of one larger movement of the Holy Spirit, within the whole church, for renewal and toward unity. The two movements together have pressed us to a closer coherence between what and how we pray and what we believe. The new material in our hymnal and worship book is the fruit of both movements, especially the liturgical, but informed by, and in some dialogue with, the ecumenical movement. If William Temple had spoken in 1980 rather than 1930, perhaps he would have spoken of "the ecumenical *and liturgical* movements" as "the great facts of our era."

A *second* learning is that the liturgical renewal movement has been a force both for unity and diversity. After our first century and more, from 1820 to about 1950, we Disciples found ourselves internally very united, reflecting cultural and social factors to be sure, but due principally to our common practice of the Lord's Supper on each Lord's Day, with the active participation of elders as well as the pastor at the Table. Looking outside ourselves, it was precisely this frequent eucharistic practice that distinguished us from our immediate ecclesiological neighbors, the churches stemming from the Calvinist Reformed tradition, as well as from the churches of the Baptist tradition, to whom we were linked by our baptismal understanding and practice. In this sense we were a sign of *diversity* in the broader Reformed tradition, but looking more broadly still, we were a sign of *unity* to Anglicans and even Roman Catholics, as a church stemming from the Reformation that had preserved the weekly celebration of the Lord's Supper as the heart of the life of the church.

What the liturgical reform movement has done over the past fifty years is to make us much more *diverse* internally, by bringing new worship materials and by encouraging the development of specific, focused worship forms for particular occasions of non-eucharistic worship. But at the same time, it has strengthened our witness to *unity* and our sense of being part of the whole church by stressing the basic patterns or structures of worship shared by many churches. And liturgical reform has strengthened our unity as a church internally by making it a unity that embraces greater diversity—first of all, of course, in our worship life, but also throughout the life of the church as a whole. And this we have experienced as the action of the Holy Spirit.

This brings me to our *third*, and final learning: liturgical renewal has taught us much about the meaning and process of renewal in the life of the church as a whole. My conviction is that most churches—and in some sense *the* church itself—have begun as movements for reform. And at any point in the life of a church, even when it has settled down into comfortable patterns of life and worship as ours had, the Holy Spirit may appeal to the church, calling it to new life.

To the extent that a church carries the memory of its origin as a renewal movement, that church has within itself the seeds of reform and renewal. The Spirit calls that church to a rediscovery of its own roots, as we discovered, encouraged by the liturgical reform movement and in the writings and witness of our founders, Alexander Campbell and Walter Scott, the vision of the Lord's Supper as a moment of Christ's actual *presence,* not just of his memory; and as we discovered that the Lord's Supper is profoundly *social* as well as personal. Here the Spirit has taken us more deeply *into* ourselves, enabling us to rediscover who we are.

But that is not the whole story, for the resources for renewal in a particular area of a church's life are not always available within that church itself. And then the Spirit calls that church to look beyond itself and its own resources, to look to other churches, to the whole church and its long tradition. And in doing that, encouraged by the liturgical renewal movement, our own church was inspired to reorder and renew our observance of the Lord's Supper, moving its position within the structure of the Lord's Day service so that the Supper was its culmination and climax, thus restoring the Supper to the center of our church's worship and life, where we had longed for it to be all along. Here the Spirit has taken us *beyond* ourselves, enabling us to see who we are called to become.

In taking us more deeply into ourselves and in calling us beyond ourselves, the liturgical movement has been a blessing for our "populist sacramental" church, and for this we give thanks to God, the Father, Son, and Holy Spirit.

125

Ermanno Genre

Polyphony and Symphony
Protestant Liturgies—A Building Site

The title of my paper immediately suggests a question: Is it proper to link the harmonious concepts of polyphony and symphony with the din of a building site? There would seem to be a clash of meanings before we even begin. I had firsthand experience of this quite recently when the people living on the floor below decided to call in the workmen to refurbish their apartment, armed with drills, hammers, and chisels and the rest of the builder's paraphernalia while I was trying hard to work in my office above, against the background of classical music. Nothing very symphonic about it! So I have to explain what I have in mind and how I intend to use these concepts that I have combined in this paper to discuss the state of the liturgy in the Protestant world. But I feel I ought to begin with a short introduction before addressing the substance of my paper, although this perhaps already touches on the substance itself.

When talking today about liturgy, and bearing in mind all the different denominations that exist, we realize at once that we can no longer speak solely about our own particular understanding of liturgy in any scientific way without taking account, with the same methodological rigor, of the debate that is taking place in the broader ecumenical context, and indeed in the broader interfaith context. Liturgical research in the past few decades has found an increasing number of common features of Christian worship that range far beyond denominational differences. Thanks to ecumenical practice, we have found common ground for our dialogue and debate that has enabled us to look at the texts, the doctrines, and traditions that once created rigid positions (and rigid minds), preventing them from sharing ideas.

We might perhaps say that there is no other area within the Catholic world that has proved so fertile and fruitful since the Second Vatican Council as liturgical research. The work carried out within worldwide Catholicism in the mid-sixties made it possible to do what was not only impossible but actually previously prohibited: dialogue, sharing, and consequently the *increasingly transversal* nature of theological research. We only need to pick up a hymnbook that we use today in our various modern languages to appreciate the innovations that have taken place: how many hymns, how many tunes by musicians from all denominations, and in particular how many Protestant hymn tunes have now become the patrimony of the whole church! And I would go further still and say that today it would be difficult to even contemplate the revival of liturgical interest in the Protestant world without that stimulus that came in the wake of Vatican II.

I would therefore like to address a number of aspects of the subject matter of my essay, starting with the current ecumenism and looking ahead to the future of this ecumenism, despite all the conflict situations that exist, realizing that I can only offer a few broad ideas relating to some of the reasons for the current liturgical renewal taking place in the Protestant world, and particularly in the churches that came into being at the Reformation. I shall therefore focus on the three concepts to which I have just referred: *polyphony, symphony,* and *the building site.*

1. THE POLYPHONY OF WORSHIP AS THE POLYPHONY OF EXISTENCE

As we all know, the Protestant churches that came into being as a result of the Reformation of the Church in the sixteenth century placed, as the centerpiece of their worship and liturgy, not some abstract concept or dogma, but the very promise of God which is revealed and which creates communion. The words of the Gospel of Matthew, "Where two or three are gathered in my name I am there in their midst" (18:20), was taken as *the criterion for the true church* which celebrates the praises of its Lord. The church, in the sense of being the body of Christians who are called together to celebrate and worship, is the criterion around which the liturgical space and time are being reorganized and which is the "actor" of the actual celebration.[1] But very early on, the very principle of the universal priesthood of all believers that was intended to animate worship was entrusted to the figure of the pastor speaking to the community that listened to him. It would certainly be an overstatement to say that Protestant worship

[1] J. F. WHITE rightly states that "People are the primary liturgical document," *Protestant Worship: Traditions in Transition* (Louisville: Westminster/John Knox, 1989) 16.

was transformed into a monologue, because the congregation at worship played an important role in the singing, and the *maître chantre* who led the singing in the Reformed churches held a very prominent position. Toward the middle of the last century, many churches instituted the office of Scripture readers, which reduced the pastoral monologue at services, but we certainly cannot yet speak of a polyphonic dimension.

When I say the "polyphony" of worship, I am not simply referring to the fact that several voices are heard, as a kind of liturgical adjustment. It not only means opening up and involving readers, men and women, or introducing musical moments and perhaps even sermons preached by several different people. The polyphony of worship is not primarily a question of aesthetics or organization, but a question of life—the life of those taking part in worship with their own questions, expectations, concerns, joys, and sufferings that they bear throughout the whole week and then bring before their God in worship and in communion with their fellow worshipers. I see polyphony as the liturgical capacity to activate the interiority of people, a dynamic that is able to make worship a moment in our life that is capable of involving the community as the whole and each and every member of it. Polyphony does not therefore mean that everybody must speak. What it does mean, however, is that a liturgy must be constructed that is capable of asking questions, activating the existences and the motivations of those taking part, giving a voice to their expectations, raising up within each of them that spark which creates unity in the faith of the many and of those who differ. In order to be able to better focus on this aspect, it may be useful to recall something that Dietrich Bonhoeffer said that illustrates this polyphonic vision of Christian worship. For Bonhoeffer, God and his eternity are to be loved in the depths of our hearts, but this must be done without earthly love being damaged or weakened, like a kind of *cantus firmus*, in relation to which the other voices in life act in a contrapuntal relationship: earthly love is one of these contrapuntal themes, wholly autonomous and yet related to the *cantus firmus*. When the *cantus firmus* is clear and distinct, the contrapuntal voices can deploy all their energies. Polyphony in music is so important and familiar to us precisely because it is the musical image of this christological fact, and hence of our Christian life.[2]

[2] D. BONHOEFFER, *Letter and Papers from Prison* (in a letter written on 20 May 1944).

I find this enlightening because it helps us to see Christian worship as part and parcel of everyday life and not something outside it, in some abstract, shapeless and artificial space. How can we talk about a "living liturgy" if it is not able to interpret and make room for the "voices of life" that make up the community that has gathered together to celebrate the name of God? What language do these "voices of life" speak if not a polyphonic language? The German churches have long used the expression *"lebendige Liturgie,"* and they also know how to practice this liturgical dynamic at the high moments of mass gatherings, such as the great *Kirchentag* rally that has been staged since the 1950s. New and previously untried forms are being created that are able to involve and create bonds of unity in faith—a polyphony of existence, because it is a polyphony of lives, presences, and intentions that the liturgy is able to take up and link together harmoniously.

In many Protestant churches this research is now in full swing, with lay groups working weekly with their pastor to prepare the Sunday liturgy, endeavoring to foster this polyphonic dimension of life that enters into the liturgy. Against this background the living liturgy means simultaneously recognizing that there is an irrepressible distance created between the liturgical text (which is necessary and essential) and the dimension of its performance, which involves the body through movements and the emotions that characterize any form of genuine participation in the liturgy. Either worship is an event or it is not worship.

2. SYMPHONY

But I have already said that it is not sufficient to put several voices together to give the liturgy a polyphonic dimension. However, there cannot be polyphony unless several voices are brought together. In worship and the liturgy these are voices which stem from real-life experience, from joy as well as suffering, and which the faith inspires and guides. It is precisely the fact of bringing together many different voices and sounds that creates the dimension of the symphony in the liturgy—in other words, a harmonious complex of sounds and voices performing together. We might say that to some degree all forms of worship, all liturgies, express a more or less harmonious symphonic dimension.

Harmony and unison are not, of course, only a matter of the music and the singing. They are equally necessary for the performance of the various parts of a liturgy, which has a beginning, a development, and a climax. And this also has to do with harmony and unison, or with disorder and being out of tune when the liturgy has not been constructed according to the rules of communication and of what we might call, with Noam Chomsky, "a generative grammar":[3] in other words, a grammar that renews the relationship and the permanent tension existing between the ordinary and the proper of the liturgy itself.

With this "generative" liturgical approach, I believe it is important to make room for lamenting. No Christian liturgy can possibly exclude the cry of suffering, the plea for justice that rises up from the earth and cries out in desperation and pain to heaven, asking why and questioning God in invocations and prayers of intercession. This "high note" is something that we find so often in the psalms, and not only does it have a rightful place in Christian liturgy but we have to ask ourselves whether there can be a Christian liturgy without this "high note," which stands out and can be heard above all the other voices and all other sounds. But this shrill note is not that of someone singing out of tune but is part of the symphony itself. Indeed, no real symphony can exist without it. This is a question that all of us have to answer: Where do we hear this shrill high note in our liturgies? Why has it been stifled? How can we restore that sound without making it over-dramatic?

The recent comprehensive volume of liturgical texts published to celebrate the fiftieth anniversary of the World Council of Churches (WCC) is called *Sinfonia Oecumenica*. Worship with the Churches in the World—Feiern mit den Kirchen der Welt—Célébration avec les Églises du monde—Comunión con las iglesias del mundo,[4] comprising just under a thousand pages in the four languages. It is a liturgical ecumenical symphony in which Basle has collected liturgical texts from every part of the Christian ecumenical universe. Ever since the 1983 Vancouver Assembly, the WCC has promoted workshops on music and liturgy in every part of the world in order to encourage liturgical renewal in the various churches with respect for all traditions and cultures, based on four essential criteria: (1) contextualization, namely, adopting the specific cultures and contexts; (2) the holistic dimension of celebration, which must involve all five senses; (3) a closer attention to the musical forms specific to each culture; (4) the appreciation of symbols and symbolic acts. These four guidelines

---

[3] N. CHOMSKY, *Syntactic Structures* (The Hague: Mouton, 1957).
[4] Gütersloh/Basle: Gütersloher Verlagshaus, 1999.

broadly sum up the approach that underlies the liturgical output of the last twenty years. We have to rediscover the innumerable hidden treasures of different liturgical traditions worldwide so that they can become the common heritage of all in a common process of liturgical ecumenical learning.[5]

This situation dates back to the very early centuries of Christianity and can be found, for example, in the writings of Clement of Alexandria (third century). In his work *Protreptikos,* he presented Christ as Orpheus, with the lute in one hand and a plectrum in the other, whose sound draws all kinds of animals to him, while nature begins to move; the plants change their positions, moved by that majestic sound, which reestablishes the harmony of Creation. The ecumenical symphony, therefore, reminds one of singing and dancing, and has a biblical reference in the parable in Luke 15:25 of the merciful father of the prodigal son. When the elder son returned from the fields, "he heard music and dancing" (Luke 15:12), the symphony of rediscovered communion of the prodigal sons and daughters that we are. But the parable also reminds us that the eldest son did not join in the music and dancing and was offended by that symphony, which he considered to be out of tune, and felt excluded from it.

Where do these discordant sounds come from? In the communities of those who are celebrating or in the lacerated interior of the first-born son? In other words, the ecumenical symphony reminds us of our denominational divisions and our inability to celebrate with those who are already in the house of the Father and who are waiting for us—waiting for us to correct our denominational dissonances and accept the symphony of the grace and love of God which precedes and which includes us. This symphony is an invitation to set aside everything that prevents the triumph of the grace of God in the midst of so many forms of human poverty and misery.

---

[5] Examples of the ongoing liturgical renewal in the European Reformed churches are *Liturgie de l'Église réformée de France,* approved by the Mazamet Synod (1996), and P. BUKOWSKI et al., *Reformierte Liturgie: Gebete und Ordnungen für die unter dem Wort versammelte Gemeinde* (Wuppertal: Foedus-Verlag/ Neukirchener Verlag, 1999). Then there is the Revised Common Lectionary used today in many Catholic and Protestant churches worldwide;see E. GENRE, "I lezionari delle Chiese della Riforma: Rapporto tra Bibbia e liturgia," *Rivista liturgica* 88, no. 6 (2001) 947–959.

3. THE BUILDING SITE AS A LITURGICAL METAPHOR

Now that we have tried to clarify these two concepts, polyphony and symphony, I would like to lead you through the hubbub of the building site without asking you to put on a hardhat or overalls or working boots. I will merely use three words that I think sum up some of the areas of research and renewal currently taking place in the Protestant churches: *rite, therapy,* and *justice.*

3.1. Rediscovered ritualism

The Reformed churches have long since overcome the suspicion with which they traditionally viewed rites and ritualism. This was a legacy of anti-ritualism which did not exist in the early days of the Protestant Reformation, but which emerged in its later history.[6]

In his *Institutio,*[7] Calvin subdivided his approach to the problem of rites into two parts: first, he launched a fierce, relentless all-out attack on the ritualism present in Roman Catholicism, denouncing its ulterior motives and deviance from the communicative potential of the gospel, and second, he clearly brought out the need for the Christian community to have its own (albeit few in number) rites. An excessive number of rites, according to Calvin, had "strangled souls," violating the conscience of believers. Calvin developed a whole series of arguments around the concept of "conscience," highlighting the power of the church when it wished to impose rites and human traditions that were not gospel-based, without any respect for the freedom of the Christian. From this point of view, ceremonies are deceptive, they are a pretense, acts of magic *(magicam incantationem),* masks without truth, farces, traps to make the ignorant people part with their money.

But this is only one aspect of the question. He launched this highly detailed and fierce criticism because it brought out the ambivalent nature of rites and hence the *need for discernment,* the need for a hermeneutic criterion, since in its genuine form a rite can and must serve for the upbuilding of the church. If the rite embodies superstition, it is because it has been wrongly used. And with that Calvin defended the fundamental function of the rite and ritualism at the service of the gospel. Calvin said that the church needed external and public constitutions and institutions in order to maintain order and decorum. In this perspective rites had a specific function, despite the

---

[6] See W. JETTER, *Symbol und Ritual: Anthropologische Elemente im Gottesdienst,* 2nd ed. (Göttingen: Vandenhoeck & Ruprecht, 1986).

[7] *The Institution of the Christian Religion.*

fact that the ritual instructions should not interfere in any way whatsoever with regard to salvation.[8]

This reference to Calvin is important in order to set out this issue properly within the context of the Reformed churches, especially because the later generations were no longer able to identify with the same degree of clarity *the positive function of rites within the liturgy*. A rift very soon emerged between the external manifestation of the faith (sacraments, ceremonies) and the internal reality in which the Spirit of God works, with the help of the preached word alone, and the attack on Roman Catholic ritualism was heightened and led to a gradual lack of appreciation of the value of the ritual dimension.

The reformed legacy of a theology of the Word with which I identify has for some time established a new relationship with the ritual dimension that characterizes the expression of the faith.[9] In itself, a rite does not deny the faith, nor does it set out to overshadow it; but it is always capable of attacking it and changing its character. Maintaining that it is necessary to properly combine rite and faith does not mean that one must deny the permanent need for a theological criticism of religion and rites. On the contrary, it means looking at it afresh and, in particular, setting it out again in a broader and more complex framework, namely, the framework in which all human creatures seek God, but in which the search for God must always come to terms both with the idol and the unpredictability and freedom of God. It is necessary for faith and rite to be articulated because the ritual dimension is inscribed in the very heart of human existence, like breathing or dreaming. Rites and human ritualism are an integral part of our existential connective tissue along the axis of communication: not everything which is communicated is true and constructive, but we cannot stop communicating (Watzlawick). That is why a rite is educable and controllable, but only up to a certain point; deep down there is an uncontrolled and uncontrollable dimension. Like speech.

Naturally, this interest in rites and ritualism within the liturgy raises numerous issues that have not yet been at all settled. What

---

[8] Ibid., IV, X, 27, 28.

[9] See W. JETTER, *Symbol und Ritual*; M. SEARLE, "Ritual," in C. JONES et al., *The Study of Liturgy*, rev. ed. (London/New York: SPCK/Oxford University Press, 1992) 51–58.; H. MOTTU, "Rites," in *Encyclopédie du Protestantisme* (Paris/Geneva: Cerf/Labor et Fides, 1995) 1338–1354; E. GENRE, "Elementi di liturgia," in E. GENRE, S. ROSTAGNO, G. TOURN, *Le Chiese della Riforma: Storia, teologia, prassi* (Cinisello Balsamo: San Paolo, 2001) 99–103.

does it mean to say that the Sunday liturgy in Christian worship is a rite?[10] This question requires a number of clarifications to more specifically establish what is meant by rite. Is there any *one* definition of a rite? Assuming that rites have to do with different forms of behavior based on different contexts, cultures, and traditions, is it possible to identify certain anthropological aspects that run right across them? The plurality of definitions of rites and human ritualism demonstrates the objective impossibility of agreeing on any one definition of rites and ritualism: rites refuse to be categorized on an exclusive basis because of their substantial *ambivalence,* the ambivalence of the rite as a source of *wealth* and as a *risk,*[11] both together, not one without the other.

3.2. *Liturgy and therapy*

A second area of this revisited building site is the therapeutic aspect of liturgy. This is by no means a novelty,[12] as such, but what is new is the reflection on it and the unprecedented nature of some of the forms it is taking.

Human life is in a state of constant tension between health and sickness. And speaking of sickness brings us necessarily into the sphere of a plurality of meanings; health is a *multidimensional* concept that cannot be restricted to one single definition that in some way tries to nail it down. The British theologian M. Wilson says that

[10] See A. N. TERRIN, *Dimensione fenomenologica e aspetti semiotici* (Brescia: Morcelliana, 1988); *Antropologia e orizzonti del sacro: culture e religione,* Leitourgía. Sezione antropologica (Assisi: Cittadella Editrice, 2001); H.-Chr. SCHMIDT-LAUBER, K.-H. BIERITZ, *Handbuch der Liturgik: Liturgiewissenchaft in Theologie und Praxis der Kirche* (Leipzig/Göttingen: Evangelische Verlagsanstalt/Vandenhoeck & Ruprecht, 1995).

[11] R. Grimes, who founded the *Journal of Ritual Studies* in 1986, suggests that the word "rite" can be used as a generic concept covering at least six different ritual types or sensitivities. Grimes defines the liturgy as the ritual action whose ultimate reference is both closely akin to magic when the participants attempt to manipulate transcendence and akin to celebration when the participants seek an encounter with the transcendent; see R. GRIMES, *Beginnings in Ritual Studies* (Washington: University of America Press, 1982) and *Ritual Criticism:. Case Studies in Its Practice. Essays on Its Theory* (Columbia: University of South Carolina Press, 1990), cited by M. SEARLE, "Ritual," 55f.

[12] See H.-J. THILO, *Die therapeutische Funktion des Gottesdienstes* (Kassel: J. Stauda, 1985); E. GENRE, *Nuovi itinerari di teologia pratica* (Turin: Claudiana, 1991) 214f. (French edition: *La relation d'aide: une pratique communautaire* [Geneva: Labor et Fides, 1997] 211f.).

health is such a true concept that it cannot be defined, and that any attempt to define it at whatever cost would "kill it."[13] And the German philosopher H.-G. Gadamer has spoken of the "concealment of health."[14] In other words, health is a dynamic process that is always exposed to the risk factor. And it is certain that in this process, in this constituent instability, there also lies our subconscious desire to defend, and at all times to seek, good health.

All the models and definitions of health, whether psychological, medical, spiritual, or religious, recognize the provisional nature of levels and states of health (the health status of a child is quite different from the health status of an elderly person). Each of us is confronted with the *growth* factor without being able to set a fixed, static point, and in the awareness that it is always growth that is limited in time. Our health is always an element that is *interdependent* with physical, psychological, social, and spiritual factors. And one might say the same thing about the concept of sickness in a general sense and the process of healing. Healing from an illness always means setting in motion a plurality and diversity of processes, a *cooperation* dynamic between the biological and the spiritual dimension of our existence.[15]

Faced with the progressive medicalization of existence, we might rightly ask whether theological thought about life and in particular pastoral theology and the liturgy have not perhaps neglected their specific task. Today medicine is concerned with numerous issues which at one time were entrusted to *caritas christiana*,[16] but which today are dealt with almost exclusively in a clinical context. The fact that in the modern age medicine has been given total responsibility

[13] M. WILSON, *Health Is for People* (London: Longmann & Todd, 1975) 117.

[14] H.-G. GADAMER, *Über die Verborgenheit der Gesundheit: Aufsätze und Vorträge* (Frankfort: Suhrkamp Verlag, 1993). Paraphrasing, he says that health is not something that shows itself; it cannot be measured, because it represents a state of intrinsic self-adjustment that no other type of control can outdo. Unlike sickness, health is never a cause of concern, and in fact we are hardly ever aware that we are healthy. It is not a condition that urges or warns us to take care of ourselves, and, if anything, entails the surprising possibility of self-neglect.

[15] See A. N. TERRIN, ed., *Liturgia e terapia: La sacramentalità a servizio dell'uomo nella sua interezza,* Caro salutis cardo. Contributi, 10 (Padua: Edizioni Messaggero, 1993). There is a great deal of work on Jesus the "healer," which I shall pass over here.

[16] "We demand of medicine today what we used to ask of religion, almost as if medicine has become our 'secular religion,' and doctors and science are the priesthood of this religion." *Janus* 1 (2001) Zadig Roma Editore, 58.

for the health-sickness-healing dimension is indicative of a void in theological reflection that is fraught with consequences. One can see this, for example, in theological anthropology, which has not managed to deal coherently with sick people jointly with sinning people (dogmatic theology seems to recognize only the sinner!). It is therefore not only a matter of attracting the interest of pastoral theology and the liturgy to this theme, but rather of proposing a substantive debate on the whole of the theological system: a vital issue in fundamental theology. The question has to do with both pastoral and diaconal training and formation within the ambit of the ministries that the church recognizes and prepares for, and with the Christian community and each and all of its individual members, who have their own personal experience of the health-sickness-healing dynamic. And here there also arises the structural relationship between all we have just said and liturgy and worship.

Today the Christian churches are suffering from a massive identity crisis. On the one hand, many of them are giving up the "ecclesial spaces" because they consider them to be meaningless or without credibility, which is pure secularization. Unfortunately, when the concept of secularization is used in theology, the responsibility of the churches is not normally taken on board, and consequently a negative judgment is passed on people lapsing from the churches without making the effort to find out why.[17] From another point of view, this detachment from the official churches is often reinvested in frequenting other religious groups with a Christian or non-Christian tradition, and sometimes into charismatic groups (which are growing very rapidly, according to the findings of sociologists of religion).[18] And it is precisely on this charismatic plane that the relationship between health, sickness, and healing becomes a central issue.[19]

The Italian sociologist Enzo Pace has defined these new movements as "religious compassion movements,"[20] emphasizing their

[17] Father Severino Pagani rightly says that the pastoral ministry of parish priests based on "total control" is finished, because it has long since "lost control of the territory, of the biographies of the people, of their consciences, of their affections, of their bodies, intelligence, work, politics." *Rivista del clero italiano*, cited in *La Repubblica* (3 June 2001) 33.

[18] See M. INTROVIGNE, ed., *Enciclopedia delle religioni in Italia* (Turin: Elle Di Ci, 2001).

[19] J. MOLTMANN, *Lo spirito della vita: Per una pneumatologia integrale*, Biblioteca di teologia contemporanea 77 (Brescia: Queriniana, 1994; original German version published in 1991) 217ff., 299ff.

[20] From my own notes, taken at a recent meeting in Padua with this author.

capacity to take on the pain of others and to lead them on to a community and liturgical plane in order to re-create well-being and combat illness and evil. In many of these charismatic groups the liturgical technique designed to set in motion the healing process is of a "trance" type: prayers and dances, involving the body and the mind, which provoke a change in the awareness and consciousness of the individuals, and it is here that the mediator tries to interpret the forces of evil in order to overcome them. And when there is a physical healing, this is at all events the consequence of the previous spiritual healing: I, a sick and suffering person, as a small human mind, must be able to become reconciled with the great mind, which is God. In this perspective, both Scripture and the liturgy are interpreted as places and opportunities for reappropriating the divinity from which we have become separated. One might say that the body, which has virtually disappeared from the liturgical attention of the institutional churches, is finding here its triumphal entry, and the healings that are manifested in these charismatic groups are interpreted as a demonstration of the ineffectiveness and the unreliability of forms of institutional mediation.[21]

I would like to recall here the experience that has been appropriately incorporated into the liturgy after a period of experimentation, not without its conflicts, in a number of Reformed churches in French-speaking Switzerland, which, after years of reflection, have managed to make a concrete response to the demand to actively involve the sick in the liturgy. It was above all the work of the Swiss theologian Walter Hollenweger, who insisted on this need for a pres-

---

[21] See CONGREGATION FOR THE DOCTRINE OF THE FAITH, "Instruction on prayers for healing," *Osservatore Romano* (24 November 2000), "as a help to local Ordinaries so that the faithful may be better guided in this area, though promoting what is good and correcting what is to be avoided." This does not seem, in my opinion, to realize that for many of these charismatic groups liturgical form is of little relevance, because they see it as ineffective. What is important to them is the effectiveness of the charisms of healing which are at work and which are legitimated by themselves. The Instruction rightly concludes that "it would be completely arbitrary to attribute a 'charism of healing' to any category of participants, for example, to the directors of the group; the only thing to do is to entrust oneself to the free decision of the Holy Spirit, who grants to some a special charism of healing in order to show the power of the grace of the Risen Christ." But it is precisely for this reason that no one institution can capture it for itself, and the problem of the "proper discernment from a liturgical perspective" remains an open question.

ence of the sick in the Sunday liturgy.[22] He has devoted close attention to this issue, emphasizing the way in which the Christian church has a dirty conscience with regard to the sick, a category normally absent from acts of worship. The Sunday liturgy only considers them in terms of praying for them. A dirty conscience of the church, which can already be seen by the fact that the missionary order issued by Jesus to his disciples in the Gospel of Matthew, "Heal the sick, raise the dead, cleanse lepers, cast out demons. You received without paying, give without pay" (Matt 10:8), is a language that is "disturbing," and this text is often readily replaced by the Gospel texts that describe the mission merely in terms of "teaching" and "baptizing" (Matt 28:19-20).

Hollenweger points out that "the place in which one can expect healing in the broadest sense of the term, but where the issue is not only discussed, is the community of Jesus Christ. *Health and sickness are not private matters, but matters that have to do with the liturgy.* The community has a gift and a task of healing."[23] He therefore considers that the sick must be able to take part in the church's liturgy, a liturgy "for the sick and for the able-bodied alike," with our Lord's Supper and with the laying-on of hands. This is by no means a novelty, because this liturgy has been maintained in the Anglican[24] and Methodist[25] traditions, but there is no doubt that this proposal, in the light of our current liturgical practice and our overall understanding of relationship between the Christian community-sickness- healing, is a salutary provocation in which the reality of sickness, particularly of incurable illness and death, are given the solidarity of the church, which as such is a body of able-bodied people and sick people awaiting healing and resurrection.

---

[22] W. J. HOLLENWEGER, *Geist und Materie: Interkulturelle Theologie III* (Munich: Kaiser, 1988) 21–35. See also numerous relevant observations on this in A. BRUSCO, S. PINTOR, *Sulle orme di Cristo medico: Manuale di teologia pastorale sanitaria,* Nuovi saggi teologici. Manuali, 1 (Bologna: EDB, 1999).

[23] Ibid., 22.23 (my emphasis).

[24] See *The Book of Common Prayer and Administration of the Sacraments and Other Rites and Ceremonies of the Church, According to the Use of the Episcopal Church* (New York: The Church Hymnal Corporation and the Seabury Press, 1979) 453ff. A Roman Catholic approach to this problem is given in A. N. TERRIN, ed., *Liturgia e terapia.*

[25] See *The Methodist Worship Book* (Petersburgh: Methodist Publishing House, 1999) 407ff.

3.3 Liturgy as a demand for justice

The third area of activity in our building site is very familiar to the Christian and Protestant tradition, but in the past few decades it has attracted particular attention and may be summed up in the word "justice." Susan E. Willhauck has said that the language of faith loses its meaning if it no longer has any recognizable references to our experience in the world,[26] and experience in the world is an experience that is constantly marked by the injustice faced by millions of human beings. Justice therefore becomes a condition for an authentic liturgy.[27] This "condition," which is mentioned by Nicolas Wolterstorff, reaches to the very essence of worship and challenges the community gathered together in terms of its vocation and its witness in the world. In other words, it is a decisive critical demand to recognize and acknowledge the distortions and the falsifications that are always possible in the churches' liturgies, a kind of preventive medicine to deal with self-referencing.

It is no coincidence that the prophetic denunciation of the worship of Israel placed the issue of law *(mischpat)* and justice *(zedaka)* at its very heart. The prophets had no intention of abolishing worship, but they placed at the center of their worship the question of law and justice as a means of restoring worship to its status of truth and authenticity:

> Take away from me the noise of your songs;
>   I will not listen to the melody of your harps.
> But let justice roll down like waters,
>   and righteousness like an ever-flowing stream. (Amos 5:23-24)

But worship and liturgy can also become, in the eyes of God, a solemn blasphemy! The prophet Jeremiah announced the destruction of the Temple because of a false sense of security and the lies and the abominations committed by the people:

> Has this house, which is called by my name, become a den of robbers in your sight?" (Jer 7:11)

asking God to prohibit intercession for the people (7:16). The prophet Isaiah denounced the distortion of the true sense of fasting:

---

[26] S. E. WILLHAUCK, "Liturgy and Education for Justice in an Age of Disbelief," in *Religious Education* 91, no. 3 (1996) 28.

[27] N. WOLTERSTORFF, "Justice as a Condition of Authentic Liturgy," *Theology Today* 48, no. 1 (1991) 6.

Is not this the fast that I choose:
    to loose the bonds of injustice,
    to undo the thongs of the yoke,
to let the oppressed go free,
    and to break every yoke?
Is it not to share your bread with the hungry,
    and bring the homeless poor into your house;
when you see the naked, to cover them,
    and not to hide yourself from your own kin?
Then shall your light break forth like the dawn,
    and your healing shall spring up quickly;
your vindicator shall go before you,
    the glory of the Lord shall be your rear guard. (Isa 58:6-8)

The prophet Hosea had no hesitation in attacking the false religious piety of the people who believed that they could "capture" the God of Israel in their liturgical formulas:

"Come, let us return to the LORD;
    for it is he who has torn, and he will heal us;
he has struck down, and he will bind us up.
After two days he will revive us;
    on the third day he will raise us up,
    that we may live before him.
Let us know, let us press on to know the LORD;
    his appearing is as sure as the dawn;
he will come to us like the showers,
    like the spring rains that water the earth."
What shall I do with you, O Ephraim?
    What shall I do with you, O Judah?
Your love is like a morning cloud,
    like the dew that goes away early.
Therefore I have hewn them by the prophets,
    I have killed them by the words of my mouth,
    and my judgment goes forth as the light.
For I desire steadfast love and not sacrifice,
    the knowledge of God rather than burnt offerings. (Hos 6:1-6)

This last text, like the other prophetic texts, shows up, with great theological clarity, the way in which the liturgy always brings with it, in the way it is formulated, the risk of perversion and self-absolution, a perverse game that is emphasized by the ritual nature of a *do ut des*. Hosea's prophetic warning is taken up twice in the New Testament by Jesus himself (Matt 9:13; 12:7); Jeremiah's invective is mentioned by Jesus in Mark's Gospel (11:17), and Isaiah's denunciation is updated by Jesus when he uses it against the scribes and Pharisees: "Woe to you, scribes and Pharisees, hypocrites! For you tithe mint, dill, and cummin, and have neglected the weightier matters of the law: justice and mercy and faith. It is these you ought to have practiced without neglecting the others" (Matt 23:23).

Justice is therefore the hermeneutic key to an authentic relationship with God, because it, and it alone, is able to take responsibility for our neighbor and for the world.

During the church's resistance against Nazism, Dietrich Bonhoeffer said that only those who had the courage to raise their voices to defend the Jews had the right to sing Gregorian chant! In every age the prophetic voice of the church makes itself heard, but it is not always perceived or listened to and often comes from outside the institutional and recognized borders; it takes forms of protest against the church's sin of omission toward the least and the oppressed. In 1966, during the Vietnam War, after President Lyndon Johnson had decided to step up the bombing and Cardinal Spellman had declared that the war was useful to defend civilization and consequently prayed for an American victory (the Good Samaritan of nations), the pacifist movements stepped up their protests everywhere. These were not limited to the streets and the squares, but took place also inside the churches. In Turin a group of young evangelicals handed out leaflets on Christmas Eve and Christmas Day to all the people entering and leaving their places of worship; they were entitled "Don't go to church, work for peace," with an explicit reference to Isaiah 1:10-18: "Don't go to church over this Christmas whoever you are. Whether you are a practicing Christian or one of those people who think it is enough to devote one hour to God at Christmas and Easter, don't go to church. Why should you go? No one is asking you to, let alone the God of Jesus Christ, who is certainly disgusted at a religiosity made up of rites and words, and is nauseated by the congregations, services worship and solemn masses which are a cover for injustice. . . ." But in addition to denunciation, they also made a proposal: "Stop being passive. Join in demonstrations for peace in Vietnam, and look around you to find out all those who you can involve to work for peace. . . . Stand by the side of the oppressed who have been downtrodden, and those who are suffering because of the injustice of man, and then go and celebrate Christmas. In that way you may perhaps receive once again the annunciation of the free forgiveness and the boundless mercy of God if this annunciation, which you have been receiving for centuries, is lived and put into practice, and not reneged upon with a religiosity of rites and words."[28]

Today, at the beginning of the new millennium, the churches are faced with and are committed to the need to address the complex issue of globalization, and since September 11, 2001, the consequences of international terrorism and the ever-present virus of new preemptive wars. But they are also strongly committed to supporting and defending human rights and the human dignity of immigrants, which recent legislation in many countries is shamefully trampling underfoot, considering human life solely in terms of economics.

This being so, the liturgical texts that are being produced today within the Christian ecumenical context (and outside it too) are transmitting new visions, new sensitivities, new words, new rites, new symbols for living in the here and now, and stimuli for exercising the function of a watchman (Ezek 3:17, etc.) in every part of the world. The liturgy can perform a powerful function of railing against injustice in the world, and in the light of God's word faithfully proclaimed and interpreted, it can point to the path of justice.

There is certainly a constant tension between liturgy and ethics, a tension which cannot be weakened and which must always be perceived by the community of believers. The perception of this tension is the sign of our vigilance and our awareness that it is something that cannot be wiped out: the church is not the kingdom of God, but merely the humble witness to that kingdom. The danger stems not from the tension between liturgy and ethics, but from the divorce between them, when they each take their own path without questioning each other, without listening to each other. And it is precisely along this path that the World Alliance of Reformed Churches (WARC) has openly confessed its culpability in relation to the oppressive economic order that causes misery, poverty, and death (Debrecen, 1997), and the twenty-third WARC General Council embarked on a process of gradual recognition, education, and confession *(processus confessionis)* within the churches at every level in relation to economic injustice and environmental destruction.[29]

[28] *Gioventù Evangelica*, 50 (1978) 3.
[29] *World Alliance of Reformed Churches Document, XXIII General Assembly, Debrecen 1997*. F. GIAMPICCOLI, ed., *Globalizzazione, Lavoro, Mezzogiorno* (Turin: Claudiana, 2001) 83ff.

It is certainly true, as Geoffrey Wainwright has said, that the world is not an easy place in which to live the doxology,[30] but there is no other world in which to express it, even when injustice becomes intolerable, as evidenced from the Apocalypse of John. The annunciation of new heavens and a new earth and the New Jerusalem that comes down from heaven (Rev 21) are concrete visions and bear witness to the fact that God does not abandon humanity and leave it to its own devices; that human injustice can and must be denounced; and that idols and idolatry can be unmasked, for they do not have the last word.

CONCLUSION

The concepts of polyphony, symphony, and the building site that I have used here show the two fundamental aspects that constitute the focus of the Protestant churches today in various ways. First, *the unity of the one church of Jesus Christ in the pluralism and diversity of its liturgical expressions*—pluralism and diversity of liturgical forms which do not contradict the unity of the faith in the same, one Lord Jesus Christ, but which are rather the tangible sign of the richness of his grace. Liturgical uniformity would signify the paralysis of the church. It would be extremely useful if we were to take up again, boldly and with determination, the work conducted by the Faith and Order Commission of the World Council of Churches, which produced the text entitled *Baptism, Eucharist and Ministry* (BEM) and the *Lima Liturgy* (1982), so that with no more ado we can share the same bread and the same wine at the one table of Christ. This one table, presided at by Christ himself and around which many of us sit (1 Cor 10:17), called to be the one and only body in the pluralism and diversity that characterize us: pluralism and diversity that must not be denied or excommunicated, but welcomed as a blessing of God.

I view with some sadness the missed opportunity for sharing the eucharistic table once again at the *Kirchentag* (Protestant) and the *Katholikentag* (Catholic) in Berlin in 2003. The doctrinal differences need to be discussed in depth, but not unilaterally. We must discover a new relationship between different practices and set aside traditional vetoes.[31] As a practical theologian, I must dissent from any rea-

[30] *Doxology: The Praise of God in Worship, Doctrine, and Life. A Systematic Theology* (New York: Oxford University Press, 1980) 42.

[31] In particular, I am saddened by the position adopted by Cardinal Kasper, the president of the Pontifical Council for the Promotion of Christian Unity, who

soning that emphasizes doctrinal differences and makes them into an absolute. I do not share the idea of people who say that it is necessary, *first of all*, to establish complete doctrinal unity and that only *afterward* will it be possible to share the same bread and the same cup. The concepts of *koinonia* and *communio* express the idea of a living communion with Christ and with our brothers and sisters in the faith, which goes much further than what are always partial and one-sided interpretations and doctrinal and ecclesiological ideas, which are too often marked by denominational disputes. I am therefore personally convinced that it is only through practical action, by *working together* to share the bread and the wine and the Eucharist ("Do this in remembrance of me") that we can free the minds and hearts that are still prisoners today of ancient disputes, of ancient, long-standing rancor and self-referencing. In the situation we are in today, which has remained stagnant for far too long, only action can liberate us: *the symbolic action performed together* can teach us to read and interpret in a new way the doctrinal differences regarding *doing something* whose essence defies any rational interpretation and requires an act of faith by individual consciences. Action, when linked to theological reflection, can also liberate and purify doctrine. And in ecumenical practice the motto "learning by doing" also applies.

---

vigorously criticized the concept of "eucharistic hospitality" at a Formation meeting for ecumenism professors, saying that he was against the idea of having one single table for *Katholikentag* and *Kirchentag* in Berlin 2003. The reasons for this stance are also to be found, with different wording, in his opening address on "The present situation and the future of the ecumenical movement" to the plenary assembly of the Pontifical Council for the Promotion of Christian Unity. See *Service d'information* 109 (2002/I-II) 22. Kasper says, among other things, that the Reformed churches have a tendency to set Jesus Christ as the head of the church against the church itself, and this attitude is repeated in connection with the Eucharist when they say that since Jesus invites everyone, the church cannot prevent eucharistic access to anyone. Consequently, any such argument is impossible for Catholics because Jesus Christ only invites people into the church through the church. In reality, however, the Reformed churches do not set off Christ against the church. They see Jesus Christ as the only Bread of Life, and the churches do not have monopoly over this bread, which is unique and one. Any real "opposition" that prevents people from meeting around the same table actually lies on the other side in those churches that unilaterally proclaim their own self-referencing authority, identifying it without any qualification with Jesus Christ. See, conversely, a Protestant interpretation favorable to the sharing of the Eucharist by people from different churches in J. ZINK, *Zum Abendmahl sind wir alle eingeladen. Warum ziehen die Kirchen Grenzen?* (Stuttgart: Kreuz Verlag, 1997).

The second aspect was briefly touched upon in my metaphor of the building site. For Protestantism, the liturgy is an open building site. Naturally, when I say "open building site,"this can be taken to mean different things. There are building sites that are open to carry out refurbishment for just a short time, but there are others that are opened regularly because a building is in constant need of repair and improvement. It is this latter case that is most suitable for the Reformed churches' understanding of liturgy. Both the liturgical commissions working in different churches and the local liturgy working groups are aware of the fact that the formulas that have been built need to be constantly rethought and reformulated.[32]

This is why liturgical texts have a fairly short life. The *proprium* of the liturgy must be created here and now, in harmony with the *ordinarium:* the liturgy is a living thing, because it participates in this tension, it thrives on an unsatisfied yearning that is the expectation that animates it. It announces new heavens and a new earth for our own world: the liturgy lives in the vision of what has yet to be revealed (1 John 3:2). Like the church, the liturgy is *semper reformanda.*

[32] See J. WHITE, *Protestant Worship,* Naturally, the concept of "transition" does not mean the progressive wiping out of tradition, but rather the constant need for it to be renewed in the light of the gospel.

146

Giulio Viviani

The Ecumenical Liturgies Celebrated by the Holy Father in Rome and in the World

"The common prayer with our brothers and sisters
who seek unity in Christ and in his Church." (*Ut Unum Sint*, 24)

I am grateful to the Centro Pro Unione for inviting me to discuss this subject and am pleased to be able to offer some data and ideas resulting from the research I conducted for my doctoral dissertation, which was presented to the Pontifical Liturgical Institute of Sant' Anselmo in 2001. My essay is somewhat different from the previous ones on liturgical renewal; what I intend to discuss is not the question of why or how the liturgical reform of the Catholic Church called for by Vatican Council II was carried out, but one of the results achieved, thanks to the work of the biblical, liturgical and ecumenical movements.

The Supreme Pontiff[1] John Paul II, in his apostolic letter *Tertio Millennio Adveniente*[2] [henceforth *TMA*], dedicated some significant passages to ecumenical prospects and in particular to prayer for Christian unity. The letter contains a passage that fully expresses the sense of the ecumenical celebrations of his pontificate:

> With regard to its *content,* this *Great Jubilee* will be, in a certain sense, like any other. But at the same time it will be different, greater than any other. For the Church respects the measurements of time: hours, days, years, centuries. She thus goes forward with every individual, helping everyone to realize how *each of these measurements of time is imbued with*

---

[1] This term designates the bishop of Rome as "Pontifex," literally "bridge-maker," that is, one who builds bridges, especially with the other churches and Christian communities, and with the other religions and humanity as a whole.

[2] JOHN PAUL II, apostolic letter *Tertio Millennio Adveniente* of His Holiness Pope John Paul II to the Bishops, Clergy and Lay Faithful on Preparation for the Jubilee of the Year 2000 (10 November 1994), *AAS* 87, no. 1 (1995) 5–41 (= *Enchiridion Vaticanum: Documenti ufficiali della Santa Sede in Latino e italiano*, vol. 14, nos. 1714–1820, cited henceforth as *EV* followed by volume number and paragraph numbers).

the presence of God and with his saving activity. In this spirit the Church rejoices, gives thanks and asks forgiveness, presenting her petitions to the Lord of history and of human consciences.

Among the most fervent petitions which the Church makes to the Lord during this important time, as the eve of the new millennium approaches, is that unity among all Christians of the various confessions[3] will increase until they reach full communion.[4]

And some paragraphs later the same document emphasizes the idea of Christian unity in a particular way:

In these last years of the millennium, the Church should invoke the Holy Spirit with ever greater insistence, imploring from him the grace of *Christian unity*. . . . It is essential not only to continue along the path of dialogue on doctrinal matters, but above all to be more committed to *prayer for Christian unity*. Such prayer has become much more intense after the Council, but it must increase still more, involving an ever greater number of Christians, in unison with the great petition of Christ before his Passion: "Father . . . that they may all be one in us" (John 17:21)."[5]

I. THE "BOOK OF UNITY" OF PAPAL ECUMENICAL CELEBRATIONS

The ecumenical celebrations of Pope John Paul II
My research has identified no less than seventy-five ecumenical celebrations [henceforth EC][6] in which Pope John Paul II participated from 1978 to November 2002.[7] Many were official or informal meet-

---

[3] Following the recommendation of the Pontifical Council for Promoting Christian Unity [henceforth PCPCU], we prefer to speak not of Christian churches or Christian communities or Christian communions, but more precisely of other "Christian confessions" [henceforth CC]. It should be noted that the PCPCU, in its "Directory for the Application of Principles and Norms on Ecumenism," *AAS* 85, no. 11 (1993) 1039–1119 (= *EV* 13, nos. 2169–2507) [henceforth *DAPNE*; original text in French], always uses the term "churches and ecclesial communities," as also does JOHN PAUL II, *Ut Unum Sint*, encyclical letter of the Holy Father John Paul II on ecumenical commitment, *AAS* 87, no. 11 (1995) 921–982 (= *EV* 14, nos. 2667–2884; [henceforth *UUS*]. For example, *DAPNE*, no. 5 (= *EV* 13, no. 2172) and *UUS*, no. 42 (= *EV* 14, no. 2743).

[4] *TMA*, no. 16 (= *EV* 14, nos. 1739, 1740).

[5] *TMA*, no. 34 (= *EV* 14, nos. 1773, 1775).

[6] See the list of EC attached below (pp. 195ff.).

[7] Of the 75 EC examined, 23 took place in Rome (of which 11 were in Vatican City) and 52 during the Holy Father's journeys (47 on his international apostolic

ings, with prayer or dialogue, held in Rome or elsewhere in the world with the representatives or delegates of other CC during these twenty-five years of his pontificate. They are explicitly recalled by the Pope himself in his encyclical letter *UUS* of 15 May 1995,[8] with a text that is also pertinent for our reflection. The Pope writes:

> I wish to mention the special experience of the Pope's pilgrimages to the various Churches in the different continents and countries of the present-day *oikoimene*. I am very conscious that it was the Second Vatican Council which led the Pope to exercise his apostolic ministry in this particular way. Even more can be said. The Council made these visits of the Pope a specific responsibility in carrying out the role of the Bishop of Rome at the service of communion. My visits have almost always included an ecumenical meeting and *common prayer with our brothers and sisters who seek unity in Christ and in his Church.*[9] With profound emotion I remember praying together with the Primate of the Anglican Communion at Canterbury Cathedral (29 May 1982); in that magnificent edifice, I saw "an eloquent witness *both to our long years of common inheritance and to the sad years of division that followed.*" Nor can I forget the meetings held in the Scandinavian and Nordic Countries (1–10 June 1989), in North and South America and in Africa, and at the headquarters of the World Council of Churches (12 June 1984), the organization committed to calling its member Churches and Ecclesial Communities 'to the goal of visible unity in one faith and in one Eucharistic fellowship expressed in worship and in common life in Christ'. And how could I ever forget taking part in the Eucharistic Liturgy in the Church of Saint George at the Ecumenical Patriarchate (30 November 1979), and the service held in Saint Peter's Basilica during the visit to Rome of my venerable Brother, Patriarch Dimitrios I (6 December 1987)? On that occasion, at the Altar of the Confession, we recited together the Nicene-Constantinopolitan Creed according to its original Greek text. It is hard to describe in a few words the unique nature of each of these occasions of prayer. Given the differing ways in which each of these meetings was conditioned by past events, each had its own special eloquence. They have all become part of the Church's memory as she is guided by the Paraclete to seek the full unity of all believers in Christ.

It is not just the Pope who has become a pilgrim. In recent years, many

---

journeys, of which there were a total of 98 as of 16 October 2002, and 5 during his pastoral visits in Italy).

[8] See *UUS*, nos. 24–25, 42, 71.

[9] The words used as the subtitle of my essay are taken from this passage.

distinguished leaders of other Churches and Ecclesial Communities have visited me in Rome, and I have been able to join them in prayer, both in public and in private. I have already mentioned the visit of the Ecumenical Patriarch Dimetrios I. I would now like to recall the prayer meeting, also held in Saint Peter's Basilica, at which I joined the Lutheran Archbishops, the Primates of Sweden and Finland, for the celebration of Vespers on the occasion of the Sixth Centenary of the Canonization of Saint Birgitta (5 October 1991). This is just one example, because awareness of the duty to pray for unity has become an integral part of the Church's life. There is no important or significant event which does not benefit from Christians coming together and praying. It is impossible for me to give a complete list of such meetings, even though each one deserves to be mentioned. Truly the Lord has taken us by the hand and is guiding us. These exchanges and these prayers have already written pages and pages of our "Book of unity," a "Book" which we must constantly return to and re-read so as to draw from it new inspiration and hope.[10]

My research has enabled me to collect, in just such a "Book of Unity," the texts of the EC of Pope John Paul II from 1978 to 1998 and to report them faithfully, so that they are not lost and made unavailable to scholars, to liturgists, and to those responsible for preparing prayer meetings with other CC. The documentation is fairly extensive and in large part unpublished; the task of collecting it was long, arduous, and painstaking. The results are offered as an academic contribution to the progress of ecumenism and as an enrichment of liturgical science.

It seemed right to include among the numerous EC typical of the present pontificate the interreligious meetings of prayer for peace held in Assisi in 1986 and in 2002 (with the prayer peculiar to Christians),[11] some eucharistic celebrations with the active participation, not just the presence, of our Orthodox brothers,[12] and some of the Good Friday *Via Crucis*[13] at the Colosseum,[14] prepared by

---

[10] *UUS*, nos. 24–25 (= *EV* 14, nos. 2712–2713). Italics in the original.

[11] With the representatives of the various religions and among Christians.

[12] EC 23, 53, 56, 62, 72, 75 in the list presented in the list below (pp. 195–198).

[13] On the history, evolution, and new forms, as also the biblical, liturgical, and theological aspects of the *Via Crucis*, or Stations of the Cross, see two brief but scholarly analyses: P. MARINI, "Presentazione," in *Via Crucis* (Vatican City: Libreria Editrice Vaticana, 1991) 3–9 (the texts were prepared by the Fathers of the Pontifical Faculty of the Marianum in Rome: Ignacio M. Calbuig Adan and Silvano M. Maggiani, O.S.M.); and C. W. VAN DUK, "Note di storia della *Via Crucis*," in *Il cammino della croce con Maria* (Brescia: Queriniana, 1988) 5–19.

distinguished representatives of the other CC (1994, 1995, 1997, 1998).[15]

The texts of the EC can be found either in the missals prepared for the Holy Father or in the leaflets specially prepared for the participants, with their peculiarities and differences in content (some texts include only part of the rubrics, the hymns are often not indicated, and there are errors).[16]

John Paul II's discourses of an ecumenical character are far more numerous. First, there are those that form part of, or are linked to, the various EC. Second, there are those given on the occasion of audiences and meetings. And third, there are all those associated with his ecumenical meetings during his apostolic journeys. It should be stressed that it was during his international journeys that the Pope held most of his ecumenical meetings. During the first twenty years of his pontificate, approximately 130 such meetings of this kind can be counted; here they are grouped together under the single term "sermons," even though they are usually designated by various terms: discourse, sermon, homily, elocution, address, greetings, message, and so on.

---

[14] On such occasions some ten thousand copies of the text of the *Via Crucis*, in an elegant edition with appropriate illustrations, are distributed free.

[15] It should be pointed out that the ecumenical aspect of the *Via Crucis* is represented not only by those who prepared the texts but by the members of the other CC who actively participated in it:

1994: His Holiness Bartholomew I, Ecumenical Patriarch of Constantinople;

1995: Sister Minke de Vries, Mother Superior of the Community of Grandchamp (Switzerland), World Alliance of the Reformed Churches;

1997: His Holiness Karekin I, Catholikos of all the Armenians;

1998: Olivier Clément, layman, theologian of the Orthodox Church; and the delegates who actively participated in the *Via Crucis*;

1994: Archimandrite Polycarpos, representative of the Patriarchate of Constantinople, who followed the Holy Father;

1995: Sister Maatje, of the Community of Grandchamp, and Father Ioann Sviridov of the Patriarchate of Moscow, who both helped the Holy Father carry the cross between some stations of the *Via Crucis*;

1997: Armenian Archbishop Nerses Bozabalian, who carried the cross between some stations;

1998: The author of the texts was supposed to participate in the *Via Crucis* but at the last moment had to withdraw due to ill health.

[16] One curious error is found in a prayer in which Pope Paul VI is cited instead of John Paul II (EC 2, at Phanar in November 1979; perhaps a text already prepared for Pope Paul VI, who visited the Patriarch on 25–26 July 1967, was recycled).

In many of the EC examined, as also on the occasion of informal meetings, the representatives or the delegates of the various CC gave a message of greeting or a sermon, a discourse, a homily, a meditation, or in other cases a message of thanks. In many cases it proved impossible to find the complete texts, either in the original language or in translation; in other cases only a résumé was published in magazines, newspapers, or official bulletins. The full texts would have permitted a more complete picture, a more "ecumenical" overall view, and a more detailed analysis.

Fruitful and interesting research

The task of searching for the texts of the celebrations and discourses was not always easy, because the presentation and definition of these meetings, especially in publications (in particular newspapers and journals of the Apostolic See) and in documentation (also Vatican documentation) often left one in uncertainty. References are made superficially to ecumenical meetings, ecumenical celebrations, and ecumenical prayers, often confusing the various forms and the structure of the Holy Father's meetings with the representatives of the other CC. The result is that we may find the definition of ecumenical meeting or ecumenical prayer being used both for an ecumenical celebration in the proper sense and for an informal meeting.[17]

[17] See, for example, the titles given to ecumenical meetings and EC in 1986, in *L'Osservatore Romano* [henceforth *OR*] or in the *Insegnamenti di Giovanni Paolo II* (which often takes its texts from *OR*):

–3 February: Meeting with the heads of the non-Catholic Christian communities in the residence of the Archbishop of Calcutta;

–21 March: Prayer meeting in the Chapel of Urban VIII ("with an ecumenical group from the Netherlands"): this was a proper EC (EC 15);

–4 October: Ecumenical prayer meeting in Lyon (EC 16);

–5 October: Meeting with guests and friends of the Taizé Community (EC 17);

–27 October: Prayer with the representatives of the Christian confessions and communities in the Cathedral of San Rufino, Assisi (EC 19);

–24 November: Ecumenical celebration in the Catholic Cathedral of the Most Holy Sacrament at Christchurch (EC 20);

–27 November: Ecumenical celebration in the Cricket Ground of Melbourne (EC 21).

This list of examples could be continued: in some cases the meetings are described as "ecumenical prayer services," whereas they were only an informal meeting including the Lord's Prayer.

Even in the *Insegnamenti di Giovanni Paolo II*, 6, 1 (1983) 674, one finds the title "At Belize, Ecumenical Concelebration," followed by the text of the homily on the theme of ecumenism given by the Holy Father during Mass with the Catholics of Belize on 9 March 1983. Such a designation is really odd, imprecise, and improper.

For the sake of precision, it is well to distinguish between an ecumenical meeting, an ecumenical prayer, and an ecumenical celebration. There are informal meetings that consist simply in the presentation to the Pope of the various delegates and a brief exchange of greetings. In other meetings there is also an exchange of written messages. In yet other cases the Holy Father reads a brief message of greeting or a longer address, and one or more representatives of the other CC may follow suit. Normally, if such a meeting occurs in a non- Catholic venue, it is up to the delegates of the Christian confession in question to begin by extending a greeting to the Pope; if it occurs in a Catholic venue (frequently, for example, in apostolic nunciatures) it may be begun by the Pope. Usually the meeting is concluded with the Lord's Prayer[18] and often, too, with a collective blessing.[19] In other cases—and these are the ones that most particularly concern us here—the meeting is a real ecumenical celebration, which may also be defined as an ecumenical prayer meeting or an ecumenical prayer service.

In collecting all the documentation, I had recourse to the Archive of the Office of the Liturgical Celebrations of the Supreme Pontiff [henceforth UCEPO],[20] especially as regards the texts of all the EC[21] in

[18] As already mentioned, at the end of his elocution the Pope generally recites the Lord's Prayer with those present. In his sermon, too, the Pope often includes prayers, perhaps by quoting the psalms. Some of his discourses conclude with or contain prayers, for example, an oration (from *Missa pro Unitate Christianorum*, C, Collecta bis, *Missale Romanum*, 812 [below: *MR*]); invocations to God (in Jewish or Moslem style); the so-called prayer "of St. Francis" ("Lord, make me an instrument of your peace"; for the text in English see *St. Francis of Assisi: Writings and Early Biographies*, ed. Marion A. Habig, [Chicago: Franciscan Herald Press, 1983, 1930]); a passage from a "Hymn of the Passion" by a local author; or a particular prayer to Mary, Mother of Divine Grace.

[19] I can affirm this, having personally participated in several apostolic journeys from 1993 onward.

[20] The Archive is housed in the First Loggia of the Apostolic Palace in Vatican City. The excellent organization of this Archive should be pointed out, especially as regards the period in which the position of Master of Papal Liturgical Celebrations has been held by Msgr. Piero Marini (Master from 24 February 1987; appointed titular bishop of Martirano on 14 February 1998 and consecrated on 19 March 1998). It is thanks to him that the liturgical texts of the Pope's various apostolic journeys are more complete and well documented than in the past. He also deserves credit for ensuring that a special missal containing the texts of the various celebrations are prepared by his assistants for each papal journey.

[21] All the texts of the EC were taken from the documentation preserved in the Archive of the UCEPO. They are all documented by the special missals for the

which the Holy Father John Paul II has taken part. The texts of the sermons of John Paul II, on the other hand, have been taken from *L'Osservatore Romano,* which is the most comprehensive source for papal discourses. All the material collected was collated with the sources in the archives of the PCPCU (in particular with the collection of the two editions of the Information Service, which contains the translation in English and French of the various discourses of an ecumenical character); of Vatican Radio and of the Vatican Press Office of the Holy See (the texts were collated with those in the bulletin published by the Vatican Press Office, which contains all the discourses of the Pontiff in their original language and often in Italian translation). A similar collating was conducted with the volumes of the *Insegnamenti di Giovanni Paolo II* and with the *AAS,* though these do not contain all the Holy Father's interventions.[22]

On the other hand, I have not taken into consideration, in the list of EC, the occasional, or at any rate "non-active," presence of "brother delegates," as may be the case in certain celebrations.[23] It should be pointed out that many celebrations peculiar to the Roman

---

apostolic journeys (EC 7, 8, 9, 10, 11, 12, 13, 20, 21, 22, 23, 24, 27, 28, 29, 21, 32, 32, 33, 34, 35, 36, 38, 39, 49, 41, 43, 46, 48, 49, 50, 54, 58, 59); by the booklets used by the participants (EC 15, 18, 19, 25, 26, 37, 42, 44, 45, 47, 51, 52, 53, 55, 56, 57, 40); and by other pamphlets or various other sources (EC 1, 2, 3, 4, 5, 6, 14, 16, 17).

[22] The incompleteness of these authoritative sources of the Apostolic See is incomprehensible (we may wonder by what criterion some discourses are chosen for inclusion in the *AAS* and others left out). The *OR* almost invariably contains the discourses both in their original languages and in Italian translation, whereas the *AAS* contains only some discourses and normally in the original language. The *Insegnamenti di Giovanni Paolo II* usually comprises the discourses in their original languages, sometimes with a facing translation, or sometimes the Italian translation alone.

[23] For example, a delegation of the patriarchate is present each year at the Mass presided over by the Holy Father in St. Peter's Basilica on the feast of Sts. Peter and Paul. This is recalled by the Pope himself in *UUS,* no. 52 (= *EV* 14, nos. 3766–2768). In recent years the one absence of the delegation took place on 29 June 1997, to the considerable and visible disappointment of the Pope: at the moment of the sign of peace; he exchanged the embrace of peace at least with Cardinal Edward Idris Cassidy, president of the PCPCU, who was present at the celebration with the eight cardinals of the so-called Cappella.

Nor have I taken into consideration any participation of the Holy Father in celebrations of other CC. For example, you will not find in this collection the celebration in the Greek Orthodox Cathedral at Phanar (Turkey) on 30 November 1979, when John Paul II participated in the celebration officiated by the then patriarch Dimetrios I (no documentation is found on this celebration in the Archive of the UCEPO).

rite, on the occasion of apostolic journeys, are attended by delegates and representatives of the other CC and other religions, especially Jews and Muslims; and it is the practice for the Holy Father to meet and greet them personally before or after the liturgical rite.

Analysis of the material gathered as contribution to ecumenical dialogue and prayer

The research undertaken, therefore, had the primary aim of assembling a collection of texts that may help to show the progress made by ecumenical activity in recent years and permit wider knowledge of what the Catholic Church has achieved in ecumenism in its relations with numerous brothers and sisters of other CC. Ecumenical prayer, and more especially ecumenical celebration, is shown in fact to be one of the essential means of ecumenical renewal. Indeed, as affirmed by Vatican II's Decree on Ecumenism *(Unitatis Redintegratio;* henceforth *UR),* it is "the soul of the whole ecumenical movement."[24]

Only those EC presided over or actively participated in by Pope John Paul II, in Rome and elsewhere in the world, in the course of his pontificate, have explicitly been taken into consideration. The material collected is, however, altogether too extensive to be able to be systematically and exhaustively analyzed. It is extremely diverse. Situations contingent on place, environment, time, and circumstance often make it difficult to reduce it to a coherent scheme. The sheer bulk of the material and the difficulty of conducting a more targeted analysis or of attempting its more precise theological study have therefore imposed some limitations.

As regards the specific content of the EC, it should be said that they devote particular attention to the proclamation of the Word of God. Moreover, the euchological texts of the EC comprise texts both of the common Christian patrimony and of the Roman liturgy, new texts, and those of other CC. They include some recurrent and essential components (Lord's Prayer,[25] penitential act, prayer of intercession, action of grace, profession of faith, formularies of blessing, hymns, musical acclamations and accompaniments, etc.). A particular aspect not to be underestimated in the EC is that of the gestures, signs, and modes of celebration; apart from the various verbal interventions and expressions (sermons and greetings), the non-verbal

---

[24] *UR,* no. 8 (= *EV* 1, no. 525). Cited repeatedly in the sermons of John Paul II.

[25] The one EC without the Lord's Prayer, curiously, is that of Taizé in 1986 (EC 17).

language of the EC is very rich (venues,[26] times, ministries, symbolic gestures, etc.[27]). Nor should the use of the ancient liturgical languages be forgotten, namely, Greek, Latin, Old Slav.

What also forcefully emerges from the EC and from the sermons of John Paul II is the ability to grasp some more explicit theological themes in the various branches of Christology, pneumatology, ecclesiology, and martyrology.

II. FROM LITURGICAL TO ECUMENICAL CELEBRATION

Liturgical celebration

In analyzing the ecumenical celebrations of John Paul II, it is important to specify their major liturgical themes. One such theme is that of prayer, a huge and not yet properly elucidated question that is still being studied, debated, and explored.[28] Another aspect, thanks to the liturgical movement and the liturgical reform promoted by Vatican Council II, is the debate on what is meant by the liturgy[29] and what is meant by liturgical celebration.[30]

[26] The 75 EC taken into consideration were held:
   37 in a Catholic venue: EC 1, 6 10, 11, 13, 14, 15, 18, 19, 20, 22, 25, 26, 29, 30, 32, 37, 38, 42, 44, 45, 46, 47, 48, 53, 54, 55, 58, 63, 65, 66, 68, 69, 73, 74, 75;
   12 in an Evangelic venue: EC 5, 9, 12, 27, 31, 34, 35, 36, 40, 41, 49, 50;
   , 5 in an Anglican venue: EC 1, 3, 4, 28, 33;
   6 in an Orthodox venue: EC 2, 8, 39, 70, 71, 72;
   2 in an ecumenical venue: EC 7, 17;
   16 in "non religious" venues: EC 16, 18, 21, 23, 24, 35, 43, 51, 52, 57, 59, 60, 61, 62, 64, 67.

[27] In particular the gesture of peace and the sign of light.

[28] See E. ANCILLI, ed., *Preghiera* (Rome: Città Nuova, 1988), vol. 2; J. CASTELLANO, "Preghiera e liturgia," in *Nuovo dizionario di liturgia* (Rome: Paoline, 1984) 1095–1111.

[29] See the classic study of C. VAGAGGINI, *Il senso teologico della liturgia: Saggio di liturgia teologica generale* (Rome: Paoline, 1965; English text: *Theological Dimensions of the Liturgy : A General Treatise on the Teology of the Liturgy*, trans. Leonard J. Doyle and W. A. Jurgens from the 4th Italian ed., rev. and augm. by the author (Collegeville: The Liturgical Press, 1976).

On the question what is and what is not, liturgy: L. SARTORI, G. BARBAGLIO, eds., *Teologia e liturgia: Rapporti interdisciplinary e metodologici. Il Convegno dell'APL, Camaldoli (4-9.09.1973)* (Bologna: EDB, 1974), in particular the article by L. SARTORI, *Teologia e liturgia*, 15–39.

[30] See, in this regard, the significant and innovative pages of Marsili in two well-known and widely disseminated studies: S. MARSILI, "Liturgia," in *Nuovo dizionario di liturgia*, 725–742, and "Liturgia e non liturgia," in *La liturgia momento nello storia della salvezza*, Anàmnesis 1 (Genoa: Marietti, 1974) 137, 56.

Vatican Council II in its Constitution on the Sacred Liturgy (*Sacrosanctum Concilium* [henceforth *SC*]) presents the liturgy as *"Iesu Christi sacerdotalis muneris exercitatio"* ("the exercise of the priestly office of Jesus Christ") and defines its spheres, content, characteristics and style.[31]

Which prayers of the church and of Christians can be defined as liturgical celebrations?[32] A reply to this question began to be sought and formulated already toward the end of the last century. It is now the fruit of the reflection and study begun by the liturgical movement and pursued during the years of Vatican Council II and the postconciliar reform.[33]

By liturgical celebrations we mean those rites, signs, and prayers regulated by norms and precepts, which the church celebrates in its role as the people of God, assembled to hear the word of God and to celebrate the sacraments, an assembly hierarchically ordered, which praises God and receives the grace that comes from God; it blesses the Lord and is blessed by the Lord. Liturgy is the worship offered to the Father by the church as Body of Christ.[34] The *Dictionary of the Ecumenical Movement* also offers a definition under the heading "liturgy." It reads: "Liturgy, or worship (and the forms it takes), is the public, common action of a Christian community in which the church is both manifested and realized."[35]

For a liturgical celebration effectively to take place, it is necessary that three fundamental characteristics be present together, namely:

–*anamnesis:* the "commemoration," or remembrance, of God's saving interventions in history, which is particularly expressed

[31] See *SC*, no. 7 (= *EV* 1, no. 11). On the nature and importance of the liturgy, ibid., nos. 5–13 (= *EV* 1, nos. 6–22).

[32] See the chapter on "La preghiera liturgica," in R. GUARDINI, *Lo spirito della liturgia* (Brescia: Morcelliana, 1980) 15–36.

[33] See the lucid and exhaustive study of A. M. TRIACCA, "'Liturgia' e 'pieta popolare': validità della loro osmosi (con riferimento alle espressioni mariane orientali)," in UCEPO, *Liturgie dell'Oriente Cristiano a Roma nell'Anno Mariano 1987–88,* Testi e studi (Vatican City: Libreria Editrice Vaticana, 1990) 1241–1300; in this article we may particularly note the difference between liturgy, devotional exercises, and popular piety, including an interesting diagram on page 1255.

[34] See B. NEUNHEUSER, "La liturgia della Chiesa come culto del Corpo di Cristo," in *Mysterion: Nella celebrazione del Mistero di Cristo la vita della Chiesa,* Quaderni di Rivista Liturgica, n.s. 5 (Leuman/Turin: LDC, 1981) 25–47.

[35] P. MEYENDORFF, "Liturgy," in N. LOSSKY et al., eds., *Dictionary of the Ecumenical Movement* [henceforth *DEM*], 2nd ed. (Geneva: WCC Publications, 2002) 702.

in the proclamation of the Word of God and in rendering thanksgiving to God with the people gathered in assembly;

–*epiclesis:* the invocation of the Paraclete, of the effective action of God, One and Triune, that is developed in the prayer of intercession and supplication;

–*methexis:* the conscious participation, active and devout presence of the believer, of the people of God, of all those who by virtue of baptism share in the common priesthood of all believers and are thus enabled to worship God.

Liturgical celebration is in essence the actualization of the paschal mystery of Christ, who offers himself to the Father for us.[36] All liturgical actions embody and prolong the fundamental act of remembrance that is the Eucharist. In this sense the Eucharist is the high point of the liturgical celebrations of the church and thus appears increasingly as the ideal of Christian unity. It cannot be celebrated with our brothers and sisters of other CC, not only for grave historical and contingent reasons, but especially due to the absence of truth in the sign which it is and which it requires of those who celebrate it.

A clearer idea of what is meant by liturgical or non-liturgical is emerging from the studies of contemporary liturgists. It can now be briefly summarized in the affirmation of "the needs of liturgical celebrations and the legitimacy of devotional exercises."[37] The liturgical celebration is therefore clearly and eminently a *locus*[38] in which an ex-

[36] Particularly significant in this regard is the text by J. CORBON, *The Wellspring of Worship* (Mahwah: Paulist Press, 1988). In relation to the eucharistic celebration, see P. LEBEAU, "Vatican II et l'espérance d'une Eucharistie œcuménique," *Nouvelle revue théologique* 101, no. 1 (1969) 23–46.

[37] Commendable for its clarity is the article of L. GIRARDI, "Azione liturgical e pii esercizi: un problema di inculturazione," in *Liturgia: itinerari di ricerca. Scienza liturgica e discipline teologiche in dialogo. Atti della XXV Settimana di Studio dell'Associazione Professori di liturgia (Salsomaggiore Terme, 25–30.08.1996)*, Bibliotheca Ephemerides liturgicae—Subsidia 91 (Rome: CVL–Edizione Liturgiche, 1997, 163–227).

[38] On the idea of the liturgical celebration as *locus theologicus*, see F. BROVELLI, "Fede e liturgia," in *Nuovo dizionario di liturgia*, 443–555; A. GRILLO, "La celebrazione liturgica come condizione di una autentica cristologia," in V. BATTAGLIA, G. BOF, eds., *Gesù di Nazaret . . . Figlio di Adamo, Figlio di Dio* (Milano: Paoline, 2000) 353–382 (in particular 380); P. TAMBURRINO, "*Lex orandi–Lex credendi*. Per un discorso liturgico nell'ecumenismo," *Rivista liturgica* 68, 3 (1981) 313–321. It should also be pointed out that this whole number (1981) 3 of the *Rivista liturgica* is devoted to liturgy and ecumenism *(Il rinnovamento liturgico nelle Chiese)*.

perience is made of communion with God. And that communion is necessarily changed into genuine communion with our brothers, or at least into a sincere desire for greater harmony with them, and into the practice of charity.

Ecumenical prayer

It may be said that only following Vatican Council II has ecumenical prayer[39] begun to be discussed and ecumenical celebrations begun to be held, in the Catholic church. Ecumenical prayer services were, of course, held before the Council, especially since Pope Leo XIII, in 1894, encouraged the practice of the octave of prayer for unity in the context of Pentecost.[40] In 1908, under the initiative of Reverend Paul Wattson, this octave was then transferred from the week following 18 January (then the feast of the Chair of St. Peter) to that following 25 January (feast of the Conversion of St. Paul).[41] The encyclical *UUS* recalls and underlines these prayer services:

> It is a source of joy to see that the many ecumenical meetings almost always include and indeed culminate in prayer. The *Week of Prayer for Christian Unity*, celebrated in January or, in some countries, around Pentecost, has become a widespread and well established tradition. But there are also many other occasions during the year when Christians are led to pray together.[42]

It is clear from these words that today when we think of the prayer for Christian unity, in the week devoted to it or on other occasions, we think not of a specific prayer of Catholics for unity, but a truly ecumenical prayer in which the faithful or representatives of the various CC participate.[43] In recent years we have passed from praying *for* others (for their conversion, for their return to the fold), considered as "separated brothers," to praying *with* others, with all the members

[39] *Cf.* T. BERGER, "Worship in the Ecumenical Movement," in *DEM. . . ., op. cit.,* 1250–1254; J. B. CARDEN, "Prayer in the Ecumenical Movement," *ibid.,* 925–927. See further, A. M. TRIACCA, "Bibbia e liturgia," in *Nuovo dizionario di liturgia . . ., op. cit.,* 175–197, with comprehensive bibliography.

[40] Information taken from PONTIFICAL COUNCIL FOR PROMOTING CHRISTIAN UNITY, *Prayer for Christian Unity 2000,* n.d.

[41] *Cf.* the booklet prepared by UCEPO for the faithful present at the celebration presided over by the Holy Father on 25 January 1988, on page 3.

[42] *UUS,* no. 24 (= *EV* 14, no. 2712).

[43] See T. F. BEST, "Week of Prayer for Christian Unity," in *DEM,* 1203.

of the various CC, with the shared aim of the common conversion to Christ. It is a prayer to the one and unifying God, in whom is found the greatest reality of communion in the distinction of three Persons. For this reason, when a celebration is placed in this dimension, it truly becomes a principle and factor of unity by the grace of God, as well as by the good will of men and women. Here we see the actual fulfillment of the words of Jesus: "Where two or three are gathered in my name, there am I in the midst of them" (Matt 18:20).

That the practice of ecumenical celebrations, at least as far as Catholics are concerned, began only in relatively recent times seems clear.[44] It was only in 1949 that the then Congregation of the Holy Office declared (finally!), in a special instruction, that "the common recitation of the Lord's Prayer is not prohibited" in ecumenical meetings.[45]

A clear transition from spiritual ecumenism to ecumenical spirituality has been perceptively noted.[46] This is also expressed in a common endeavor and genuine collaboration in preparing the texts not only for the prayers and celebrations of the Week of Prayer for Christian Unity but also, as the present research has shown, for the EC with the presence of the Pope, the bishop of Rome.

The origins of ecumenical celebrations

The precursors of the pontifical EC may be identified in the first approaches made to the representatives and delegates of the "separated brethren" by Pope John XXIII, on the occasion of the convening and holding of the first Session of Vatican Council II. The sessions of the Council were also attended, in some moments of prayer, by the "fraternal delegates" of other CC, not in an active role but undoubtedly participating in and attentive to what was happening.[47] But it was especially after the Council that the decisive, even if not immediately confident, steps were taken for ecumenical prayer services, ecumenical study, and dialogue, and then ecumenical celebrations themselves.

[44] See B. FISCHER, "Liturgical Reforms," *DEM*, 697–701.

[45] Cited in R. BEAUPÈRE, *L'ecumenismo* (Brescia: Queriniana, 1993). An interesting historical excursus on the development of the ecumenical prayer can be found in the same book, 36–39.

[46] See S. SPINSANTI, "Ecumenismo spirituale," in *Nuovo dizionario di spiritualità* (Rome: Paoline, 1982) 460–478.

[47] Interesting, in this regard, is, for example, the testimony in M.-D. CHENU, *Diario del Vaticano II: Note quotidiane al Concilio 1962–1963* (Bologna: Il Mulino, 1996) 35.

Interesting in this regard is the document of the Joint Working Group between the Catholic church and the World Council of Churches in 1966, in which it is affirmed—and this also goes for the EC under consideration—that "the rapid development of the ecumenical movement obliges us to reflect together on common prayer and common liturgical action. . . . During the Week of Prayer for Christian Unity, the faithful of all confessions meet together before the Lord. Further developments along these lines require common study."[48]

The consciousness of such a need had by this time been felt. Christians of the various confessions were beginning to pray together for their unity and their common witness in the world of one faith, one baptism, one Lord, and one God the Father.[49] The Council had already acknowledged this when, in its Decree on Ecumenism, it had clearly affirmed, with reference to the spiritual dimension and prayer:

> This change of heart and holiness of life, along with public and private prayer for the unity of Christians, should be regarded as the soul of the whole ecumenical movement, and merits the name "spiritual ecumenism."
>
> It is a recognized custom for Catholics to meet for frequent recourse to that prayer for the unity of the Church with which the Savior himself on the eve of his death so fervently appealed to his Father: "That they may all be one." (John 17:20)
>
> In certain circumstances, such as in prayer services "for unity" and during ecumenical gatherings, it is allowable, indeed desirable that Catholics should join in prayer with their separated brethren. Such prayers in common are certainly a very effective means of petitioning for the grace of unity, and they are a genuine expression of the ties that still bind Catholics to their separated brethren. "For where two or three are gathered together in my name, there are I in the midst of them." (Matt 18:20)
>
> Yet worship in common *(communicatio in sacris)* is not to be considered as a means to be used indiscriminately for the restoration of unity among Christians. There are two main principles upon which the practice of such common worship depends: first, that of the unity of the

[48] JOINT WORKING GROUP BETWEEN THE CATHOLIC CHURCH AND THE WORLD COUNCIL OF CHURCHES, "First Official Report," February 1966, no. 8. Cited 21 July 2003. Online: http://www.prounione.urbe.it/dia-int/jwg/doc/e_jwg_02.html.

[49] See in this regard the already cited articles in the *DEM* (see notes 39, 43, 44 above): "Worship in the Ecumenical Movement," "Prayer in the Ecumenical Movement," "Week of Prayer for Christian Unity," "Liturgical Reforms."

Church which ought to be expressed; and second, that of the sharing in the means of grace. The expression of unity very generally forbids common worship. Grace to be obtained sometimes commends it. The concrete course to be adopted when all the circumstances of time, place, and persons have been duly considered is left to the prudent decision of the local episcopal authority, unless the bishops' conference according to its own statutes or the Holy See has determined otherwise.[50]

This is a seminal text, in which principles are enunciated, guidelines laid down, but especially in which the way is opened, with due caution but without excessive fears, to ecumenical celebration as an effective (one might almost say "quasi -sacramental") means to invoke from God the gift of unity for all those who profess themselves Christians.[51] The decree recognizes that praying with the separated brethren of other CC is not only permissible but desirable: a hope, an incitement, a new prospect for EC. Catholics were beginning, as mentioned above, not only to pray *for* others (the separated brethren of other CC) but also, and in an irreversible way, to pray *with* others, the representatives and members of the various CC, both in the dioceses and at the national level and at the level of the Apostolic See itself.

The ecumenical celebrations of Pope Paul VI

Already under Pope Paul VI[52] there had been occasions, other than audiences and meetings, in which ecumenical prayer services with the brethren of other CC were held. The archive of the UCEPO contains documentation of some ecumenical celebrations presided over by Pope Paul VI. They represent altogether four fine testimonies of EC:[53] a first celebration was on the occasion of the visit of the Ecumenical Patriarch of Constantinople Athenagoras I in 1967; another on the occasion of the meeting with the Catholicos of all the Armeni-

---

[50] *UR*, no. 8 (=*EV* 1, nos. 525–328).

[51] In the years following Vatican II's Decree on Ecumenism, an ecumenical directory was published in two successive parts: SECRETARIATUS AD CHRISTIANORUM UNITATEM FOVENDAM, *Directorium ad Ea quae a Concilio Vaticano II de re oecumenica promulgata sunt exequenda*, in *EV* 2, nos. 1194–1292; the first part, general in scope, dated 14 May 1967; the second part dedicated to ecumenism in higher education, dated 16 April 1970. Nos. 21–37 of the document are devoted to EC (= *EV* 2, nos. 1214–1230).

[52] See the interesting publication of G. MONZIO COMPAGNONI, ed., *Montini Giovanni Battista—Paolo VI. L'Ottavario per l'unità dei Cristiani. Documenti e discorsi (1955–1978)*, Quaderni dell'Istituto 12 (Rome/Brescia: Studium-Istituto Paolo VI, 1998).

ans Vasken I in 1970; a prayer meeting for Christian unity was held with the Diocese of Rome in 1973; and, lastly, an ecumenical celebration marked the visit of Dr. Donald Coggan, Anglican Primate, in 1977. It does not seem out of place here to recall these significant testimonies, but also to enable comparisons to be drawn with the EC of Pope John Paul II. It seems particularly important to point out a courageous and peculiar ritual sequence provided by Paul VI to the EC of 1967, 1970, and 1977 by the insertion in them of two examples of a particular "eucharistic prayer," a prayer both of praise and thanksgiving and blessing *(eulogia)*. They are two texts of great theological richness, very precise both in substance and form. From the text of the first of these two "eucharistic prayers" a preface was derived with the title *"De unitate corporis Christi, quod est Ecclesia,"* which is found in the Holy Mass *"Pro unitate christianorum"* of the Roman Missal.[54]

Analogies with this style, this action of praise and thanksgiving, even if only in the form of translations of these texts, can be found in prayer meetings proposed and realized for the Week of Prayer for Christian Unity.[55] Curiously these texts do not occur in any of the seventy-five EC of Pope John Paul II, in which ample scope is given to the dimension of the liturgy of the Word, but very little to celebration of the "eucharistic" type, unless in the form of some liturgical prayer of blessing, praise, and thanksgiving.

III. THE EXPERIENCE OF THE ECUMENICAL CELEBRATIONS OF JOHN PAUL II

An experience of communion and prayer

The EC, both in Rome and more particularly those during the apostolic journeys of John Paul II, are typical of the meetings with the

[53] The texts are taken from the booklets prepared for the use of the participants and from other documentation in the UCEPO Archive.

[54] See *Missae et orationese pro variis necessitatibus,* no. 13, A, in *MR,* 808 (*MRit,* 797). The same text is also found in the *Missale Ambrosianum* (Milan, 1981) and in the *Messale Ambrosiano* (Milan, 1976) 625, with one or two minor variants.

[55] These texts of *eulogia* can be found in some prayer leaflets in the archive of the Office for Ecumenism of the Archdiocese of Trent. For example, the leaflet prepared for an ecumenical celebration in the historic Basilica of San Vigilio, on 25 January 1974, contains an Italian translation of the action of praise and thanksgiving of 26 October 1967. I personally recall this and other EC, particularly those held in the Church of the Holy Trinity, the church from which the inaugural procession of the Council of Trent set out.

"separated brethren," better defined as the representatives of the other CC.[56] In many cases the meetings in question were simply meetings limited to an exchange of greetings and speeches given by one or two representative of the delegations present and the Pope; they cannot therefore be called celebrations in the strict sense, even though they normally make provision for the recitation of common prayer (usually the Lord's Prayer) at the end. In some cases a brief supplication, or a passage of Holy Scripture, is added to this; in other cases there is also a blessing. These meetings can more properly described as ecumenical celebrations or ecumenical services if they take place in a church or in a place specially prepared for prayer with an assembly and with a celebratory structure that takes the form either of a moment of prayer or a celebration of the Word.

An examination of the recommendations for liturgical celebrations prepared by the UCEPO for the Holy Father's apostolic journeys and furnished to the local ecclesiastical authorities shows that they comprise, apart from the celebration of Mass, two liturgical sequences, defined either as a "Liturgy of the Word" *(Celebratio verbi Dei)* or a "Moment of Prayer" *(Conventus orationis).*[57] The difference between

---

[56] The *DAPNE* speaks in general of members, delegates, and ministers of other churches or communities.

[57] In the case of Liturgies of the Word, the ritual structure normally makes provision for:

"the same order as the Liturgy of the Word of the Mass:
a) The Holy Father begins with the sign of the cross and addresses a liturgical greeting to the assembly.
b) The Ordinary addresses a tribute to the Holy Father.
c) The Holy Father recites the oration (of the day, of the patron or titular saint, or another suitable prayer).
d) Reading from the Old or New Testament (if desired and if time permits a responsorial psalm and a Gospel passage may also be suitably added).
e) Homily or discourse of the Holy Father.
f) Prayer of the faithful, with a maximum of six invocations, concluded with the recitation or singing of the Lord's Prayer.
g) Final oration by the Holy Father.
h) Apostolic Blessing.

If provision is made for the offering of gifts, these may be presented immediately after the prayer of the faithful, before the blessing.

As regards other, shorter celebrations (for example, for a visit to the cathedral), the following scheme is advised:
–Sign of the cross
–Liturgical greeting of the Holy Father

them is determined by the needs of the planned program, by the organization of the visit, by the local situation, or by the time available for the celebration. Ecumenical services, even if they have not always respected this scheme in its entirety and have sometimes included other features (for example, penitential act, exchange of peace, etc.), are, however, fundamentally linked to these two forms of celebration, called respectively "Liturgy of the Word" and "Moment [or also Meeting] of Prayer."

Can such liturgies be defined as celebrations? And on the basis of what criteria? These are questions frequently raised, especially by those who fear that these occasions of prayer may create confusion, give rise to a kind of eirenicism, or even syncretism, or are too "Protestant" in character. An answer to such questions and such fears emerges from the texts of the EC themselves: they reveal both in structure and content the essential elements required to be considered genuine liturgical actions.

The ritual structure of ecumenical celebrations

An analysis of the ritual structure of the celebrations being examined here shows their specific ritual nature as liturgies, devotional exercises, popular devotions, etc. Some of them can undoubtedly be considered liturgical actions (Holy Mass and Liturgy of the Hours, *Moleben*). Others are clearly devotional exercises *(Via Crucis)*. But can all the rest be considered liturgical celebrations? Certainly not those brief periods of prayer we have included among the EC, at least for purposes of documentation. But the EC, which are also called "Celebration of the Word of God" or, as we have seen in the recommendations of the UCEPO, "Liturgy of the Word," have a ritual structure often similar to, if not identical with, the first part of the Mass. Referring to what is said by the *Ordo Lectionum Missae* [henceforth *OLM*] regarding the Liturgy of the Word,[58] it seems that these EC can be

---

–Oration of the titular of the church or other suitable oration
–Brief welcoming address by the local ecclesiastical authority
–Discourse or welcome by the Supreme Pontiff
–Hymn or recitation of the Lord's Prayer
–Apostolic Blessing.

UCEPO, *"Indicazione e norme per le Celebrazione Liturgiche presiedute dal Santo Padre in occasione della Visita Pastorale a un Paese od a una Diocesi fuori Roma"* [typescript for internal use].

[58] See *Ordo Lectionum Missae,* in *Missale Romanum ex decreto Sacrosancti Œcumenici Concilii Vaticani II instauratum auctoritate Pauli PP. VI promulgatum,* editio

defined as liturgical actions in the proper sense, since they have all the requisites both of form and content.[59]

The author of the article on "Ecumenism" in the recently published *Dizionario di omiletica*, analyzing the experience of ecumenism and its liturgical expression in recent years, writes as follows:

> The category of the "paraliturgical" and that of the occasional sermon or discourse has in fact been abandoned, at least on the Catholic side, in favor of the definitive, and perhaps irreversible, adoption of the descriptive name "liturgical celebration" and homily, a name which is so charged with patristic suggestion and revived, and in some sense imposed, by the liturgical reform promoted by Vatican Council II.[60]

Other questions are posed as regards the person/persons who should preside over such celebrations: can ministers of other CC be admitted as the officiant or co-officiant of liturgical celebrations?[61] And what texts may be used or what texts are unsuitable, to ensure that the *lex orandi* be also *lex credendi*? An answer to such questions is not easy. In the following I will try to offer at least some reflections and elucidations on the matter, but the questions remain open.

As mentioned above, the liturgical schemes adopted for EC are those of the celebration of the Word of God, following the scheme of the first part of the Mass: initial rites and liturgy of the Word. Wholly absent from the EC of this pontificate, on the other hand, is the proposal of *eulogia*, of a "eucharistic prayer," of which traces can be found, as we have seen, in the EC of Pope Paul VI.

The peculiar and specific characteristics of the EC to be examined here are:

    –an initial welcome addressed to the Holy Father by one or
    more representatives of the delegations the other CC present;

---

typica altera (Vatican City: Libreria Editrice Vaticana, 1981), nos. 1–10); see also, *mutatis mutandis,* what is said for the Liturgy of the Word in the Mass, *ibid.,* nos. 11–57. See also *Introductio Generalis,* in *Missale Romanorum ex decreto Sacrosancti Œcumenici Concilii Vaticani II instauratum auctoritate Paulo PP. VI promulgatum, editio typica* (Vatican City: Libreria Editrice Vaticana, 1975) nos. 9, 33–47.

[59] See A.M. TRIACCA, "Valore teologico delle 'Liturgia della Parola,'" *Rivista di liturgia* 73, no. 5 (1986) 616–632, an article particularly suggestive and informative in this regard.

[60] B. AMATA, "Ecumenismo," in *Dizionario di omiletica* (Leumann/Gorle: LDC/Velar, 1984) 416.

[61] See *DAPNE,* nos. 111–121 (= *EV* 13, nos. 2386–2300).

1. the common listening to the Word of God;
2. homily of the Holy Father;
3. prayer culminating in the Lord's Prayer;
4. the exchange of peace;
5. the final blessing.

There are no rigid or preestablished schemes for such celebrations. A certain degree of freedom is left in the choice and sequence of the various elements, while at the same time respecting the normal structure of a celebration of the Word of God.

Normally, rites belonging to other confessions are not adopted in full,[62] even though the practice is recommended by the *DAPNE:* "In some situations, the official prayer of a church may be preferred to ecumenical services specially prepared for the occasion."[63] In the seventy-five celebrations examined, wide scope is clearly given to the typically Latin ritual of the Catholic church, though it should be said that on the Pope's more recent apostolic journeys this situation has been somewhat modified and improved.

The Pope himself, conscious of the problem, did not hesitate to say, in the Anglican cathedral of Bulawayo in Zimbabwe (1988):

> Although common worship may not be possible in many cases, nevertheless prayer services such as this one today play an important part in helping to restore unity among the followers of Jesus. The annual Week of Prayer for Christian Unity is one initiative in this regard which deserves special commendation and support. And in our own Communions, we have an obligation to *follow the example of Christ* in praying: 'May they all be one' (John 17:21). Above all, we must never lose confidence in what the Spirit of God can accomplish in our own day. For as the Angel Gabriel said to the Virgin Mary, *'nothing is impossible to God'* (Luke 1:37). Let our hearts then be alive with faith and always steadfast in hope."[64]

---

[62] That may be the case of the *Akathistos* or *Moleben* rites of the Oriental churches, both Orthodox and in communion with Rome (EC 39). In other cases the active presence of the Pope at a rite celebrated by ministers of other CC, for example, the Orthodox Divine Liturgy in Romania (EC 61) or without his active participation, for example, at Fanar on 30 November 1979.

[63] *DAPNE*, no. 117 (= *EV* 13, no. 2396).

[64] JOHN PAUL II, "Sermon for the ecumenical meeting in the Anglican Cathedral of Bulawayo," 12 September 1988, *OR* 14 September 1988, 5 (weekly edition in English, 19 September 1988, 11).

The problem is how to find, in consultation with the delegates of the other CC, the procedures that may permit all the participants to pray together, by drawing on what it is that unites us, what it is that we share as a common patrimony, but without betraying the truth. In this regard, we may appropriately cite what is outlined, in a very lucid way, in a special Appendix to the above-mentioned "First Report of the Joint Working Group between the Catholic Church and the WCC," published in 1966.[65] Already during those early years of the ecumenical movement, it was affirmed that "it is essential for the ecumenical movement that Christians may meet in common prayer and understand that dialogue and collaboration may only be developed on condition that this common foundation be developed."[66] Numerous recommendations are therefore made for ecumenical meetings, especially as regards "religious services." Worth emphasizing in this text are the following remarks that seem precisely to fit this study on the EC: "Common prayer . . . ought not to give the impression that such a community exists where it unfortunately does not."[67]

So the criterion is the truth of the liturgical sign. An EC may only be held if there truly is at least an effort to achieve communion, a striving toward a certain form of *one* community of brothers and sisters who believe in Christ. Ecumenical celebration is not, nor can it be, a kind of "scenic representation," a façade raised for the occasion. It is not an apparently happy parenthesis in a situation in which the various CC continue to ignore each other.

> 1. "As far as possible the various traditions represented at a gathering should have the opportunity to participate actively in worship, even if practical considerations seem to make it difficult."[68]

Unfortunately, in the EC examined, sufficient attention is not always paid to this presence, which is often only passive, but which must become genuinely active and participative. To this end, a far more intensive and cooperative effort of preparation is needed, and

---

[65] JOINT WORKING GROUP BETWEEN THE CATHOLIC CHURCH AND THE WORLD COUNCIL OF CHURCHES, "First Official Report," nos. 8.17–18, Appendix.

[66] Ibid., Appendix, no. 1.

[67] Ibid., Appendix, no. 2.

[68] Ibid., Appendix, no. 7.1.

that requires time, energy, and personnel. Scope must be given to specific texts, ministers, and rites representative of the liturgical tradition of the various CC.

2. "There are various forms of worship which must be distinguished:
a) Services in which representatives of several traditions participate. It is important that such services are prepared together and are carried out in a representative way. The celebration of the Eucharist is normally excluded at such occasions.
b) Services composed in a form which can be adopted by the members of any church tradition, e.g., prayers of adoration, Bible readings, prayers of intercession, etc.
c) Services which are conducted for all those participants in the meeting by one or several members of one church according to the rules of this church. . . .
d) Eucharistic services which are held by one church within the context of a meeting."[69]

This series of examples of the various possible forms of celebration is closely matched in the papal EC considered the present study. The findings of the present research have shown that the sense and letter of these recommendations are generally respected in the preparation and conduct of the EC of this pontificate.

In a homily given in Los Angeles in 1987, John Paul II clearly explained that "this sharing can take the form of coming together as brothers and sisters to pray to God in ways which safeguard the uniqueness of each religious tradition."[70] In other words, the Pope invites respect for the various CC in the search for what is already the common patrimony of them all and for what may become so with a more courageous eye to the future.

Classification of the various ecumenical celebrations

To give an idea of what might be called a certain creativity or perhaps even confusion in the material collected, it is enough to scan the simple listing in chronological order of the titles given to the 75 EC in the list below. The great variety of titles in a variety of languages

---

[69] Ibid., Appendix, no. 7.2.

[70] JOHN PAUL II, "Sermon for the meeting with non-Christians at the Japanese Cultural Center in Los Angeles," 16 September 1987, *OR* 18 September 1987, 8 (weekly edition in English, 28 September 1987, 7).

used may be noted .[71] It is a listing that presents the reality of the situation, a quite precise frame of reference that also reveals the attention to the various sensibilities in the field of ecumenism. It should be noted that the adjective "ecumenical" recurs in the majority of the titles of the EC, especially the most important ones. In the present study, the following types of celebration and rite have been taken into consideration (the numbers correspond to the chronological list of the celebrations below):

1. 50 Liturgies of the Word	EC 1, 3, 5, 7, 9, 10, 12, 13, 14, 15, 16, 17, 18, 19, 20, 21, 22, 23, 27, 28, 29, 30, 31, 32, 33, 34, 35, 36, 40, 41, 43, 44, 46, 47, 48, 49 50, 54, 58, 59, 64, 65, 67, 68, 69, 70, 71, 72, 73;
2. 6 Prayer Meetings	EC 2, 4, 6, 8, 24, 38;
3. 7 Vespers	EC 11, 25, 37, 42, 55, 63, 74;
4. 4 *Via Crucis*	EC 51, 52, 57, 60;
5. 6 Eucharistic Celebrations	EC 26, 53, 56, 62, 72, 75;
6. 1 Divine Liturgy	EC 61;
7. 1 *Ora media* [Sext]	EC 45;
8. 1 *Moleben*	EC 39.

In the six prayer meetings listed above, there was no proclamation of the Word of God, to which space was given to all the other celebrations. In the great majority of cases, therefore, the EC in question can be described as liturgies of the Word, celebrations of the Word of God with a specific liturgical character of their own.

Liturgy and rites of the ecumenical celebrations

The ritual organization of the EC normally comprises some fixed points and other variables according to the scheme already presented above.[72] It may more precisely be tabulated as follows:

---

[71] The titles in Latin have a raison d'être of their own. The missals prepared by UCEPO usually contain, for convenience, all the rubrics in Latin (and hence the titles too), unless the missals in question are entirely composed in the better known modern languages (Italian, English, Spanish. French, German and Portuguese, also Polish in certain cases). In the booklets for the faithful printed in Rome, the rubrics are normally in Italian.

[72] See the recommendations of UCEPO cited above (see note 20).

Initial rites

    1. welcome

    2. processional hymn

    3. sign of the cross and liturgical greeting

    4. greeting (or greetings)

    5. penitential act

    6. prayer of thanksgiving

    7. oration

Liturgy of the Word

    8. readings with psalms and hymns

    9. homily

    10. prayer of the faithful

    11. Lord's Prayer

    12. oration

Final rites

    13. sign of peace

    14. exchange of gifts

    15. words of thanksgiving

    16. blessing

    17. final hymn or musical piece

The space given to the mode of celebration based on the sanctification of time is also worth noting; on six occasions, in fact, the texts of the Liturgy of the Hours were used for common prayer (EC 11, 25, 37, 42, 45, 55). Great respect is also normally paid to the liturgical year, though bearing in mind that the EC usually do not coincide with occasions of particular solemnity in the church calendar.

Some remarks made in an ecumenical document published in 1984 are indicative for this reflection on the EC, in their dimension of celebration of the Word:

> Apart from liturgical celebrations that comprise the proclamation of the Word and the sacrament, right from the start there have been liturgies in church that have concentrated on prayer, readings, proclamation of the Word. *Prayer liturgies* have their own fixed place in the daily life of male and female religious communities, of monastic communities, but they may also be liturgical celebrations of the local community. In Catholic and Evangelic communities homiletic liturgies *(Predigtgottesdienste)* are regularly held on certain days or at particular times of the liturgical year. In the Lutheran Evangelical Church the main service of the community, held on Sunday, may be a homiletic liturgy.

Liturgies of the Word and liturgies of prayer are an actualization of the Lord's promise: "Where two or three are gathered in my name, there am I in the midst of them" (Matt 18:20); the Lord's promise, "He who hears you hears me" (Luke 10:16), also holds good for the proclamation of the Word of God in such liturgies. The proclamation of the Word always has a missionary dimension, also by virtue of the fact that it dissolves and transcends the confines of the church. That's why such liturgies of the Word, unlike the Eucharist or penance, are also open to non-baptized persons. Our prayer and homiletic liturgies, however, are normally liturgical celebrations common to all Christians, in which the congregation listens to the Word of God, praises the one and triune God, and intercedes for the whole world. The fact that we, members of the Roman Catholic Church and of the Lutheran Evangelical Church, may participate together in such liturgies is therefore not only an expression of the missionary dimension but also the realization of a communion in and under Jesus Christ in the celebration of the liturgy.[73]

So by EC we mean those prayer meetings that rightfully form part of the ecumenical process[74] and have very precise characteristics both in terms of ritual and content, as described above. The decree *UR* refers to such celebrations when it explicitly affirms:

Taking part in this movement, which is called ecumenical, are those who invoke the Triune God and confess Jesus as Lord and Savior. They do this not merely as individuals, but also as members of the corporate groups in which they have heard the Gospel and which each regards as his Church and indeed, God's. And yet, almost everyone, though in different ways, longs for the one visible Church of God, a Church truly universal and sent forth to the whole world that the world may be converted to the Gospel and so be saved, to the glory of God.

The sacred Council gladly notes all this. It has already declared its teaching on the Church and now, moved by a desire for the restoration of unity among all the followers of Christ, it wishes to set before all Catholics guidelines, helps and methods, by which they too can respond to the grace of this divine call.[75]

---

[73] BILATERALE ARBEITSGRUPPE DER DEUTSCHEN BISCHOFSKONFERENZ UND DER KIRCHENLEITUNG DER VEREINIGTEN EVANGELISCH-LUTHERISCHEN KIRCHEN DEUTSCHLANDS, *Kirchengemeinschaft in Wort und Sakrament* (Paderborn/Hannover: Bonifacius/Lutherisches Verlagshaus, 1985) nos. 22–23.

[74] See P. TAMBURRINO, "Ecumenismo," in *Nuovo dizionario di liturgia*, 410–428.

[75] *UR*, no. 1 (= *EV* 1, nos. 495–496).

The EC of Pope John Paul II can certainly be placed in this context and conform to this style: they are genuine liturgical celebrations.

The legitimacy of ecumenical celebrations

It may be said that the legitimacy of such meetings springs from the gospel itself. Jesus himself promised to be present where two or more are gathered and pray together in his name (Matt 18:19-20), and the Lord himself set us an example with his prayer, reported by St. John in his account of the Last Supper: "that they may all be one" (John 17:20-23). "The ecumenical prayer," as a member of the Church of England has put it, "was anticipated by Jesus in the Lord's Prayer, developed by his disciples in the great prayer of unity in John 17 and newly extended to embrace all mankind in the diffusion of the Gospel beginning at Pentecost. It is a prayer offered for the unity of the whole Church of Christ and for the good of the world that he came to save."[76]

The legitimacy and, I would go further, the duty of such EC are already enunciated by Vatican Council II, which, in its Decree on Ecumenism, presents Christ as the model of how to pray to the Father for the unity of all those who believe in him:

> Before offering himself up as a spotless victim upon the altar of the cross, he prayed to his Father for those who believe: "that all may be one, as you, Father, are in me, and I in you; I pray that they may be one in us, that the world may believe that you sent me" (John 17:21). In his Church he instituted the wonderful sacrament of the Eucharist by which the unity of the Church is both signified and brought about. He gave his followers a new commandment to love one another, and promised the Spirit, their Advocate, who, as Lord and life-giver, should remain with them forever.[77]

The same document, as already mentioned above, gave impulse, value, and warranty to this ecumenical prayer, which it authoritatively defined as "the soul of the whole ecumenical movement."[78] Having pointed out the liturgical legitimacy of the EC, we may confirm that such EC should be considered a legitimate and necessary prayer of the church. The legitimacy of the EC is also confirmed by the declarations of Pope John Paul II, as documented in his sermons,

---

[76] J. B. CARDEN, *Prayer in the Ecumenical Movement*, 925.

[77] *UR*, no. 2 (= *EV* 1, no. 497).

[78] Ibid., no. 8 (= *EV* 1, no. 525).

and particularly by his encyclical letter *UUS*.[79] For example, in Malawi, on the occasion of his apostolic journey in 1989, John Paul II presented the value of ecumenical prayer as follows:

> We are all convinced that *common prayer* is not only fundamental to the search for Christian unity, but also important in nourishing the very ecumenical activity in which we are engaged. In prayer we learn to open ourselves to God and to others. In common prayer for Christian unity we experience the Christian identity arising from our common Baptism, but at the same time we experience the pain of division. In that very prayer, however, we are encouraged by the Spirit of Christ, who prays within us (*cf.* Rom 8:26), to go forth and work together for the unity of all his followers. The Week of Prayer for Christian Unity and other occasions during the year offer wonderful opportunities for prayer leading to greater mutual understanding, esteem and love.[80]

The legitimacy of the EC may therefore be reaffirmed, first and foremost, as prayers, but also in general as liturgical prayers, insofar as they respect the fundamental characteristics and essential requirements of a liturgical celebration and more specifically a celebration of the Word of God, as I have tried to describe. It should be emphasized, therefore, that these celebrations are not just an occasion to pray with others, under the guidance and responsibility of the pastors. They are in the first place an act of worship which, like any genuine liturgical rite, entails an ascending movement (prayer of supplication, thanksgiving, request for forgiveness) and an event of blessing from on high (listening to the Word of God, acceptance of divine grace). So what is performed also in the EC is the dynamic inherent in Christian worship: *anamnesis* and *epiclesis* are decidedly aimed at *metexis*, at the witness vital for the progress of unity.

The opportunity of ecumenical celebrations

The opportunity offered by EC consists in the fact that we cannot limit ourselves just to an ecumenism confined to meetings or dialogue, as if it merely had a cultural or elitist value; it is not an event reserved for just a few experts. In the case of the Apostolic See, it would be minimalist for the Pope to limit himself to granting "audi-

[79] See *UUS*, nos. 24–25, 42 (= *EV* 14, nos. 2712–2713, 2743).

[80] JOHN PAUL II, "Sermon at the meeting with representatives of other confessions and religions in Our Lady of Wisdom School in Blantyre," 5 May 1989, *OR* May 1989, 5 (weekly edition in English, 29 May 1989, 22).

ences" to representatives of the other CC. The Pope himself said so, speaking in Nairobi in 1980:

> Whenever possible, then, let us find ways of engaging in acts of common witness, be it in joint Bible work, in promoting human rights, in meeting human needs, in theological dialogue, in praying together when opportunity allows—as happens in so welcome a manner today—or in speaking to others about Jesus Christ and his salvation.[81]

Also, on the occasion of his journey to Japan in 1981, John Paul II said:

> How much I would encourage you to engage in this on the occasion of the annual Week of Prayer for Christian Unity, joining Christians throughout the world in a great act of intercession that can open hearts and lives to the reconciling power of Christ! In such an atmosphere of prayer, theological dialogue can flourish, and we can face, in accordance with our ecumenical responsibility, those difficult questions that still keep us apart. Moreover, it is fervent prayer which will enlighten us to see and strengthen us to use the opportunities that are ours to bear a common witness to Jesus Christ and to his Gospel.[82]

And, again, during his homily on the theme of ecumenism at Mass in Belize, on 9 March 1983, the Holy Father said:

> All of you, dear brothers and sisters, together with the members of the Catholic Church must work and pray so that the unity which Christ desires for his followers will be fully realized *in truth and charity*. . . . Thus, we have learned that when we engage in *work for Christian Unity*, we are accomplishing the will of our Lord. Moreover, we have learned that prayer through, with and in Christ is the *main source* of this unity. Since prayer for Christian unity, and, if possible, common prayer for Christian unity, is an essential element of our ecumenical work, let us then be faithful to this prayer. Prayer cannot be what it should be without what the Second Vatican Council calls a change of heart. (*UR* 7)[83]

---

[81] JOHN PAUL II, "Sermon for the meeting with exponents of the other Christian confessions at Nairobi," 7 May 1980, *OR* 9 May 1980, 3 (weekly edition in English, 26 May 1980, 17).

[82] JOHN PAUL II, "Sermon at the meeting with representatives of non-Catholic Christian Churches at the apostolic Nunciature in Tokyo," 24 February 1981, *OR* 25 February 1981, 2 (weekly edition in English, 9 March 1981, 8).

[83] JOHN PAUL II, "Sermon for the concelebration for Christian unity, at the international airport of Belize," 9 March 1983, *OR* 11 March 1983, 4 (weekly edition in English, 3 May 1983, 10).

Praying together becomes a genuine exercise of ecumenism: it turns ecumenism from theory to practice, from an ideal into a reality. Ecumenical prayer is ecumenism in practice. One may think not just of the meeting together to pray, in itself a great thing, open to the breath of the Spirit of God, but also of all the work that goes into preparing the EC, which entails meetings, study, exchange, appraisal, etc. This is emphasized by the decree *UR* itself:

> Today, in many parts of the world, under the influence of the grace of the Holy Spirit, many efforts are being made in prayer, word and action to attain that fullness of unity which Jesus Christ desires. The sacred Council exhorts, therefore, all Catholic faithful to recognize the signs of the times, and to take an active and intelligent part in the work of ecumenism.[84]

When the third European Ecumenical Meeting, promoted by the Conference of European Churches (KEK) and by the Council of the European Episcopal Conferences (CEEC) was held at Riva del Garda (Trent) in 1984, on the theme "Confessing together our faith, source of hope," one of the characteristics that most impressed the participants was the experience of praying together with the various local Catholic parish communities that welcomed them during the meeting.[85] This is also the experience of the many believers of the various CC and particularly of the Catholics who have participated in the EC that have been held in Rome or in various parts of the world during the Pope's apostolic journeys.

The opportunity provided by the EC also consists in the fact that the need to prepare them together offers a chance to meet and get to know one another better, and make progress along the road of ecumenism. But even in the strictly liturgical field, unexpected roads of mutual understanding and enrichment are opened up to better understand the liturgy of the church in its variety of rites and expressions, to celebrate it in a more authentic way, and to experience it more fully. "The Second Vatican Council made it clear that elements present among other Christians can contribute to the edification of Catholics."[86]

---

[84] *UR*, no. 4 (= *EV* 1, no. 508).

[85] Texts and reports in *Rivista Diocesana Tridentina* 90 (1984) 622–635, 702–703. The quotation on page 635, from an article written by Cardinal Roger Etchegaray, is interesting: "Rarely has an ecumenical assembly of church leaders been supported in so brotherly a manner by the people of God."

[86] *UUS*, no. 48 (= *EV* 14, no. 2756), introducing the quotation of *UR*, no. 4, cited above.

The symbolic value of ecumenical celebrations

As regards the value of EC, we may cite what is stated in a part of a document on the conversion of the churches, published by the Groupe des Dombes (3 September 1990). The long quotation in question eloquently expresses what seems to emerge from our analysis of the EC as a sign of a new journey of the church on the road of ecumenism:

> Ecumenical conversion is underway in the church, by three converging routes: symbolic gestures, documents on doctrinal dialogue and finally acts or decisions that commit the Churches.
>
> The scope of symbolic gestures is wide because of the representative value of those who make them. and because they express visibly and emotively the evolving conversion. Who could remain unmoved by the pilgrimage of Pope Paul VI and the Patriarch Athenagoras in the land of Jesus in January 1964, which culminated in their fraternal embrace of reconciliation? Does that event not take us back to the brotherly extension of "the right hand of fellowship" between Paul and Peter, "as a sign of communion" in that same Jerusalem? (Gal 2:9)? In 1975, Pope Paul VI made the unheard-of and astonishing gesture of kneeling before Metropolitan Meliton, the envoy of Patriarch Dimitrios, to kiss his feet. Considering that the Vatican protocol—not so long ago—required those favored with an audience to kiss the feet of the pope (which almost caused the meeting between the Orthodox Patriarch Joseph II and Pope Eugene IV to fall through on the eve of the Council of Florence), how can we fail to rejoice that so ambiguous a gesture of homage to authority should be reversed and suddenly find its evangelical significance, that of Jesus washing the feet of his disciples and inviting them to wash each other's feet?
>
> Among symbolic gestures we may also recall the confession of Paul VI at the beginning of his pontificate, addressed to all the "separated" Christians: "If we are in any way to blame for that separation, we humbly beg God's forgiveness and ask pardon too of our brothers who feel themselves to have been injured by us. For our part, we willingly forgive the injuries which the Catholic Church has suffered, and forget the grief endured during the long series of dissensions and separations. May the heavenly Father deign to hear our prayer and grant us true brotherly peace!"[87]
>
> The major meetings between church leaders are also symbolic gestures of conversion and reconciliation. The decision of Michael Ramsey, Archbishop of Canterbury, to go to the Vatican to meet Paul VI (1966)

---

[87] These words all the more relevant as they relate to what is affirmed by John Paul II in *TMA*, nos. 33–35 (= *EV* 14, nos. 1770–1776).

is one of these. On that occasion the Pope presented him with his pastoral ring. Likewise the visit of Pope Paul VI to the World Council of Churches in Geneva (1969), followed by the WCC's invitation to John Paul II WCC (1983) and the latter's visit to the Lutheran Church in Rome (1983) on the occasion of the 500th anniversary of the birth of Luther. And how many more! In a category of its own, which is not part of the ecumenical process in the strict sense, the Assisi encounter (1986), in which the representatives of the great religions of humanity met together to pray for peace in the world, was also a common gesture of conversion. For Christians also have to experience together a conversion to charity and respect towards their brothers and sisters who are believers of other faiths.[88]

Symbolic gestures do not take place only at the top. And even these were made possible thanks to the numerous gestures of conversion which Christians who are still separated had made at the grassroots. Usually these latter gestures have value only for those who experience them. Thus it is impossible to list them here, whether they were made by individuals, local congregations or regional leaders. . . . These symbolic gestures which are the product of a conversion become in turn generators of the spirit of conversion. They encourage and embolden Christians of every confession to be involved in a similar process. As such these gestures are indispensable for the dynamics of unity.[89]

Again, in the context of the opportunities offered by such celebrations, it is worth quoting a paragraph of *DAPNE*, which declares as follows:

In some situations, the official prayer of a Church may be preferred to ecumenical services specially prepared for the occasion. Participation in such celebrations such as Morning and Evening Prayer, special vigils, etc., will enable persons of different liturgical traditions—Catholic, Eastern, Anglican, and Protestant—to understand each other's community prayer better and to share more deeply in traditions which often have developed from common roots.[90]

---

[88] Elsewhere in the document it is noted that the meeting of Assisi in 1986 may be considered a real ecumenical meeting for the Christians present, who met together twice to pray together: the first in the Cathedral of San Rufino, for an EC in the proper sense with the Holy Father (EC 19), the second in the Christian prayer in the presence of the representatives of the other religions in the esplanade in front of the Basilica of San Francesco (EC 18). The same was the case in 2002 (EC 73).

[89] GROUPE DES DOMBES, *For the Conversion of the Churches* (Original title: *Pour la conversion des Églises*, 1991), translated from the French by James Greig (Geneva: WCC Publications 1993), nos. 135–139, 141, pp. 58–60.

[90] *DAPNE*, no. 117 (= EV 13, no. 2396).

In this perspective our research has shown the attention paid to the specific communities and situations of the EC in question. The majority of the EC examined can be identified as "Liturgies of the Word" or "Celebrations of the Word," their style and characteristics particularly adapted to Protestants, Anglicans, and Catholics. But there are other celebrations typical of each CC. Thus EC 2, 8, 39, 63 and 74 are clearly of Eastern character. Others are based on the Roman rite: EC 11, 25, 37, 42, 55, 63, 74 (Vespers); 45 (Sext); 26, 53, 56, 62, 72, 75 (Mass); 51, 52, 67 and 60 (*Via Crucis*). Other EC are tailored to the ecclesial communities of the Reformation, both Evangelical-Lutheran (EC 5, 9, 12, 27, 31, 34, 36, 40, 41, 49, 50) and Anglican (EC 3, 4, 28, 33).

In this regard, four annotations and a brief conclusion of Prof. P. Jesús Castellano Cervera, O.C.D., pertinent to the analysis we are conducting may be quoted. He writes, commenting on two EC of 1991 (among those examined for the present research), namely, EC 42 and 44:

> 1. La liturgia romana, con sus estructuras celebrativas, tiene una gran capacidad de integrar armónicamente muchos elementos y de darles el sentido de la unidad y del equilibrio. Lo demuestran estas dos celebraciónes.
>
> 2. La liturgia tiene la capacidad de acoger los sentimientos de un momento vivido por la Iglesia, de evangelizarlos a la luz de la palabra, de darles cauces expresivos a través de la oración y de los símbolos.
>
> 3. La liturgia tiene una fuerza particular para impulsar el ecumenismo y juntar a los hermanos en torno al Padre, con una misma palabra que invita a la conversión y una plegaria ardiente que expresa a la vez nuestra impotencia y nuestros deseos.
>
> 4. Una efectiva y sana creatividad, sobre todo en el ámbito de la Liturgia de la palabra y de la oración, no sólo es posible sino con frecuencia necesaria. Es suficiente dejar che la liturgia misma inspire y oriente, y que una atención a los valores del patrimonio eclesial, en este caso a nivel ecuménico, puedan encontrar su colocación armónica.
>
> En nuestro caso, lo podemos decir sin triunfalismo, estas dos celebraciónes papales han sido ejemplares en el doble sentido de la palabra. Celebraciónes que presentan un esmerado equilibrio, celebraciónes que se pueden imitar.[91]

These words may be extended to the great majority of the celebrations considered here, and suggest the exemplary and symbolic value of the EC of this pontificate.

[91] J. CASTELLANO, "Liturgia y ecumenismo ne la hora de la neuva evangelización. Dos celebraciónes ecuménicas pontificias ejemplares," *Phase* 32 (1992) 161.

Ecumenical celebrations as ways of promoting mutual understanding and acceptance

If the first historic meeting in Assisi and other meetings in the various parts of the world between Catholics and representatives of the various religions generated some difficulty and some apprehension, not to say misgivings or downright opposition, the ecumenical meetings between the various confessions led by and participated in by the Holy Father John Paul II have usually aroused less apprehension among the faithful. At times the misgivings of the past were caused by superficial misunderstandings on the part of some faithful (or some non-practicing Catholics). But some degree of consciousness on the matter has now been achieved at the level of priests and faithful long active also in the ecumenical ministry, which has led Catholic parishes and dioceses to engage with the representatives and brothers of other CC. Ecumenical prayer meetings, both those at the "pontifical" level and those at the more modest diocesan and parish level, have been a real school in this field.

In certain cases the sensibility of the faithful at the grassroots level and of the local Christian communities is stronger and more advanced than that of the hierarchy of the various Churches and ecclesial communities. What has happened as a result of some festivities and celebrations associated with popular devotion, of the "hearing" and praying of the people of God, which have then become an integral part of the liturgy and of the church, has also perhaps happened in our context too.[92]

Nor should we forget the enrichment many Catholic communities have derived from the discovery and adoption of elements of the Eastern Liturgies,[93] from the content of many hymns and chorales of the Reformation, and from a greater consciousness of the attention to

---

[92] An instance is the cry of the faithful who invoked unity in Romania in 1999.

[93] I refer not just to the extensive and complex use of icons but also to the texts and feasts of the rites of the Eastern churches. Truly stimulating for the ecumenical enterprise was John Paul II's exhortation: "The Church must breathe with her two lungs!" (those of East and West), in *UUS*, no. 54 (= *EV* 14, no. 2774). The point is also made by A. CAZZAGO, "'Respirare con due polmoni.' Sull'origine di una imagine fortunata," in *Communio*, 157–162 (1998), January-February, 58–68, where he also cites an address of John Paul II to the Roman Curia on 28 June 1980: "We need to learn to breathe once again with two lungs, that of the West and that of the East," *OR* 29 June 1980, 2. A similar affirmation, and the same metaphor of the two lungs, is found in JOHN PAUL II's encyclical *Redemptoris Mater*, no. 34 (= EV 10, nos. 1272–1421).

be given to the proclamation of the Word of God according to the style of the Evangelical communities.

The apostolic journeys of Pope John Paul II, with their moments of meeting and especially of prayer with the brothers of other CC, have, in a particular way, contributed greatly to this growing consciousness and this enrichment, both in the individual local churches visited and at a more universal level; they have added to the resonance of the papal magisterium throughout the whole church. In many cases the Holy Father's meeting with the representatives of the other CC has given an impetus to the ecumenical process already begun in some particular churches and given heart to those who have not yet embarked on this road with courage. The words spoken by the Pope at Accra (Ghana) in May 1980 can be taken as a hope in this context:

> All of us realize the great value that prayer has in accomplishing what is humanly difficult or even impossible. . . . Hence, this meeting inspires us to pray together, to raise our hearts in unison to "the Father of mercies and God of all comfort." (2 Cor 1:3)[94]

Lastly, mention should be made of all those small but basic experiences of ecumenical prayer that have characterized countless marriages and families with members belonging to different CC. This ecumenism, peculiar to the people of God, has given rise to many experiences that have permitted the believers of different Christian confessions to learn how to pray together at various levels, culminating in the pontifical celebrations that are the focus of this study. It cannot therefore be forgotten that numerous "ecumenical" documents, especially at the level of local dialogue, have been dedicated to the ecumenical prayer of families.[95]

---

[94] JOHN PAUL II, "Sermon at the meeting with heads of other Christian denominations in Independence Square in Accra," 8 May 1980, OR 10 May 1980, 2 (weekly edition in English, 2 June 1980, 7).

[95] The following texts are of particular interest in this context: JOINT CATHOLIC-PROTESTANT COMMITTEE OF FRANCE, "The ecumenical celebration of the baptism of children. A Note," in EŒ 2, nos. 538, 557; JOINT CATHOLIC-EVANGELICAL ECUMENICAL COMMISSION IN GERMANY, "Joint recommendations of the churches for the pastoral care of marriages and families of different confessions," December 1981, ibid., nos. 1241–1300, GERMAN EPISCOPAL CONFERENCE—COUNCIL OF THE EVANGELICAL CHURCH IN GERMANY, "Joint Document On Mixed Marriages," Bonn/Hannover, 1 January 1985, ibid., nos. 1467–1481.

III. PROSPECTS FOR ECUMENICAL CELEBRATIONS

Positive and negative aspects

The collection of the EC of the pontificate of John Paul II, which the present research has made possible, has a validity in itself. It throws light on the past history of ecumenism. But it may also contribute to its future.

The texts of the EC examined here do not always give proof of spiritual liveliness; indeed, at times they seem rather prosaic and superficial. In some EC one has the impression that the exercise in itself was rather academic and very *soft*. Having personally participated in some occasions, I admit that I took away from them a certain disappointment, perhaps because my expectations had been too high.

What does seem interesting in the EC, however, is the use of elements and texts of the various traditions, even if in too limited a way: some hymn or prayer from the Evangelical-Lutheran or Anglican tradition; some Eastern litany. Little is drawn from the heritage of the various CC, and the signs, or rather the evocative and prophetic signs, are fairly limited. The involvement of the "separated brethren," especially in the preparation of the liturgy but also in the service itself, is normally rather timid and uncertain.

One negative aspect, a considerable one, that the EC may give rise to is that of considering such EC an end in themselves: everything ends there. The encyclical *UUS* itself points this out when it says:

> Relations between Christians are not aimed merely at mutual knowledge, common prayer and dialogue. They presuppose and from now on call for every possible form of practical cooperation at all levels: pastoral, cultural and social, as well as that of witnessing to the Gospel message. . . . In the eyes of the world, cooperation among Christians becomes a form of common Christian witness and a means of evangelization which benefits all involved.[96]

The positive contribution made by the EC and their priority in the ecumenical process are recognized by John Paul II himself, who has repeatedly expressed in his sermons the joy of being able to pray together with other Christian brothers and "confessing with them that Jesus Christ in the son of God."[97] The experience of the EC in his apos-

---

[96] *UUS*, no. 40 (= *EV* 14, nos. 2737–2740).

[97] At Dublin in 1979. But also on other occasions the Pope has expressed his thoughts on the matter:

tolic journeys, as we have already been able to see, expresses the Holy Father's faith in the ecumenical journey sustained by prayer. He said so as he knelt in prayer with the Christians in Madagascar (1989):

> The frequent participation of the faithful in ecumenical prayer meetings is proof that concern for unity is not just something for those who are in a position of responsibility for a few organizations. All over the world, everywhere, the fruits of the ecumenical movement can be observed. Serious doctrinal differences still exist and sometimes new problems arise among Christians. However along the road we have already traveled and in the reality of prayer and today's joint collaboration, we find reasons for hope for the journey we still must make.[98]

The experience of the first postconciliar years and that of the pontificate of John Paul II lead us to reconsider the EC from various points of view, both in terms of content and in terms of the mode of their celebration. In this sense, we need to bear in mind what the *DAPNE* prescribes in this regard. In chapter 4, "Communion in Life and Spiritual Activity Among the Baptized," after having spoken of the sacrament of baptism, it dedicates some paragraphs to the question of "sharing spiritual activities and resources" and enunciates

---

–Porto Alegre, 1980: "more intensively and more faithfully seeking full union . . . also by means of prayer";
–Mainz, 1980: "let us begin with the most important dialogue, with the most important work, let us pray!":
–Manila, 1981: "the central point is personal conversion, the holiness of life and prayer for Christian unity";
–Khersatz, 1984: "let us do the most important thing: let us pray constantly. I wish to invite you just now to join with me in a common prayer from which everything ought to start out and in which we ought to find ourselves unanimous for the greater glory of God and for the salvation of the world";
–Melbourne, 1986: "it's a joy for me to be with you . . . to pray together and reflect on the gifts of God in unity and in peace";
–Buenos Aires, 1987: "to express our will for communion and our act of thanksgiving to God for the many gifts we have received from his goodness";
–Columbia, 1987: "it is important for all of us to understand how far the conversion of the heart depends on prayer, and how far prayer contributes to unity;
–Antananarivo, 1989: "praying and joining together to listen to the Holy Spirit";
–Kingston, 1993: "this in fact is a moment of grace, a gift of the infinite love of our Redeemer."
[98] JOHN PAUL II, "Sermon the participants in the ecumenical meeting in the cathedral of Antananarivo," 29 April 1989, *OR* 1 May 1989, 7 (weekly edition in English, 15 May 1989, 5).

some valuable principles, the fruit of the experience of the ecumenical journey.[99] Similarly, *UUS*, speaking of the "primacy of prayer," makes some remarks full of appropriate proposals and recommendations born from the experience of the EC.[100]

Worth noting is the considerable development of the meetings with other CC and of the EC in more recent years, despite the fact that this period is thought of by many as one of "ecumenical frost." It's enough to think of the EC and meetings during the Holy Year in Rome (EC 65, 67, 68),[101] at São Paulo in Brazil in 2001 (EC 69 and during the international journeys to Romania, Georgia, Egypt (Sinai), the Holy Land, Syria, Ukraine, Armenia, Azerbaijan and Bulgaria.[102]

Greater use of texts derived from the various Christian confessions and from the Bible

An essential condition for the greater effectiveness of the EC is a more convinced use of common prayer texts, both those taken from the Bible and those that are the common patrimony of the early years of Christianity. This suggestion is also found in a very precise and interesting proposal in the *DAPNE*, when it affirms:

> Churches and ecclesial Communities whose members live within a culturally homogeneous area should draw up together, where possible, a text of the most important Christian prayers (the Lord's Prayer, Apostles' Creed, Nicene-Constantinopolitan Creed, a Trinitarian Doxology, the Glory to God in the Highest). This would be for regular use by all the Churches, and ecclesial Communities or at least for use when they pray together on ecumenical occasions. Agreement on a version of the Psalter for liturgical use, or at least of some of the more frequently used psalms would also be desirable; a similar agreement for common Scriptural readings for liturgical use should also be explored. The use of liturgical and other prayers that come from the period of the undivided Church can help to foster an ecumenical sense. Common hymn books, or at least common collection of hymns to be included in the

---

[99] See *DAPNE*, nos. 102–142 (= EV, nos. 2373–2423), bearing in mind the just comments of Triacca, in A. M. TRIACCA, "Vita liturgica-sacramentale: contesto ecclesiale del collaudo dell'ecumenismo," *Ephemerides liturgica* 110, no. 1 (1996) 3–50.

[100] *UUS*, nos. 21–27 (= EV 14, nos. 2705–2717).

[101] JOHN PAUL II, apostolic letter *Novo Millenio Ineunte* of His Holiness Pope John Paul II to the Bishops, Clergy and Lay Faithful at the Close of the Great Jubilee of the Year 2000, no. 12.

[102] In Georgia and in Bulgaria there were no ecumenical celebrations, but the Pope visited the Orthodox patriarchal cathedrals in both countries.

hymn books of the different Churches and ecclesial Communities, as well as cooperation in developing liturgical music, are also to be recommended. When Christians pray together, with one voice, their common witness reaches to heaven as well as being heard on earth.[103]

The value of these recommendations is all the greater if we consider that in many cases the pontifical celebrations are used as a model for other celebrations at various levels— national, diocesan, and parish, both Catholic and of the other CC. In this sense the collection of John Paul II's EC may be of help, though bearing in mind the many limitations of the EC presented, due to the precarious circumstances in which many of them arose, even though presided over by the Holy Father.

The document on ecumenical formation published by the Joint Working Group between the Catholic Church and the World Council of Churches of 20 May 1993 underlined, among other things, the importance of a knowledge of "the spiritual texts, prayers and songs of other churches."[104] The encyclical *UUS* makes a similar point in relation to the value of the ritual of the Eastern churches, whose "great liturgical and spiritual tradition" was acknowledged by the Council.[105] That tradition could be turned to more profitably.

A greater effort should also be made to avoid repetitiveness, often motivated in ecclesial circles by the fear of creating further work or causing further difficulties: the principle that what has already been done is always worth repeating may, in practice, encourage passive stagnation or an eirenic attitude out of place in genuine ecumenical endeavor.

Prayer of praise and contemplation seems rather unaccountably lacking in the celebrations examined. Space is given instead, almost exclusively, to the prayer of intercession and frequently to the request for forgiveness. The form of EC followed during the pontificate of Pope Paul VI, as mentioned above, devoted ample space to *eulogia*. Why, we may wonder, was this style of EC abandoned?

---

[103] *DAPNE,* no. 187 (= EV 13, no. 2472).

[104] JOINT WORKING GROUP BETWEEN THE CATHOLIC CHURCH AND THE WORLD COUNCIL OF CHURCHES, "Ecumenical Formation. Ecumenical Reflections and Suggestions," 20 May 1993, no. 15. Cited 21 July 2003: Online: http://www.prounione.urbe.it/dia-int/jwg/doc/e_jwg_n7dd.html.

[105] *UUS,* no. 50 (= *EV* 14, no. 2762); cf. *UR,* nos. 14–15.

Nor does a further recommendation of *DAPNE* seem out of place. It recommends the commemoration of the sacrament of baptism, as was done in exemplary fashion in the EC at Canterbury in 1982:

> According to the local situation and as occasion may arise, Catholics may, in common celebration with other Christians, commemorate the baptism which unites them, by renewing the engagement to undertake a full Christian life which they have assumed in the promises of their baptism, and by pledging to cooperate with the grace of the Holy Spirit in striving to heal the divisions that exist among Christians.[106]

Nor can we fail to hope for a more abundant use of Holy Scripture in the EC. The proclamation of the Word of God must be shown to be truly central, not so much for its quantity as for its quality, also in the style and modalities of the celebration. The choice of the passages of Holy Scripture in the EC examined here seems very limited and repetitive; many other suitable and significant passages could be chosen. No use is even made of those proposed by the *OLM* for eucharistic celebrations *"ad diversa"* for Christian unity.[107] Apart from those already used in the EC described, a whole series of other suitable scriptural passages could be proposed.

Positive aspects of ecumenical celebrations that need to be fostered
Along with due criticism, it is right that explicit appreciation of the positive aspects of the EC examined be expressed. The fact that we have been able to collect seventy-five EC distributed throughout the current pontificate is in itself a positive sign for the ecumenical process. But it is also an important liturgical experience, conducted in conformity with the indications and guidelines of the postconciliar liturgical reform.

Many positive features have emerged from our analysis of the EC. From various points of view, and in particular from those of a liturgical and theological character, it should be underlined that careful attention to the truth of the gospel and to the situation of the church in history can be found in them. The abundant proclamation of the Word of God, the use of ancient prayer texts, whether common to all the churches or not, effectively reveal the centrality given to God, to God's presence, to God's work. The involvement of the representa-

---

[106] *DAPNE*, no. 96 (= *EV* 13, no. 2359).
[107] See *OLM*, in *MR*, nos. 867–871, 398–400.

tives and delegates of the various CC, the organization of the minis-
terial role, and the attention given to the assembly clearly indicate the
importance attached to recognizing ourselves in the one church of
Christ, albeit in the human experience of division. Many small gestures
and signs remain as symbols in the personal and community memory of ecumenical progress on the journey that leads to full communion in the one Lord. The use of churches and venues of the various
CC is emblematic of this journey undertaken in mutual recognition
and respect, without confusion or syncretism, and in the common
willingness to listen to each other and especially to meet together,
brothers and sisters, children of the one Father, in unanimous prayers.

A more involving preparation

What is also needed is that greater attention be paid to a common
preparation that may more greatly involve the representatives of the
other CC and ensure a stronger presence of elements of their traditions.
In this regard, the *DAPNE* expresses itself in a clear and precise way:

> Representatives of the Churches, ecclesial Communities or other
> groups concerned should cooperate and prepare together such prayer.
> They should decide among themselves the way in which each is to
> take part, choose the themes and select the Scripture readings, hymns
> and prayers.[108]

The Pope, too, insists on the need to form Christians, especially
church leaders, to prepare them for this service to ecumenism represented by the EC. He said so in Manila in 1981:

> That's why it is so urgent that at every level Christians be prepared to
> work actively and to pray for the restoration of full communion. The
> effort of theological dialogue is an integral part of this, but its very soul
> is personal conversion, holiness of life and prayer for Christian unity.
> (*cf. UR* 8)[109]

The impression one gets from the texts examined is that a real effort was not always made together to prepare really shared EC. In
many cases those responsible were satisfied with not disappointing

---

[108] *DAPNE,* no. 111 (= *EV* 13, no. 2386).

[109] JOHN PAUL II, "Sermon at the meeting with representatives of other Christian Churches at the Apostolic Nunciature in Manila," 21 February 1981, *OR* 22
February 1981 (weekly edition in English, 2 March 1981, 15).

the one side or the other, though without forging something new together, without seeking a greater involvement. It will be increasingly essential in the future for the EC to be conceived and studied in advance, with genuine commitment and participation not just in the celebration itself, but even more so in its preparation in a truly ecumenical and community spirit. To this end there is a need for people better prepared in knowledge of the liturgies of the various CC. The danger of improvisation or a purely token or superficial involvement may hinder authentic progress in the communion of prayer. The great goal of a single Eucharist, albeit in diversity of ritual, underlines the duty to pay greater attention to the preparation of the EC, and unfortunately the risks of a failure to do so.

A new approach to ecumenical celebration

Emblematic of the need for a new approach to ecumenical celebration is the by now traditional celebration of 25 January in the Basilica of St. Paul's Outside the Walls to mark the closing of the Week of Prayer for Christian Unity, with a Catholic Mass presided over by the Holy Father.[110] The celebration in question concludes the various

---

[110] The point may be documented by reporting the type of celebrations for the Week of Prayer for Christian Unity during this pontificate:

- –1979 and 1980: No celebration;
- –23 January 1981: A liturgy of the Word:
- –25 January 1982: Vespers and Holy Mass, presided over by the Pope (Basilica of St. Paul's Outside the Walls);
- –25 January 1983: Holy Mass and beatification of Trappist Sister M. Gabriella Sagheddu, presided over by the Pope (Basilica of St. Paul's Outside the Walls);
- –25 January 1984: Vespers presided over by the Holy Father in the Jubilee Year of the Redemption (Basilica of St. Paul's Outside the Walls);
- –25 January 1985/86/87/88/89: Holy Mass presided over by the Pope (basilica of St. Paul's outside the Walls):
- –25 January 1990: The Pope was in Africa; Mass was celebrated in his stead by Cardinal Johannes Willebrands (Basilica of St. Paul's Outside the Walls);
- –25 January 1991/92/93: Mass presided over by the Pope (Basilica of St. Paul's Outside the Walls);
- –25 January 1994: The Pope celebrated Mass in the Vatican Basilica for peace in the Balkans;
- –25 January 1995: The Pope had just returned from a journey to the Far East; Mass was celebrated in his stead by Cardinal Edward Idris Cassidy (Basilica of St. Paul's Outside the Walls—Protestant choir: "Mailänder Kantorei");
- –25 January 1996: Holy Mass presided over by the Pope (Basilica of St. Paul's Outside the Walls—"Viva Vox" choir from Helsinki);

events of the diocese of Rome during the week and is realized in collaboration with the PCPCU and the abbey of St. Paul's. Always present at the rite are some delegates of other CC, but they play no active part, not even—at least in recent years—at the sign of peace. Some Orthodox students sometimes collaborate, at the invitation of the PCPCU, in the proclamation of the intentions of the prayer of the faithful. So in this situation one cannot in any way speak of EC in the proper sense. It seems almost a return to the practice of praying *for* the "separated brethren" rather than *with* the brethren of other CC.

The courage is lacking for an exemplary ecumenical celebration for all the CC and in particular for the various Catholic dioceses that look to the pontifical celebrations as a model to follow. In a particular way, in our time television and the Internet immediately transmit the papal celebrations, together with the texts and signs used in them throughout the world. It is therefore of great importance to focus all our attention and care on the preparation and meticulous realization of each celebration, especially those of an ecumenical nature. Some steps forward, it must be recognized, have been made in recent years, since the Jubilee of 2000.

One of the most explicit absences in the EC—and the reason for it is understandable—is that of the Blessed Virgin Mary, the Mother of the Lord. Yet, especially with our Orthodox brethren, it would have been, and would still be, possible to begin experiences of Marian

---

–25 January 1997: Holy Mass presided over by the Pope (Basilica of St. Paul's Outside the Walls) with the Catholicos (EC 56);

–25 January 1998: The Pope was in Cuba; the Mass was celebrated in his stead by Cardinal Edward Idris Cassidy (Basilica of St. Paul's Outside the Walls);

–25 January 1999: The Pope was in America; Mass celebrated in his name by Cardinal Edward Idris Cassidy (Basilica of St. Paul's Outside the Walls);

–25 January 2000: The Pope presided over the EC of 18 January 2000; Cardinal Roger Etchegaray presided over Vespers (Basilica of St. Paul's Outside the Walls);

–25 January 2001: The Pope presided over an ecumenical celebration of the Word with the representatives of the other churches and ecclesial communities (Basilica of St. Paul's Outside the Walls);

–25 January 2002: On the day following the meeting with the Pope in Assisi; Vespers officiated by Cardinal Walter Kasper.

These celebrations were fairly well prepared from a liturgical viewpoint but not too well from an ecumenical viewpoint. In particular, an attempt is made for the Mass each year to prepare a good prayer for the faithful, whereas the hymns are rather too "Roman" (e.g., *Adoro te devote, Ave verum . . .*).

ecumenical prayer. Here too, perhaps, we need to be a little bolder in trying to unite our various spiritual patrimonies and also in demonstrating, in joint preparation, what is meant, also on the part of Catholics, by authentic Marian worship (not distorted by devotions or "visions" which often dominate public opinion but which are not the genuine Marian prayer of the church).

Steps should also be taken to reformulate the style of officiating at the EC by involving with greater courage, as has been done occasionally in the past, the Holy Father and the delegates of the other CC.

In hoping for a renewal of the EC and progress in ecumenical endeavor, we can still derive illumination from the words written over thirty years ago in Vatican II's Decree on Ecumenism, which has lost none of its relevance and is still able to inspire decisions and guidelines for the various ecumenical proposals and activities. The decree declares:

> Church renewal therefore has notable ecumenical importance. Already this renewal is taking place in various spheres of the Church's life: the biblical and liturgical movements, the preaching of the Word of God and catechetics, the apostolate of the laity, new forms of religious life and the spirituality of married life, and the Church's social teaching and activity. All these should be considered as promises and guarantees for the future progress of ecumenism.[111]

To conclude these reflections, we cite the suggestions expressed with clarity and lucidity in one of the articles of the *Dizionario di omiletica:*

> Those ecumenical celebrations that have now become almost universal, and have become customary particularly during the Week of Prayer for Christian Unity, therefore need to be reconsidered. They should not remain an isolated event, divorced from the celebrations of the liturgical year, but should find, for example, their culmination in the solemn Easter liturgy of Good Friday and in that of the Epiphany (Baptism) of the Lord, which is no less effective and charged with significance. They would therefore lead from the universal vocation to the faith, to the Lord's prayer that they may all be one (see John 19:20), redeemed by his blood.[112]

---

[111] *UR*, no. 6 (= EV 1, no. 521). See the interesting observations of Triacca in A. M. TRIACCA, *Vita liturgico-sacramentale: contesto ecclesiale*, 22.

[112] B. AMATA, *Ecumenismo*, 419.

Ecumenical celebrations and the life of communion in the ecumenical process

It does not seem out of place to recall, lastly, an appeal made by the Pope himself for the EC not to be divorced from a concrete commitment of Christian life, of witness and charity that spring from prayer. The passage is taken from a homily in Edmonton (Canada) in 1984:

> Since true *prayer overflows into generous service,* we are not unmindful this evening of the great needs of our brothers and sisters who suffer throughout the world. In faithful response to the Lord, whose Holy Spirit has inspired the ecumenical movement, not only do we want to pray together and to enter into theological dialogue, but we also engage in efforts of joint collaboration to promote a more just and peaceful world.[113]

And in the United States some years later (1987), the Pope observed with great objectivity:

> In speaking of the priority of internal renewal and prayer in the ecumenical task, I do not intend in any way to minimize other important factors such as our *common Christian service* to those in need or our *common study* carried out in theological dialogues.[114]

At the end of our analysis of the EC, the message inherent in the liturgy rings out loudly and clearly: Practice what is celebrated. The participants in the EC are asked to translate into the concrete circumstances of their daily life the truth of the Word of God they have heard, the obligations of the prayer they have recited, and the gift of the experience they have shared. But above all, there is the consciousness that the search for communion and unity is a gift of God, as the Pope himself eloquently points out:

> The contemporary Church is profoundly conscious that only on the basis of the mercy of God will she be able to carry out the tasks that derive from the teaching of the Second Vatican Council, and, in the first place, the ecumenical task which aims at uniting all those who confess Christ. As she makes many efforts in this direction, the Church confesses with humility that only that *love* which is more powerful than the

[113] JOHN PAUL II, "Sermon for the ecumenical prayer meeting at St. Joseph's Cathedral in Edmonton," 16 September 1984, *OR* 17/18 September 1984, 7 (weekly edition in English, 8 October 1984, 13).

[114] JOHN PAUL II, "Sermon for the ecumenical meeting with the other Christian communities at the University of South Carolina at Columbia," 11 September 1987, *OR* 13 September 1987, 7 (weekly edition in English, 14 September 1987, 9).

weakness of human divisions *can definitively bring about that unity* which Christ implored from the Father and which the Spirit never ceases to beseech for us "with sighs too deep for words. (Rom 8:26)[115]

A rich and valuable documentation at the service of ecumenism

It is not easy to draw this account to a close by offering some conclusions that can make any claim to completeness. The subject is too vast, the material examined too prolific, the period examined too close to the writer to be able to evaluate it. Others will be able to do so better than I, in a more authoritative and precise way, perhaps helped by this collection itself and this exposition of data and documentation. "It is now clear," wrote Cipriano Vagaggini almost forty years ago, "that the liturgy is one of the central areas in which separated Christians can draw close to each other again."[116] With this in mind, I have tried to place at the disposal of scholars, liturgists, and promoters of ecumenism a collection of the EC and sermons addressed by Pope John Paul II in his meetings with the brothers and sisters of other CC. It is the first collection of this type and one that also offers a synchronic picture of the question. I have also tried to analyze the material, with all the necessary limitations, in a study that continuously opened various new avenues of research.

The presence of Pope John Paul II at these 75 EC offers, it may be said, a historic perspective and guides the journey of the third millennium of the Christian era on the irreversible road of ecumenism, of the search for the unity of the believers in Christ.

A spirituality as the basis of ecumenical celebrations

In conclusion, the importance should be emphasized of the "ecumenical spirituality in common prayer and other forms as the underpinning of ecumenical formation [that] invites all to conversion and change of heart which is the very soul of the work for restoring unity."[117] It seems appropriate to further underline a very important concept that is well expressed by the *DAPNE,* which says, with reference to Vatican II's Decree on Ecumenism:

---

[115] JOHN PAUL II, encyclical letter *Dives in Misericordia* of the Supreme Pontiff John Paul II on the Mercy of God, 30 November 1980, no. 13, *AAS* 72, no. 9, 1980) 1221 (= *EV* 7, no. 936).

[116] C. VAGAGGINI, *Il senso teologico della liturgia,* 776.

[117] JOINT WORKING GROUP BETWEEN THE CATHOLIC CHURCH AND THE WORLD COUNCIL OF CHURCHES, *"Ecumenical formation,"* no. 15.

The Council affirms that this unity by no means requires the sacrifice of the rich diversity of spirituality, discipline, liturgical rites and elaborations of revealed truth that has grown up among Christians in the measure that this diversity remains faithful to the apostolic Tradition.[118]

John Paul II concluded his reflections in a memorable sermon at Debrecen (Hungary) as follows:

In this time of change, the willingness of Christian communities to work together in restoring Europe to its Christian foundations is of special value. However, the task before Hungary and before Europe is greater than anything that our material and cultural resources alone can attain. *Prayer is vital.* Our Savior promised that where two or three are gathered in his name, He is there among them (*cf.* Matt 18:19-20).

If not just two or three, but thousands of believers, who have been separated too long, are reunited in mutual love and common invocation, surely Christ will bless their efforts. If then we who are still divided can learn to pray together for our continual conversion and for the conversion of our non-believing brothers and sisters who do not yet know God, but are searching for the truth, our heavenly Father will not refuse to grant us his Spirit, his forgiveness and his grace (*cf.* Luke 11:9-13).

Dear brothers and sisters in Christ, *this very meeting is already a stage on the way towards the goal of unity.* The "signs of the times" tell us that the Spirit of the Lord is exhorting us to continue our course. Our immediate duty is to hear the exhortation of St. Paul: to lead a life worthy of the calling which we have received, "with all lowliness and meekness, with patience, forbearing one another in love, eager to maintain the unity of the Spirit in the bond of peace" (Eph 4:2-4). This is the hope and commitment which lie before us. This is the path of our growing together in sound faith and effective love. May God, who began a good work in us, bring it to completion! (*cf.* Phil 1:6).[119]

The analysis conducted in this study offers many perspectives both for ecumenical renewal and for a truly catholic (universal) Christian spirituality.[120] The biblical and euchological texts and the theological

---

[118] *DAPNE*, no. 20 (= *EV* 13, no. 2188), referring to *UR*, nos. 4, 15–16 (= *EV* 1, nos. 514–516, 547–552).

[119] JOHN PAUL II, "Sermon during the ecumenical celebration in the Calvinist church at Debrecen," 18 August 1991, *OR* 19–20 August 1991, 8 (weekly edition in English, 9 September 1991, 5).

[120] See S. SPINSANTI, "Ecumenismo spirituale," in *Nuovo Dizionario di spiritualità*, 460–478. See also the valuable suggestions in O. WAHL, "Una celebrazione liturgica 'ecumenica': Attualità della pericope di Abramo e Melchisedech (Gen 14,

themes of the sermons suggest avenues of reflection and provide the foundation for a new ecumenical proposal of spirituality that is open to and enriched by the values and riches of the different traditions of the various CC. There is a need for those endowed with solid theological formation, and able to fuse the various sensibilities with the truth of the gospel and of the Tradition, to offer a genuine soul to ecumenism and especially to the preparation and realization of the EC.

Outwardly, it does not seem, from the findings of this research, that any great steps forward in the ecumenical process have been made in recent years. The EC have clearly multiplied. Mutual understanding, mutual esteem, and a willingness to collaborate have undoubtedly grown. But there does not seem to have been a growth, a maturation, a development of the *lex orandi* in its relation to the *lex credendi*.

At least as regards the EC, it may undoubtedly be affirmed that they have now become a normal and consolidated event, not only of the ecumenical movement but also of the life of the Christian community. They are performed in the recognition that the liturgy is above all adoration of the one God, who is the source of unity. The liturgy is glorification of God, as "common prayer of brothers." It is liturgy "made" for God and not for ourselves, because only in him is found and transmitted to us "the unity in Christ and in the church." And as the late Don Achille Maria Triacca, S.D.B., who guided this research, wrote: "It is in the liturgy that we are led to discover, in its essential lines, all the power of transformation of the Holy Spirit. Just as the liturgical assembly of the faithful needs celebrations to join together ever more closely in unity with Christ, so the study and practice of the liturgy in its various manifestations is the best means of forging unity among the various Christians.[121]

18-20)," in G. COFFELE, ed., *Dilexit Ecclesiam: Studi in onore del Prof. Donato Valentini* (Rome: LAS, 1999) 409–421.

[121] A. M. TRIACCA, *Le "Conferenze San Sergio." Settimane ecumeniche di studi liturgici. Origini, finalità, tematiche, valutazioni, indici,* Bibliotheca *Ephemerides Liturgicae*—Subsidia 76 (Roma: CLV–Edizioni Liturgiche, 1994) 48.

NO.	DATE	PLACE	CELEBRATION
	1978:		No ecumenical celebration
	1979:		
01.	07 October	WASHINGTON	Ecumenical service of prayer
02.	29 November	ISTANBUL	Cérémonie religieuse en la Cathédrale Patriarcale
	1980:		No ecumenical celebration
	1981:		No ecumenical celebration
	1982:		
03.	29 May	CANTERBURY	Celebration of faith
04.	30 May	LIVERPOOL	United Service
	1983:		
05.	11 December	ROME	Evangelisch-lutherischer Wort gottesdienst
	1984:		
06.	26 February	BARI	Prayer for Christian Unity
07.	12 June	GENEVA	Service of Worship in the Ecumenical Center
08.	12 June	GENEVA	Cérémonie religieuse en l'église
09.	14 June	BERN-KEHRSATZ	Gottesdienst
10.	14 September	TORONTO	Ecumenical Service
11.	16 September	EDMONTON	Evening Prayer
	1985:		
12.	13 May	UTRECHT	Œcumenische Gebedsdienst
13.	18 May	MECHELEN	*Officium Œcumenicum*
14.	05 December	VATICAN CITY	Prayer
	1986:		
15.	21 March	VATICAN CITY	Gebedsdienst
16.	04 October	LYON	Célébration œcuménique de prière
17.	05 October	TAIZÉ	Prière
18.	27 October	ASSISI	I. In prayer for peace, with representatives of churches and ecclesial communities and of world religions at the invitation of Pope John Paul II

NO.	DATE	PLACE	CELEBRATION
19.			II. In prayer for peace: the Christian prayer for peace

NO.	DATE	PLACE	CELEBRATION
20.	24 November	CHRISTCHURCH	Ecumenical Service
21.	27 November	MELBOURNE	Ecumenical Service

1987:

22.	04 May	AUGSBURG	Ökumenischer Gottesdienst
23.	11 September	COLUMBIA	Service of Christian Witness
24.	19 September	DETROIT	Meeting with Ecumenical Representatives
25.	05 December	ROME	Vespers with Ecumenical Patriarch Dimitrios I
26.	06 December	VATICAN CITY	Mass with the Patriarch

1988:

27.	26 June	SALZBURG	Ökumenischer Gottesdienst
28.	12 September	BULAWAYO	Ecumenical Meeting of Prayer
29.	15 September	MASERU	Celebration of the Word
30.	18 September	MAPUTO	Celebration of the Word
31.	09 October	STRASBOURG	Prière commune

1989:

32.	29 April	ANTANANARIVO	Rencontre œcuménique de prière
33.	04 May	LUSAKA	Celebration of the Word
34.	02 June	TRONDHEIM	Ecumenical Service
35.	03 June	THINGVELLIR	Ecumenical Service
36.	09 June	UPPSALA	Ecumenical Service
37.	30 September	ROME	First Vespers with the Anglican Primate

1990:

38.	27 May	MDINA	Ecumenical Meeting

1991:

39.	05 June	BIAŁYSTOK	Nabozenstwo-Molebien
40.	09 June	WARSAW	Modlitewne spotkanie ekumeniczne
41.	18 August	DEBRECEN	*Celebratio Verbi Dei*
42.	05 October	VATICAN CITY	Celebrazione ecumenica
43.	18 October	FLORIANOPOLIS	Encontro ecumenico
44.	07 December	VATICAN CITY	Celebrazione ecumenica

NO.	DATE	PLACE	CELEBRATION
	1992:		
45.	23 April	VATICAN CITY	Ora Sesta
46.	07 June	LUANDA	Encontro ecumenico
	1993:		
47.	09 January	ASSISI	Prayer Vigil for peace in Europe
48.	10 August	KINGSTON	Ecumenical Prayer
49.	08 September	RIGA	*Liturgia œcumenica Verbi*
50.	10 September	TALLIN	*Liturgia œcumenica Verbi*
	1994:		
51.	01 April	ROME	Good Friday *Via Crucis*
	1995:		
52.	14 April	ROME	Good Friday *Via Crucis*
53.	29 June	VATICAN CITY	Mass with the Patriarch
	1996:		
54.	22 June	PADERBORN	Ökumenischer Gottesdienst
55.	05 December	ROME	Vespers with the Anglican Primate
	1997:		
56.	25 January	ROME	Mass with the Catholicos of Cilicia
57.	28 March	ROME	Good Friday *Via Crucis*
58.	27 April	PRAGUE	*Liturgia œcumenica Verbi*
59.	31 May	WROCŁAW	*Liturgia œcumenica Verbi*
	1998:		
60.	10 April	ROME	Good Friday *Via Crucis*
	1999:		
61.	09 May	BUCHAREST	Divine Liturgy presided over by the Romanian Patriarch
62.	09 May	BUCHAREST	Eucharistic Celebration presided over by the Holy Father
63.	13 November	VATICAN CITY	Ecumenical Celebration—Vespers
64.	10 June	DROHICZYN	*Celebratio œcumenica Verbi Dei*
	2000:		
65.	18 January	ROME	Opening Holy Door Basilica of St. Paul
66.	25 January	CAIRO	Ecumenical Meeting

NO.	DATE	PLACE	CELEBRATION
67.	07 May	ROME	Ecumenical Commemoration witnesses of the faith in the 20th century
68.	10 November	VATICAN CITY	Ecumenical celebration (Karekin II)
	2001:		
69.	25 January	ROME	Ecumenical Celebration of the Word
70.	05 May	DAMASCUS	Ecumenical Meeting
71.	06 May	DAMASCUS	Meeting with Clergy and Religious
72.	25-27 September	ARMENIA	(Six "celebrations" with the Catholicos: reduced to one so as not to exaggerate the number)
	2002:		
73.	24 January	ASSISI	Together for Peace— In prayer for Peace
74.	04 October	VATICAN CITY	Ecumenical Celebration of Vespers
75.	13 October	VATICAN CITY	Mass with Romanian Patriarch Theoctist

Robert F. Taft, S.J.

Mass Without the Consecration? The Historic Agreement on the Eucharist Between the Catholic Church and the Assyrian Church of the East Promulgated 26 October 2001[1]

[1] Annual 2002 Paul Wattson–Lurana White Lecture at the Centro pro Unione, Rome, originally scheduled for 12 December 2002, but postponed until 20 March 2003 because of illness. I am indebted to Prof. Dr. Gabriele Winkler of Tübingen for reading a draft of this paper and suggesting numerous suggestions and corrections.

Abbreviations used in the notes:

BELS 19: B. D. SPINKS, ed., *The Sacrifice of Praise: Studies on the Themes of Thanksgiving and Redemption in the Central Prayers of the Eucharistic and Baptismal Liturgies.* Bibliotheca *Ephemerides Liturgicae,* Subsidia 19 (Rome: CLV–Edizioni Liturgiche, 1981).

CPG: M. GEERARD, F. GLORIE, eds., *Clavis Patrum Graecorum,* 5 vols., and M. GEERARD, J. NORET, eds., *Supplementum,* Corpus Christianorum (Turnhout: Brepols, 1974–1998).

CPL: Clavis Patrum Latinorum, E. DEKKERS, E. GAAR, eds., Corpus Christianorum, Series Latina (Steenbrugge: Abbatia Santi Petri, 1995).

CSEL: Corpus Scriptorum Ecclesiasticorum Latinorum

DOL: INTERNATIONAL COMMISSION ON ENGLISH IN THE LITURGY, *Documents on the Liturgy 1963–1979: Conciliar, Papal and Curial Texts* (Collegeville: Liturgical Press, 1982).

Dz: H. DENZINGER, A. SCHÖNMETZER, *Enchiridion symbolorum definitionum et declarationum de rebus fidei et morum,* 33rd ed. (Freiburg/B.: Herder, 1965).

EDIL 1: R. KACZYNSKI, ed., *Enchiridion documentorum instaurationis liturgicae,* vol. 1; 1963–1973 (Turin/Rome: Marietti/CLV–Edizioni Liturgiche, 1976).

JTS: The Journal of Theological Studies

OCA: Orientalia Christiana Analecta

OCP: Orientalia Christiana Periodica

OKS: Ostkirchliche Studien

PE: A. HÄNGGI, I. PAHL, *Prex eucharistica,* vol. I: *Textus e variis liturgiis antiquioribus selecti,* 3rd ed. by A. GERHARDS and H. BRAKMANN, eds., Spicilegium Friburgense 12 (Freiburg, Switzerland: Éditions Universitaires, 1998).

SC: Sources chrétiennes

SL: Studia liturgica

My deliberately provocative title, "Mass Without the Consecration?" I owe to a high-ranking Catholic prelate who, upon hearing of the epoch-making decree of the Holy See recognizing the validity of the eucharistic sacrifice celebrated according to the original redaction of the Anaphora of Addai and Mari—that is, without the Words of Institution—exclaimed in perplexity, "But how can there be Mass without the consecration?" The answer, of course, is that there cannot be. But that does not solve the problem; it just shifts the question to "What, then, is the consecration, if not the traditional Institution Narrative, which all three Synoptic Gospels[2] and 1 Corinthians 11:23-26 attribute to Jesus?"

The 26 October 2001 Agreement

One of the basic tasks of the Catholic theologian is to provide the theological underpinnings to explain and justify authentic decisions of the Supreme Magisterium. That is my aim here. For the historic agreement on the Eucharist between the Catholic Church and the Assyrian Church of the East is surely one such authentic decision, approved by the Pontifical Council for Promoting Christian Unity, the Congregation for the Oriental Churches, the Congregation for the Doctrine of the Faith, and Pope John Paul II himself. This decision tells Catholics who fulfill the stated conditions and receive Holy Communion at an Assyrian Eucharist using the Anaphora of Addai and Mari that they are receiving the one true Body and Blood of Christ, as at a Catholic Eucharist.

Let us look at what this audacious agreement says, how it came about, and what made its approval possible. The text, entitled "Guidelines for Admission to the Eucharist Between the Chaldean Church and the Assyrian Church of the East," was promulgated on 26 October 2001 but bears the date of its approval 20 July 2001. I consider this the most remarkable Catholic magisterial document since Vatican II. The purpose of this mutual agreement is pastoral: to ensure that the faithful of two Sister Churches that spring from the same ancient apostolic tradition not be deprived of the Bread of Life through the unavailability of a minister of their own Church. But

---

[2] Matt 26:26-29; Mark 14:22-25; Luke 22:19-21. The Johannine tradition paraphrases it in John 6:51.

200

pastoral in the context of two Sister Churches means also common, that is, mutual: what kind of an agreement can be called an agreement if it is one-sided?

The Problem

The Catholic side, however, was faced with a problem that could only be resolved by the Supreme Magisterium: in the light of Catholic teaching on the importance of the words of Institution in the eucharistic consecration, how can the Catholic Church authorize its faithful to receive Holy Communion at a liturgy lacking these central words? The problem, of course, comes not just from the fact that Addai and Mari does not have these words. If Addai and Mari had been written yesterday, Rome would have said, "Let's use a traditional text containing the Words of Jesus." But that is the precise point: *Addai and Mari is traditional.* Scholars are unanimous that it is one of the most ancient anaphoras extant, a prayer believed to have been in continuous use in the age-old East-Syrian Christendom of Mesopotamia from time immemorial. As such, it merited the respect Rome has always had for Tradition with a capital "T."

With that context in mind, the Pontifical Council for Promoting Christian Unity subjected the question to the study of experts. A preparatory document dated 23 May 1998, entitled "Pastoral Disposition for Eucharistic Hospitality Between the Assyrian Church and the Catholic Church," was prepared, proposing that the Catholic Church recognize the validity of the Anaphora of Addai and Mari and giving the reasons why. This extraordinarily well-formulated document was then circulated among Catholic scholars deemed expert in the field. It was sent to twenty-six, I was told, an unusually large number. This was only prudent, considering the enormous significance and audacity of what was being proposed: a decision that would, in effect, overturn the centuries-old clichés of Catholic manual theology concerning the eucharistic consecration. I received my copy of the working paper from the Congregation for the Oriental Churches, of which I am a consultor for liturgy, accompanied by a letter of 28 May 1998, signed by the then Prefect, His Eminence Achille Cardinal Silvestrini and Subsecretary Msgr. Claudio Gugerotti.

The document discussed the pastoral and ecumenical context, as well as what it calls the *dogmatic question* concerning the validity of Addai and Mari, a question, the document reveals, that in three letters from 1994 to 1997, the Vatican Congregation for the Doctrine of the Faith had repeatedly insisted needed further investigation. This dogmatic question is the focus of my interest here.

The document takes a forthright and courageous stand in favor of recognizing the validity of Addai and Mari, arguing, *inter alia,* from the apostolicity of the East-Syrian tradition and from Addai and Mari itself, placing its lack of an Institution Narrative in the context of the history of the Eucharistic Prayer, as well as in relation to the Assyrian eucharistic tradition concerning the Institution Narrative as reflected in the other two East-Syrian anaphoras that do have the Institution.

The argumentation, fully *au courant* theologically and liturgically, can be summed up as follows:

1. The Catholic Magisterium teaches that the traditional practices of our Eastern Sister Churches are worthy of all veneration and respect.
2. Scholars are unanimous that Addai and Mari is one of the most ancient extant anaphoras still in use.
3. The consensus of the latest scholarship is that Addai and Mari in its original form never had the Institution Narrative. Contrary to earlier opinion, this is not a *hapax:* there are several other early Eucharistic Prayers that have no Words of Institution.[3]
4. Though Addai and Mari may lack the institution *ad litteram,* it contains it virtually, in explicit, if oblique, references to the eucharistic Institution, to the Last Supper, to the Body and Blood and sacrifice of Christ, and to the oblation of the Church, thereby clearly demonstrating the intention of repeating what Jesus did, in obedience to his command: "Do this in memory of me."
5. This clear intention to express the links joining the Last Supper, the eucharistic Institution, the sacrifice of the Cross, and the oblation of the Church is confirmed by the other Assyrian anaphoras, by all the East-Syrian liturgical commentators, as well as by the peculiar Assyrian tradition of the *malka,* or Holy Leaven, added to the eucharistic loaves as a sign of historical continuity with the Last Supper.

The final document sums up the doctrinal decision as follows:

In the first place, the Anaphora of Addai and Mari is one of the most ancient anaphoras, dating back to the time of the very early

[3] See below at notes 10–20.

Church; it was composed and used with the clear intention of celebrating the Eucharist in full continuity with the Last Supper and according to the intention of the Church; its validity was never officially contested, neither in the Christian East nor in the Christian West.

Secondly, the Catholic Church recognizes the Assyrian Church of the East as a true particular Church, built upon orthodox faith and apostolic succession. The Assyrian Church of the East has also preserved full eucharistic faith in the presence of our Lord under the species of bread and wine and in the sacrificial character of the Eucharist. In the Assyrian Church of the East, though not in full communion with the Catholic Church, are thus to be found *"true sacraments, and above all, by apostolic succession, the priesthood and the Eucharist"* (Vatican II, Decree on Ecumenism, *Unitatis Redintegratio*, no. 15).

Finally, the words of Eucharistic Institution are indeed present in the Anaphora of Addai and Mari, not in a coherent narrative way and *ad litteram,* but rather in a dispersed euchological way, that is, integrated in successive prayers of thanksgiving, praise, and intercession.

These three paragraphs reflect the progress in Catholic liturgical scholarship and ecumenical thinking that provided the historical and theological basis for such an agreement.

Ecumenical Scholarship

Let us begin with ecumenical scholarship.[4] All scholarship worthy of the name is historico-critical, objective, fair, and representatively comprehensive. But *ecumenical* scholarship is not content with these purely natural virtues of honesty and fairness that one should be able to expect from any true scholar. Ecumenical scholarship takes things a long step further. I consider ecumenical scholarship a new and

---

[4] Here and elsewhere below in this paper I resume some ideas expressed earlier in R. F. TAFT, "Ecumenical Scholarship and the Catholic-Orthodox Epiclesis Dispute," *OKS* 45 (1996) 201–226, here 202–204; *id.,* "Understanding the Byzantine Anaphoral Oblation," in N. MITCHELL, J. BALDOVIN, eds., *Rule of Prayer, Rule of Faith: Essays in Honor of Aidan Kavanagh, O.S.B.,* A Pueblo Book (Collegeville: The Liturgical Press, 1996) 32–55; *id.,* "The Epiclesis Question in the Light of the Orthodox and Catholic Lex orandi Traditions," in B. NASSIF, ed., *New Perspectives on Historical Theology: Essays in Memory of John Meyendorff* (Grand Rapids/Cambridge: William B. Eerdmans, 1996) 210–237. For an essay on the "ecumenical method" *ante factum* as well as *ante vocabulum,* see C. LIALINE, "De la méthode irénique," *Irénikon* 15 (1938) 1–28, 131–153, 236–255, 450–459.

specifically Christian way of studying Christian tradition in order to reconcile and unite, rather than to confute and dominate. Its deliberate intention is to emphasize the common tradition underlying differences, which, though real, may be the accidental product of history, culture, language, rather than essential differences in the doctrine of the apostolic faith. Of course, to remain scholarly, this effort must be carried out realistically, without in any way glossing over real differences. But even in recognizing differences, ecumenical scholarship seeks to describe the beliefs, traditions, and usages of other confessions in ways their own objective spokespersons would recognize as reliable and fair.

So ecumenical scholarship seeks not confrontation but agreement and understanding. It strives to enter into the other's point of view, to understand it insofar as possible with sympathy and agreement. It is a contest in reverse, a contest of love, one in which the parties seek to understand and justify, not their own point of view, but that of their interlocutor. Such an effort and method, far from being baseless romanticism, is rooted in generally accepted evangelical and Catholic theological principles:

1. The theological foundation for this method is our faith that the Holy Spirit is with God's Church, protecting the integrity of its witness, above all in the centuries of its undivided unity. Since some of the issues that divide us go right back to those centuries, one must ineluctably conclude that these differences do not affect the substance of the apostolic faith. For if they did, then, contrary to Jesus' promise (Matt 16:18), the "gates of hell" would indeed have prevailed against the Church.
2. Secondly, the Catholic Church recognizes the Eastern Churches to be the historic apostolic Christianity of the East, and Sister Churches of the Catholic Church. Consequently, no view of Christian tradition can be considered anything but partial that does not take full account of the age-old, traditional teaching of these Sister Churches. Any theology must be measured not only against the common tradition of the undivided Church, but also against the ongoing witness of the Spirit-guided apostolic Christendom of the East. That does not mean that East or West has never been wrong. It does mean that neither can be ignored.
3. An authentic magisterium cannot contradict itself. Therefore, without denying the legitimate development of doctrine, in the

case of apparently conflicting traditions of East and West, preferential consideration must be given to the witness of the undivided Church. This is especially true with respect to later polemics resulting from unilateral departures from or developments out of the common tradition during the period of divided Christendom.

4. Those who have unilaterally modified a commonly accepted tradition of the undivided Church bear the principal responsibility for any divisions caused thereby. So it is incumbent first of all on them to seek an acceptable solution to that problem. This is especially true when those developments, albeit legitimate, may be perceived by others as a narrowing of the tradition or have been forged in the crucible of polemics, never a reliable pedagogue.

5. Within a single Church, any legitimate view of its own particular tradition must encompass the complete spectrum of its witnesses throughout the whole continuum of its history, and not just its most recent or currently popular expression.

6. Finally, doctrinal formulations produced in the heat of polemics must be construed narrowly, within the strict compass of the errors they were meant to confute. In 1551, when Session 13, chapter 3–4 and canon 4 of the Council of Trent (1545–1563) defined that "immediately after the consecration *(statim post consecrationem),*" and "by the consecration *(per consecrationem),*" and "once the consecration is accomplished *(peracta consecratione),*" the bread and wine become the Body and Blood of Christ (Dz §§1640, 1642, 1654), it was combating those who denied that transformation, not making a statement about its "moment" or "formula."[5]

If we bear all these principles in mind, it should be immediately obvious that the Catholic Church could not but seek a positive solution to the perceived problem of the validity of Addai and Mari. From a historical and ecumenical point of view, on what legitimate theological and ecclesiological basis could Rome argue that an Apostolic Church whose Urancient principal anaphora had been in continuous use since time immemorial without ever being condemned by anyone, not by any Father of the Church, nor by any local or provincial synod, nor by ecumenical council nor catholicos nor patriarch nor pope—on what basis would one dare to infer, even implicitly,

[5] N. P. TANNER, ed., *Decrees of the Ecumenical Councils*, 2 vols. (London/Washington: Sheed & Ward/Georgetown University Press, 1990) 2:695–697.

that such an ancient Apostolic Church did not and had never had a valid eucharistic sacrifice? This is not mere rhetoric—it is ecclesiology: the implications of such a negative verdict would be staggering.

A Missing Institution Narrative?

In addition to the ecumenical principles just enumerated, the elements that rendered such a positive solution feasible result from the consensus of the best in contemporary Catholic scholarship on the Eucharist and its theology. Earlier Catholic scholarship on Addai and Mari tended to argue *a priori* that since there could be no Eucharist without the Words of Institution, the original text of Addai and Mari must perforce have once had those words. The prominent seventeenth-century French Catholic scholar of Eastern liturgies Eusèbe Renaudot (1613–1679) wrote that an anaphora without the Words of Institution was "totally unheard of in antiquity and contrary to the discipline . . . of all Churches."[6] In such a climate of opinion, scholarly research and debate concerned just where these Words of Institution must have been and how they got removed.

But already half a century ago in Catholic scholarship, rumblings began to be heard against such arguments, which Alphonse Raes, S.J. (1896–1983) labeled an "apriorisme" and "insuffisantes."[7] Contemporary scholarship also completely rejects such an approach and has no patience with theories based on suppositions of what must or must not have been. Today's scholar starts with what is and attempts to explain it—not explain it away. So scholarly opinion tends to respect a text as it is, and presumes that to be its pristine form until the contrary is proven.[8] This prejudice in favor of the text is reinforced, in the case of Addai and Mari, by the unanimity of the manuscript tradition: not a single witness to this anaphora contains the Institution Account. Had the Institution Narrative once been part of the text only to be excised at a later date, it is unlikely that there would be

---

[6] ". . . inauditum prorsus antiquitus, & contra omnium Ecclesiarum . . . disciplinam": *Liturgiarum orientalium collectio*, 2 vols. (Paris: 1716) 2:579; Frankfurt/London: J. Baer, 1847) 2:573.

[7] "Le récit de l'institution eucharistique dans l'anaphore chaldéenne et malabare des Apôtres," *OCP* 10 (1944) 216–226, here 220, 225.

[8] For an extensive bibliography of scholarship on Addai and Mari until 1992, see A. GELSTON, *The Eucharistic Prayer of Addai and Mari* (Oxford/New York: Clarendon Press/Oxford University Press, 1992) 126–130, as well as his discussion, 5–28; to which add the more recent collected studies of B. D. SPINKS, *Worship. Prayers from the East* (Washington: The Pastoral Press, 1993), hereafter cited *Prayers from the East*.

not one single manuscript witness to the earlier redaction nor any other reminiscence of the matter in the literature of the tradition. That silence would hardly have been possible in the light of the importance the classical East-Syrian liturgical commentators give to the Institution Narrative in their eucharistic theology.[9]

Furthermore, although theories on the origins and evolution of the pristine anaphora remain in flux, one point of growing agreement among representative scholars, Catholic and non, is that the Institution Narrative is a later embolism—that is, interpolation—into the earliest Eucharistic Prayers. For *pace* Renaudot's mistaken assertion, not only Addai and Mari but several other early Eucharistic Prayers do, in fact, lack these words.[10] Those generally listed include the 1st/2nd-century *Didache,* 9–10[11] and the dependent *Apostolic Constitutions* (ca. 380), VII, 25:1–4;[12] the 2nd/3rd-century apocryphal *Acts of John,* 85–86, 109–110 and *Acts of Thomas,* 27, 49–50, 133, 158;[13] the *Martyrdom of Polycarp* (†167), 14;[14] the 4/5th-century *Papyrus Strasbourg* Gr. 254;[15] the Eucharistic Prayer on two 7/8th-century Coptic Ostraca, *British Library Nr.* 32 799 and *Nr.* 33

---

[9] The relevant texts are cited and commented by S.Y.H. JAMMO, "Gabriel Qatraya et son commentaire sur la liturgie chaldéenne," *OCP* 32 (1966) 39–52; see B. D. SPINKS, "Addai and Mari and the Institution Narrative: The Tantalising Evidence of Gabriel Qatraya," *Ephemerides Liturgicae* 98 (1984) 60–67 = *id., Prayers from the East,* 37–45.

[10] Among innumerable modern studies on this issue, in addition to those cited below apropos of Addai and Mari, see, for example, G. J. CUMING, "The Shape of the Anaphora," *Studia Patristica* 20 (1989) 333–345; G. DIX, *The Shape of the Liturgy* (London: Dacre Press, 1945) 197–198; J.R.K. FENWICK, *Fourth Century Anaphoral Construction Techniques,* Grove Liturgical Studies 45 (Bramcote: Grove Books, 1986); C. GIRAUDO, *Eucaristia per la Chiesa: Prospettive teologiche sull'eucaristia a partire dalla "lex orandi,"* Aloisiana 22 (Rome/Brescia: Gregorian University Press/Morcelliana, 1989) 345ff. E. J. KILMARTIN, "*Sacrificium laudis:* Content and Function of Early Eucharistic Prayers," *Theological Studies* 35 (1974) 268–287, here 277–278, 280; L. LIGIER, "The Origins of the Eucharistic Prayer: From the Last Supper to the Eucharist," *SL* 9 (1973) 161–185, esp. 179; and, for a contrary opinion, E. YARNOLD, "Anaphoras without Institution Narratives?" *Studia Patristica* 30 (1997) 395–410.

[11] *SC* 248:180 = *PE* 66.

[12] *SC* 336:52–55.

[13] *PE* 74–79.

[14] F. HALKIN, *Bibliotheca hagiographica Graeca,* 3rd ed., Subsidia Hagiographica 8a (Brussels: Société des Bollandistes, 1957) §1556; H. MUSURILLO, ed., *The Acts of the Christian Martyrs,* Oxford Early Christian Texts (Oxford: Clarendon Press, 1972) 12–15.

[15] *PE* 116–119.

050;[16] and the Ethiopic Anaphora of the Apostles, as Gabriele Winkler has recently demonstrated.[17] Furthermore, it seems probable that ca. 150, Justin Martyr's Eucharistic Prayer did not have them either.[18] In addition, Cyrille Vogel lists six Eucharistic Prayers in the apocrypha without any trace of an Institution Narrative,[19] and at least twenty-one later Syriac anaphoras either lack the Words of Institution completely (8 anaphoras) or partly (4), or give them in a form considered defective (9)—for example, in indirect discourse.[20]

Already in 1928, Anglican liturgical scholar Edward C. Ratcliff challenged the notion that Addai and Mari once had the Institution Narrative,[21] and later (1950) argued that the *Sanctus* was the conclusion to the primitive anaphoras,[22] a possibility raised earlier (1938) by the great German Benedictine Orientalist and comparative liturgiolo-

[16] H. QUECKE, "Das anaphorische Dankgebet auf den koptischen Ostraka, B.M Nr. 32 799 und 33 050 neu herausgegeben," *OCP* 37, no. 9 (1971) 391–405; *cf.* K. GAMBER, "Das koptische Ostraka London B.M Nr. 32 799 und 33 050 und seine liturgiegeschichtliche Bedeutung," *OKS* 21 (1972) 298–308.

[17] G. WINKLER, *Das Sanctus: Über den Ursprung und die Anfänge des Sanctus und sein Fortwirken, OCA* 267 (Rome: Pontificio Istituto Orientale, 2002) 162–168, 171–172; see also 85–86, 92–93, 96, 128, 143; *eadem*, "A New Witness to the Missing Institution Narrative," in M. E. JOHNSON, L. E. PHILLIPS, eds., *Studia Liturgica Diversa: Essays in Honor of Paul F. Bradshaw Studies in Church Music and Liturgy* (Portland: The Oregon Catholic Press) 117–128.

[18] *Apology,* I, 65, 67 = *PE* 70.

[19] C. VOGEL, "Anaphores eucharistiques préconstantiniennes. Formes non traditionelles," *Augustinianum* 20 (1980) 401–410.

[20] A. RAES, "Les paroles de la consécration dans les anaphores syriens," *OCP* 3 (1937) 486–504; C. GIRAUDO, *Eucaristia per la Chiesa,* 350–359.

[21] E. C. RATCLIFF, "The Original Form of the Anaphora of Addai and Mari: A Suggestion," *JTL* 30 (1928) 23–32 = *id., Liturgical Studies,* A. H. COURATIN, D. H. TRIPP, eds., (London: SPCK, 1976) 80–90 (see. also other relevant studies in the same anthology of his works). On Addai and Mari see also S.Y.H. JAMMO, "The Quddasha of the Apostles Addai and Mari and the Narrative of the Eucharistic Institution," in *Syriac Dialogue* (Vienna: Pro Oriente, 1994) 167–181; P. HOFRICHTER, "The Anaphora of Addai and Mari in the Church of the East— Eucharist without Institution Narrative," ibid., 182–191; most recently S.Y.H. JAMMO, "The Anaphora of the Apostles Addai and Mari: A Study of Structure and Historical Background," *OCP* 68 (2002) 5–35.

[22] E. C. RATCLIFF, "The Sanctus and the Pattern of the Early Anaphora," I: *The Journal of Ecclesiastical History* I (1950) 29–36; II: ibid., 125–134 = id., *Liturgical Studies,* 18–40. Ratcliff repeats his ideas in a letter of 23 October 1961, to A. Couratin, published in "The Thanksgiving: An Essay by Arthur Couratin," ed. by D. H. TRIPP in *BELS* 19:23–24. On Ratcliff's views, see also B. D. SPINKS, "The

gist Hieronymus Engberding, who had proposed that the presanctus of the Urtext behind the Greek Anaphora of St. John Chrysostom and the related Syriac Anaphora of the Apostles was once a complete Eucharistic Prayer.[23] Other authors like the French Jesuit Louis Ligier, professor of liturgy at the Pontifical Oriental Institute and Gregorian University in Rome, resumed and developed this idea. In Ligier's hypothesis, the Institution/Anamnesis block in the anaphora would be a later embolism framed by the general thanksgiving and its common concluding acclamation, "In all and for all we hymn you, we bless you, we thank you, and we pray to you, Our God."[24] The *Sanctus*, in turn, would be a still later enrichment of this structure.[25] Gabriele Winkler of Tübingen has carried this research further, proposing that the *Sanctus* was present from the beginning in such ancient anaphoras as UrBasil[26] and the Syriac (Addai and Mari) and Ethiopic

---

Cleansed Leper's Thankoffering before the Lord: Edward Craddock Ratcliff and the Pattern of the Early Anaphora," *BELS* 19:161–178; *id.*, *The Sanctus in the Eucharistic Prayer* (Cambridge: Cambridge University Press, 1991) 4–7. See also the more recent summary of views and discussion in R. F. TAFT, "The Interpolation of the Sanctus into the Anaphora: When and Where? A Review of the Dossier," Part I, *OCP* 57 (1991) 281–308; Part II, *OCP* 58 (1992) 82–121, here I:291–298; *id.*, *Liturgy in Byzantium and Beyond*, Variorum Collected Studies Series, CS493, (Aldershot/Brookfield: Variorum, 1995) ch. IX; *id.*, *Il Sanctus nell'anafora. Un riesame della questione* (Rome: Edizioni Orientalia Christiana, 1999); on the latter, see the critical review of G. WINKLER in *Oriens Christianus* 85 (2001) 283–284, and her seminal new study *Das Sanctus*.

[23] H. ENGBERDING, "Die syrische Anaphora der zwölf Apostel und ihre Paralleltexte einander gegenübergestellt und mit neuen Untersuchungen zur Urgeschichte der Chrysostomosliturgie begleitet," *Oriens Christianus* 34 = ser. 3, vol. 12 (1938) 213–247, here 239, 241.

[24] For the text referred to, see F. E. BRIGHTMAN, *Liturgies Eastern and Western* (Oxford: Clarendon Press, 1896) 88.10–16, 178.18–19, 329.9–10, 438.12–14; G. J. CUMING, *The Liturgy of St. Mark,* edited from the manuscripts with a commentary, *OCA* 234 (Rome: Pontificium Institutum Studiorum Orientalium, 1990) 43.9; A. GERHARDS, *Die griechische Gregoriosanaphora: Ein Beitrag zur Geschichte des Eucharistischen Hochgebets,* Liturgiewissenschaftliche Quellen und Forschungen 65 (Münster: Aschendorff, 1984) 34.193–194; *PE* 226, 236, 267, 271, 287, 290, 296, 305, 307, 312, 317, 322, 329, 335, 339, 352, 364, 377, 384, 393; see. J.-M. HANSSENS, *Institutiones liturgicae de ritibus orientalibus*, vols. II–III (Rome: Università Gregoriana, 1930, 1932) 3:451–452 §1321.

[25] L. LIGIER, "The Origins of the Eucharistic Prayer: From the Last Supper to the Eucharist," *SL* 9 (1973) 161–185, esp. 167, 171ff, 177–180, 183.

[26] G. WINKLER, *Die Basilius-Anaphora. Edition der beiden armenischen Redaktionen und der relevanten Fragmente, Übersetzung und Zusamnenschau aller Versionen im*

anaphoras. Neither of the latter two, however, originally had an Institution Narrative.[27] Finally, present expert opinion on the *Apostolic Tradition* holds that the Institution and Anamnesis/Oblation may have been added to its anaphora later, not earlier than the fourth century.[28] *So there is not a single extant pre-Nicene Eucharistic Prayer that one can prove contained the Words of Institution,* and today many scholars maintain that the most primitive, original Eucharistic Prayers were short, self-contained benedictions without Institution Narrative or Epiclesis, comparable to the *Didache* 10 and the papyrus *Strasbourg 254.*[29]

Licht der orientalischen Überlieferungen, Anaphorae Orientales 2 = Anaphorae Armeniacae 2 (Rome) in press.

[27] G. WINKLER, *Das Sanctus,* 130–133, 167–168, 171–172; and these articles in press: *eadem,* "Beobachtungen zu den im *ante Sanctus* angeführten Engeln," *Theologische Quartalschrift* 183 (2003) 213–238, here 214 note 6; *eadem,* "Über die Bedeutung des Sanctus-Benedictus und seine Wurzeln in der Qeduššâ," *Studi sull' Oriente cristiano,* 8/1 (2004) 91–100; and, most recently, *eadem,* "A New Witness to the Missing Institution Narrative."

[28] P. F. BRADSHAW, "A Paschal Root to the Anaphora of the Apostolic Tradition? A Response to Enrico Mazza," *Studia Patristica* 35 (2001) 257–265; *id.* and M. E. JOHNSON, L. E. PHILLIPS, *The Apostolic Tradition: A Commentary,* Hermeneia (Minneapolis: Fortress Press, 2002) 45–48; J. F. BALDOVIN, "The Apostolic Tradition? Of Hippolytus? Of Rome?" The Sir Daniel & Countess Bernardine Murphy Donohue Chair in Eastern Catholic Theology at the Pontifical Oriental Institute, Rome, Annual Lecture, 13 March 2003 (in press *Theological Studies*).

[29] See. S.Y.H. JAMMO, "The Anaphora of the Apostles Addai and Mari," 11–18; M. ARRANZ, "L'esegesi dei testi liturgici: un'apertura metodologica per orizzonti nuovi," *Rassegna di teologia* 32 (1991) 86–92, here esp. 89–90; W. H. BATES, "Thanksgiving and Intercession in the Liturgy of St. Mark," *BELS* 19:112–119; G. J. CUMING, "The Anaphora of St. Mark: A Study in Development," *Le Muséon* 95 (1982) 115–129, 122–123, 128; KILMARTIN, *"Sacrificium laudis,"* 268–287; G. KRETSCHMAR, *Studien zur frühchristlichen Trinitätstheologie,* Beitrage zur historischen Theologie 21 (Tübingen: J.C.B. Mohr, 1956) 148; E. C. RATCLIFF, "The Original Form of the Anaphora of Addai and Mari: A Suggestion," *JTS* 30 (1929) 23–32 = *id., Liturgical Studies,* 80–90, 23–32; H. WEGMAN, "Une anaphore incomplète? Les fragments sur Papyrus Strasbourg Gr. 254," in R. van den BROEK, M. J. VERMASEREN, eds., *Studies in Gnosticism and Hellenistic Religions* (Leiden: E. J. Brill, 1981) 432–450; *id.,* "Généalogie hypothétique de la prière eucharistique," *Questions liturgiques* 61 (1980) 263–278. For a summary of research on the origins of the anaphora up to the dates of the respective publications, see T. J. TALLEY, "The Eucharistic Prayer of the Ancient Church according to Recent Research: Results and Reflections," *SL* 11 (1976) 138–158; G. J. CUMING, "The Early Eucharistic Liturgies in Recent Research," *BELS* 19:65–69; to which must be added the recent works of C. GIRAUDO, *La struttura letteraria della preghiera eucaristica. Saggio sulla genesi letteraria di una forma. Toda veterotestamentaria, b^eraka giudaica, anafora*

All this shows that scholarship on the Eucharistic Prayer has been rich and intensive for a generation, and even if some remain skeptical of one or another hypothesis or conclusions,[30] there is consensus on at least one point: I know of not one single reputable contemporary scholar on the topic, Catholic or non-Catholic, who would hold it as certain that the Words of Institution were an integral part of the earliest Eucharistic Prayers over the gifts. Jesuit Cesare Giraudo, one of the major figures in the area by anyone's criteria, calls it "una questione aperta" whether the original Eucharist included Jesus' Words.[31] Anthony Gelston, summing up the contemporary consensus, notes

> the not inconsiderable evidence that the wording of the Christian Eucharistic prayer remained far from fixed until at least the beginning of the third century. There is no hint of a tradition that the actual content of Jesus' thanksgiving at the Last Supper was remembered, transmitted, and repeated at the celebration of the Eucharist. What was done in remembrance of Jesus was the offering of thanks, but not according to a fixed formula.[32]

Interpreting the Tradition: Theologia prima—Theologia secunda

How, then, are we to interpret liturgical texts? What do our anaphoras mean? They mean what they say. It is axiomatic in contemporary liturgical theology to distinguish between *theologia prima* and *theologia secunda*. *Theologia prima*, or first-level theology, is the faith expressed in the liturgical life of the Church antecedent to speculative questioning of its theoretical implications, prior to its systematization in the dogmatic

---

cristiana, Analecta Biblica 92 (Rome: Biblical Institute Press, 1981); *id.*, *Eucaristia per la Chiesa*; *id.*, "Le récit de l'institution dans la prière eucharistique a-t-il des antécédents? Quelques aperçus sur la prière liturgique et la dynamique de son embolisme," *Nouvelle revue théologique* 106 (1984) 513–536; *id.*, "Vers un traité de l'Eucharistie à la fois ancien et nouveau. La théologie de l'Eucharistie à travers l'école de la «lex orandi»," *Nouvelle revue théologique* 112 (1990) 870–887.

[30] E.g., B. D. SPINKS, *The Sanctus in the Eucharistic Prayer* (Cambridge: Cambridge University Press, 1991) 104, 108; *id.*, "A Complete Anaphora? A Note on Strasbourg Gr. 254," *The Heythrop Journal* 25 (1984) 51–59; J. MAGNE, "L'anaphore nestorienne dite d'Addée et Mari et l'anaphore maronite dite de Pierre III: Étude comparative," *OCP* 53 (1987) 144–145. Most recently, Winkler concurred with Spinks' assessment in his study *The Sanctus*. See her analysis of the Syriac and Ethiopic evidence in *Das Sanctus*; in her forthcoming study on the Basil Anaphora (note 26 above); and in *eadem*, "A New Witness to the Missing Institution Narrative."

[31] GIRAUDO, *Eucaristia per la Chiesa*, 329. See the whole discussion there, 329–360.

[32] GELSTON, *The Eucharistic Prayer of Addai and Mari*, 5.

propositions of *theologia secunda,* or systematic reflection on the lived mystery of the Church. Liturgical language, the language of *theologia prima,* is typological, metaphorical, more redolent of Bible and prayer than of school and thesis, more patristic than scholastic, more impressionistic than systematic, more suggestive than probative. In a word, it is symbolic and evocative, not philosophical and ontological.

Now although it is perfectly obvious, indeed necessary, that doctrine will acquire theological refinements, especially in the heat of dogmatic controversy, it should be equally obvious that such refinements cannot be read back into texts composed long before the problems arose that led to those precisions. To pounce upon ancient anaphoral texts and exploit them tendentiously in today's theological controversies is an anachronistic procedure devoid of any legitimacy.

If we turn now to the pristine Latin *theologia prima* as expressed in the ancient Roman *Canon Missae,* we find a movement which, far from justifying a hylomorphic scholastic *theologia secunda,* fits better with the pre-scholastic theology of the Latin Fathers. Less smooth and unified in its redactional structure than the Antiochene anaphoral type, the Roman Canon does not first recite the Institution Narrative, then elucidate its meaning. Rather, it imbeds Jesus' words in a series of discrete prayers for the sanctification and acceptance of the oblation (which, theologically, are of course the same thing). Now some of these prayers even before the Words of Institution speak of the species in terms that can only refer to the Body and Blood of Christ as if the gifts were already consecrated and, conversely, after the Words of Institution speak in a way that could seem to imply the gifts are not yet consecrated.

Only the wooden-headed literalist totally innocent of the proleptic and reflexive nature of liturgical discourse could find anything surprising about this. Such seeming contradictions—and similar apparent contradictions can be found in the Fathers of the Church who comment on the Eucharistic Prayer—result from the fact that before the Middle Ages no one tried to identify a "moment of consecration" apart from the anaphoral prayer over the gifts in its entirety.

In his *De officiis ecclesiae,* I, 15, St. Isidore (ca. 560–†636), bishop of Seville from 600 to 636, says that the consecration occurs in the canon, which he calls the "sixth prayer" of the "ordo of the Mass and prayers by which the sacrifices offered to God are consecrated."[33]

---

[33] I, 15.1; PL 83:752A (= *CPL* §11207): "Ordo . . . missae et orationum quibus oblata Deo sacrificia consecrantur."

From the context it is clear that he is referring to the entire section of the anaphora following the preface that extends from the *Sanctus* to the Our Father inclusive (the entire text in Appendix I below, p. 225).

> Then [comes] *the sixth prayer* [of the Eucharist], from which results the formation of the sacrament as an oblation that is offered to God, sanctified through the Holy Spirit, formed into the Body and Blood of Christ. The last of these is the prayer by which our Lord instructed his disciples to pray, saying: "*Our Father, who art in heaven.*"[34]

St. Isidore is usually considered the "last of the Latin Fathers," so right through to the end of the patristic period the view was current in Latin theology (1) that the eucharistic consecration was the work of the Holy Spirit, and (2) that the prayer that effected it was the canon or anaphora without further specifying one of its component parts as the "form" of the sacrament or the "moment of consecration." St. Fulgentius of Ruspe (ca. 468–†533)[35] and numerous other pre-scholastic Latin authors teach the same doctrine.[36]

Nor is this view substantially different from that of the early medieval Latin commentators. Peter Lombard (ca. 1095–†1160), speaking of the *Supplices* (Roman Canon §6 in Appendix I below), says in his *Sentences*, IV, 13: "It is called 'Missa' that the heavenly messenger might come to consecrate the life-giving body, according to the expression of the priest: 'Almighty God, bid that this be borne by the hand of your holy angel to your altar on high . . . .'"[37]

Even more explicitly, shortly after A.D. 1215, John Teutonicus's comment on the same prayer says: "'Bid,' that is: *make*. 'Be borne,' that is: *be transubstantiated*. Or: 'be borne,' that is, be assumed, that is: *be changed.* . . ." The inclusion of this text in the *Glossa ordinaria ad*

---

[34] I, 15.2; PL 83:753AB: "Porro *sexta [oratio]* exhinc succedit conformatio sacramenti, ut oblatio, quae Deo offertur, sanctificata per Spiritum sanctum, Christi corpori ac sanguini conformetur. Harum ultima est oratio, qua Dominus noster discipulos suos orare instituit, dicens: *Pater noster, qui es in coelis.*"

[35] *Ad Monimum*, II, 6 and 9–10 (= CPL §814), PL 65:184–185, 187–188.

[36] J. R. GEISELMANN, *Die Abendmahlslehre an der Wende des christlichen Spätantike zum Frühmittelalter: Isidor von Sevilla und das Sakrament der Eucharistie* (München: M. Hüber, 1933) 198–224; Y. CONGAR, *Je crois en l'Esprit Saint*, 3 vols. (Paris: Cerf, 1979–1980) 3:320–330.

[37] PL 192:868: "*Missa* enim dicitur, eo quod coelestis nuntius ad consecrandum vivificum corpus adveniat, juxta dictum sacerdotis: *Omnipotens Deus, jube haec perferri per manus sancti angeli tui in sublime altare tuum*, etc."

Decretum Gratiani, shows how common and acceptable such a view must have been. Note, please, that these authoritative medieval Latin commentators are speaking about a consecratory prayer said *after the Words of Institution* in the Roman Canon (Appendix I below, §6).[38]

In modern times, no less an authority on the Roman Eucharist than the great Josef A. Jungmann, S.J., sums up the original tradition of the undivided Church as follows: "In general Christian antiquity, even until way into the Middle Ages, manifested no particular interest regarding the determination of the precise moment of the consecration. Often reference was made merely to the entire Eucharistic prayer."[39]

Already in the seventeenth century, the famous Bossuet (1627–1704) raised his voice in favor of a similar sanity. He says:

> The intent of liturgies, and, in general, of consecratory prayers, is not to focus our attention on precise moments, but to have us attend to the action in its entirety and to its complete effect. . . . It is to render more vivid what is being done that the Church speaks at each moment as though it were accomplishing the entire action then and there, without asking whether the action has already been accomplished or is perhaps still to be accomplished.[40]

Dom Charles Chardon, O.S.B., in his *Histoire des sacrements* (Paris: 1745), expressed a similarly balanced view:

> Despite this diversity [over the form or moment of consecration] there was formerly no dispute over this subject. The Greeks and Latins were convinced that the species [of bread and wine] were changed into the Body and Blood of our Savior in virtue of the words of the Canon of the Mass, without examining the precise moment at which this change occurred, nor just which of the words [of the anaphora] effected it as

---

[38] "Jube, id est: *fac.* Perferri, id est: *transsubstantiari.* Vel: perferri, id est sursum efferri, id est *converti.* . . ." *Decretum de consecratione* 2, 72, in *Glossa ordinaria* (Rome: 1582) 2:1813, cited by S. Salaville, *SC* 4 bis:322.

[39] J. A. JUNGMANN, *The Mass of the Roman Rite. Missarum sollemnia,* 2 vols. (New York: Benziger Brothers, 1951, 1955) 2:203–204 note 9. He goes on to say, "It is Florus Diaconus [of Lyons, †860], *De actione miss.,* c. 60 (PL 119:52f.), in the Carolingian period, who with particular stress brought out the significance of the words of consecration; *ille in suis sacerdotibus quotidie loquitur.*"

[40] J.-B. BOSSUET, *Explication de quelques difficultés sur les prières de la messe à un nouveau catholique,* F. LACHAT, ed., *Œuvres* 17 (Paris: L. Vivès, 1864) 74–75, trans. in R. CABIÉ, *The Eucharist* = A. G. MARTIMORT, ed., *The Church at Prayer,* vol. 2, new edition (Collegeville: The Liturgical Press, 1986) 147.

over against other [words]. One side said the change was effected by the prayer and invocation of the priest; the others said that it was the result of the words of Our Lord when he instituted this august sacrament. And they in no way believed that these different ways of expressing themselves were opposed to each other (and indeed they are not, as would be easy to show). But we shall leave that to the theologians to treat. . . .[41]

Later Scholasticism vs. the Earlier Tradition

The later Western narrowing of the perspective, ultimately doctrinalized in the scholastic hylomorphic *materia/forma* theory of the eucharistic consecration, contrasts sharply with the *theologia prima* of the Roman Canon and its earlier Latin interpreters, which views, in turn, were fully consonant with traditional Eastern doctrine. The new Latin theology was sanctioned doctrinally by Benedict XII's (1334–1342) *Libellus "Cum dudum" ad Armenos* 66 in A.D. 1341 (Dz §1017) and by the A.D. 1439 *Decretum pro Armeniis* (Dz §1321; see §1017) and the A.D. 1442 *Decretum pro Iacobitis* (Dz §1352) in the aftermath of the Council of Florence.[42]

Even more restrictive was the teaching formulated by Pius VII (1800–1823) in his brief *Adorabile Eucharistiae* of 9 May 1822 (Dz §2718), addressed to the Melkite Catholic patriarch and hierarchy, condemning

> *that new opinion* proposed by schismatic men which teaches that the form by which this lifegiving . . . sacrament is accomplished consists not in the words of Jesus Christ alone which both Latin and Greek priests use in the consecration, but that for the perfect and complete consecration, there should be added that formula of prayers which among us [Latins] precede the above-mentioned words [of Jesus], but in your [Byzantine] liturgy follow them.[43]

[41] I translate it from the re-edition of J.-P. MIGNE, *Theologiae cursus completus,* 28 vols. (Paris 1839–1843) 20:249.

[42] N. P. TANNER, *Decrees of the Ecumenical Councils* 1:546–547, 581. On the council and its aftermath, see J. GILL, *The Council of Florence* (Cambridge: Cambridge University Press, 1959) 116, 265–267, 272–278, 280– 281, 284–286, 292.

[43] ". . . *novam illam opinionem* a schismaticis hominibus propugnatam qua docetur formarn, qua vivificum hoc . . . sacramenturn perficitur, non in solis Iesu Christi verbis consistere, quibus sacerdotes tam Latini quam Graeci in consecratione utuntur, sed ad perfectam consurnmatamque consecrationern addi oportere earn precurn formulam, quae memorata verba apud Nos praecurrit, in vestra autem liturgia subsequitur" (emphasis added).

I will leave to the dogmaticians what "theological note" they wish to assign this exclusively Latin teaching, construed in its narrowest popular understanding that the *Verba Domini,* they alone and nothing else, are the so-called "words of consecration" of the Mass. Suffice it to say that what His Holiness is pleased to call a "new opinion" was taught explicitly from the fourth century by saints and Fathers of the undivided Church like St. Cyril/John II of Jerusalem (*post* 380),[44] St. John Chrysostom (ca. 340/350–†407),[45] and St. John Damascene (ca. 650/675–†753/754)[46] in the East, along with St. Isidore of Seville (ca. 560–†636) in the West.[47] Since all these sainted gentlemen are venerated in the liturgical calendar of the Catholic Church, to be consistent we must apply here the old adage "Let the rule of prayer determine the rule of faith *(lex orandi legem statuat credendi)."*

As for the *Decretum pro Armeniis,* it certainly does not recommend itself by the fact that it also proclaims the *traditio instrumentorum* to be the sacramental matter of holy orders (Dz §1326), a teaching not only no longer held today (Dz §§3858–3860), but one that *even in its own day* was flatly false, contradicting the clear facts of liturgical history. More important, it also departed from and contradicted age-old Catholic teaching, which had never impugned the validity of ordination rites of Churches with no *traditio instrumentorum* like that of the Latins. So one must either reject that decree, or if your theory of magisterium obliges you to squirm to salvage it by arguing that it envisaged only the medieval Latin ordination rite, in which the *traditio*

---

[44] *Mystagogic Catechesis,* 5, 7, see 1, 7; 3, 3, SC 126bis:94, 124, 154; regarding date and authorship, 177–187. See also THEODORE OF MOPSUESTIA, *Homily* 16, 12: R. TONNEAU, R. DEVREESSE, *Les homélies catéchétiques de Théodore de Mopsueste,* Studi e testi 145 (Vatican: Biblioteca Apostolica Vaticana, 1949) 553.

[45] See below at notes 65–69.

[46] *Expositio fidei,* 86:163–166, B. KOTTER, ed., *Die Schriften des Johannes von Damaskos,* 5 vols., Patristische Texte und Studien 7, 12, 17, 22, 29 (Berlin/New York: W. de Gruyter, 1969–1988) 2:197 = *De fide orthodoxa,* IV, 13, PG 94:1152C–1153B; English translation from St. John of Damascus, *Writings,* trans. F. H. CHASE, JR., The Fathers of the Church 37 (Washington: The Catholic University Press, 1981) 360–361. See also the texts cited below at notes 56–57 and the excellent study of N. ARMITAGE, "The Eucharistic Theology of the *Exact Exposition of the Orthodox Faith (De Fide Orthodoxa)* of St. John Damascene," OKS 44 (1995) 292–308; R. TAFT, "Ecumenical Scholarship and the Catholic-Orthodox Epiclesis Dispute," 210; *id.,* "Understanding the Byzantine Anaphoral Oblation," 47–55; *id.,* "The Epiclesis Question in the Light of the Orthodox and Catholic Lex orandi Traditions," 225–237.

[47] See above at notes 33–34.

had assumed a significant place, then intellectual honesty would require saying the same for its teaching on the Words of Institution. For the decree assigns them an exclusive importance they had assumed only in the Latin West. More significant for me is the fact that the decree sanctions a culturally and temporally conditioned, medieval scholastic theology of the sacraments that can in no wise claim to be traditional to the teaching of the undivided Church. Here we are talking not about magisterial teaching but the undeniable facts of history available to anyone able to read Latin and Greek.

The Entire Eucharistic Prayer as Formula of Consecration

So these doctrinal statements of the past must be understood not only in their historical context but also in the light of contemporary Catholic teaching, which of late has come to take a considerably broader view of what comprises the eucharistic consecration. A steady stream of Catholic theologians have moved toward the view that the formula of eucharistic consecration comprises the prayer over the gifts in its entirety.[48] I do not have space to list these theologians here; those interested can find their teaching in Vincentian Father John H. McKenna's thorough review of the question.[49]

The most recent study by the late (+2003) Dom Burkhard Neunheuser, O.S.B., monk of Maria Laach and professor of the Pontifical Liturgical Institute Sant'Anselmo in Rome, furnishes not only the most explicit and emphatic justification of this return to the original tradition of the undivided Church but does so with full respect for traditional Catholic teaching on the centrality of the Words of Institution within the anaphoral context.[50] As Neunheuser is careful to point out, this renewal is already found reflected in official Catholic texts in the aftermath of Vatican II. The 18 November 1969 *Institutio Generalis Missalis Romani*, §54, concerning the reformed Roman Missal, says of the Eucharistic Prayer: "Now begins the summit and center of the

---

[48] See esp. Y. CONGAR, *Je crois en l'Esprit Saint*, 3:309ff.

[49] J. H. McKENNA, *Eucharist and Holy Spirit: The Eucharistic Epiclesis in 20th Century Theology*, Alcuin Club Collections 57 (Great Wakering: Mayhew-McCrimmon, 1975); also *id.*, "Eucharistic Prayer: Epiclesis," in A. HEINZ, H. RENNINGS, eds., *Gratias agamus:. Studien zum eucharistischen Hochgebet. Für Balthasar Fischer*, Pastoralliturgische Reihe in Verbindung mit der Zeitschrift "Gottesdienst" (Freiburg/Basel/Vienna: Herder, 1992) 283–291.

[50] B. NEUNHEUSER, "Das Eucharistische Hochgebet als Konsekrationsgebet," in A. HEINZ, H. RENNINGS, *Gratias agamus*, 315–326.

whole celebration, namely the Eucharistic Prayer itself, *that is, the prayer of thanksgiving and sanctification.*"[51] "Sanctification," of course, means in this context "eucharistic consecration." And although Paul VI continues to use the outdated scholastic terminology of matter and form of the sacrament in his 18 June 1968 apostolic constitution *Pontificalis Romani* recognitio, he does so in a broad, non-scholastic context: the "matter" of the sacrament is the imposition of hands;[52] "the form consists in the words of the very prayer of consecration,"[53] and not some isolated formula within it. This broader vision is also reflected in how the new *Catechism of the Catholic Church* refers to the anaphora: "with the eucharistic prayer, the prayer, namely, *of thanksgiving and consecration, we come to the heart and culmination of the celebration.*"[54]

This renewal found ecumenical agreement in Part I, no. 6, of the July 1982 Munich Statement of the Orthodox-Catholic Joint Commission for Theological Dialogue: "the eucharistic mystery is accomplished in the prayer which joins together the words by which the word made flesh instituted the sacrament and the epiclesis in which the church, moved by faith, entreats the Father, through the Son, to send the Spirit."[55] It is also reflected in what the new *Catechism of the Catholic Church* has to say about the eucharistic consecration: "In the Institution Narrative, by the words and action of Christ and the power of the Holy Spirit, His Body and Blood are made sacramentally present under the species of bread and wine."[56]

This view that the prayer of consecration is the entire core of the anaphora, not just some segment of it set apart as an isolated "for-

[51] "Prex eucharistica. Nunc centrum et culmen totius celebrationis habet, ipsa nempe Prex eucharistica, *prex scilicet gratiarum actionis et sanctificationis*": *EDIL* §1449 (emphasis added); cf. §1450; *DOL* §1444, cf. §1445; B. NEUNHEUSER, "Das Eucharistische Hochgebet als Konsekrationsgebet," 321.

[52] *EDIL* §§1084–1085 = *DOL* §§2608–2609.

[53] *EDIL* §§1085–1087 = *DOL* §§2609–2611: "forma constat verbis eiusdem precationis consecratoriae."

[54] *Catechismus Catholicae Ecclesiae, Typica Latina editio* (Vatican: Libreria Editrice Vaticana, 1997) §1352, emphasis added.

[55] JOINT COMMISSION FOR THEOLOGICAL DIALOGUE BETWEEN THE CATHOLIC CHURCH AND THE ORTHODOX CHURCH, "The Mystery of the Church and the Eucharist in the Light of the Mystery of the Holy Trinity," *Information Service* 49 (1982/II–III) 108; *Origins* 12 (12 April 1982) 158; French text in La *documentation catholique* 79 (1982 = No. 1838, 17 October) 942; *Episkepsis*, no. 277 (July–August 1982) 13.

mula," is, I think, more faithful to the earlier common tradition of the undivided Church. Several patristic texts lend themselves to this interpretation, using the term "epiclesis" for the whole prayer over the gifts. Among the earliest second-century witnesses to the Eucharist in the period following the New Testament, Justin's *Apology*, I, 65–67, written ca. A.D. 150, testifies to a prayer over the gifts. After that prayer, the gifts were no longer "ordinary food or ordinary drink but . . . flesh and blood of that same Jesus who was made flesh" (I, 66).[57] From the same period (ca. 185), Irenaeus, *Adversus haereses*, IV, 18.5, calls this consecration prayer "the invocation *(tēn epiklēsin)* of God."[58] And although Cyril/John II of Jerusalem, *Mystagogic Catechesis (post* 380) 3, 3 and 5, 7), also uses the term "epiclesis" in its present, restricted sense,[59] in another passage, *Mystagogic Catechesis* 1, 7, the word is usually interpreted as referring to the entire anaphora: "Before the holy epiclesis of the adorable Trinity the bread and wine of the eucharist was ordinary bread and wine, whereas after the epiclesis the bread becomes the body of Christ and the wine the blood of Christ."[60] That, in my view, should suffice for a common profession of our faith in the eucharistic consecration. The rest can be left to theology.

---

[56] *Catechismus Catholicae Ecclesiae*, §1375.

[57] *PE* 68–72.

[58] *SC* 264:611; see also *Adv. haer.*, 1, 13.2, *SC* 264:190–191. Indeed, "epiclesis" is commonly used for the entire prayer over the gifts even in sources as late as the fourth century: Hippolytus, *Refutatio omnium haeresium (Philosophoumena)*, VI, 39:2, PG 16.3:3258 (= *CPG* §1899; on its disputed authenticity, see *CPG* §1870); Firmilian of Caesarea, cited in Cyprian, *Ep.* 75, 10, *CSEL* 3.2:818—translation and discussion of this text with relevant literature in A. BOULEY, *From Freedom to Formula: The Evolution of the Eucharistic Prayer from Oral Improvisation to Written Texts*, Catholic University of America Studies in Christian Antiquity 21 (Washington: The Catholic University of America Press, 1981) 143–145; G. A. MICHELL, "Firmilian and Eucharistic Consecration," *JTS* 5 (1954) 215–220; *Didaskalia*, VI, 22:2: *Didascalia apostolorum*. The Syriac Version translated and accompanied by the Verona fragments, with an introduction and notes, by R. H. CONNOLLY (Oxford: Clarendon Press, 1929) 252–253. See J. W. TYRER, "The Meaning of *epiklesis*," *JTS* 25 (1923–1924) 139–150, esp. 142–145, 148; O. CASEL, "Neuere Beiträge zur Epiklesenfrage," *Jahrbuch für Liturgiewissenschaft* 4 (1924) 169–178, esp. 170–171. Some authors would also include in this list BASIL, *De Spiritu sancto*, 27, *SC* 17bis:480 = PG 32:188 (= *CPG* §2839). But I agree with GELSTON (*The Eucharistic Prayer of Addai and Mari*, 15–17) that Basil is probably referring to the epiclesis in the narrow sense of the term.

[59] *SC* 126bis:124, 154.

[60] *SC* 126bis:94.

The Words of Institution as Consecratory

As we have seen, both before and after the scholastic interval and the dispute between East and West over the epiclesis,[61] reputable Catholic theologians rejected theologies that would isolate the Institution Narrative from its essential setting within the anaphora. Does that mean that the Words of Institution are not consecratory? Not at all. For the Fathers of the Church they are indeed consecratory, for they are words eternally efficacious in the mouth of Jesus. The classic Latin doctrine on the Words of Institution as "words of consecration" can be traced back to St. Ambrose (339–397), who states the teaching unambiguously (though not restrictively—that is, *sensu aiente*, not *sensu negante*) in his *De sacramentis*, IV, 4.14-17,[62] 5.21-23, and *De mysteriis*, IX, 52-54.[63] But Ambrose is not speaking of the words as a "formula." Not until the twelfth century do the scholastics formulate the thesis that the Words of Institution are the essential "form of the sacrament" that *alone* effect the consecration of the bread and wine.[64]

That more narrow view is not the authentic tradition of the Fathers of the Church. St. John Chrysostom (ca. 340/350–†407), for instance, attributes consecratory efficacy both to the Words of Institution and to the epiclesis. Chrysostom states in at least seven different homilies that what happens in the Eucharist happens by the power of the Holy Spirit,[65] a teaching common to both the Greek and Latin

---

[61] On East-West issues in eucharistic theology from two of the major recent Catholic theologians writing on the issue, in addition to my studies above in note 4 and others cited in this present essay, see E. J. KILMARTIN, "The Active Role of Christ and the Holy Spirit in the Sanctification of the Eucharistic Elements," *Theological Studies* 45 (1984) 225–253, esp. 235ff.; C. GIRAUDO, "L'epiclesi eucaristica: Proposta per una soluzione «ortodossa» della controversia fra Oriente e Occidente," *Rassegna di teologia* 41 (2000) 5–24. On Kilmartin's liturgical theology, see most recently the excellent study of J. M. HALL, *We Have the Mind of Christ: The Holy Spirit and Liturgical Memory in the Thought of Edward J. Kilmartin*, A Pueblo Book (Collegeville: The Liturgical Press, 2001).

[62] Cited below at note 71.

[63] *SC* 25bis:110, 114, 186–188 = *CSEL* 73:51–53, 55–56, 112–113 (= *CPL* §§154–155).

[64] J. R. GEISELMANN, *Abendmahlslehre*, 192–194, 144–147; J. J. HUGHES, "Eucharistic Sacrifice: Transcending the Reformation Deadlock," *Worship* 13 (1969) 540; J. A. JUNGMANN, *The Mass of the Roman Rite*, cited above at note 39.

[65] *De sacerdotio*, III, 4:40–50; VI, 4:34–44, *SC* 272:142–146, 316 = *PG* 48:642–645, 681; *CPG* §4316); *Oratio de beato Philogonio*, 3, *PG* 48:753 (= *CPG* §4319); *De resurr. mortuorum* 8, *PG* 50:432 (= *CPG* §4340); *In pentec. hom.*, 1, 4, *PG* 50:458–459 (= *CPG* §4343); *In Ioh. hom.*, 45, 2, *PG* 59:253 (= *CPG* §4425); *In I Cor hom.*, 24, 5, *PG* 61:204

Churches. In at least one instance it is clear Chrysostom is talking about the epiclesis. But in his *Homily on the Betrayal of Judas* (*De proditione Judae hom.*, 1 /2, 6), he attributes the consecration to Christ in the Words of Institution:

> It is not man who causes what is present to become the body and blood of Christ, but Christ himself, who was crucified for us. The priest is the representative when he pronounces those words, but the power and the grace are those of the Lord. "This is my body," he says. This word changes the things that lie before us; and just as that sentence, "increase and multiply," once spoken, extends through all time and gives to our nature the power to reproduce itself; likewise that saying, "This is my body," once uttered, from that time to the present day, and even until Christ's coming, makes the sacrifice complete at every table in the churches.[66]

Note that Chrysostom assigns consecratory power *not to the priest's liturgical repetition* of Jesus' words now, but *to the historical institution itself*, that is, to the original utterance of Jesus whose force extends to all subsequent eucharistic celebrations.[67]

In the eighth century St. John Damascene, "last of the Greek Fathers" (ca. 675–753/754), teaches the exact same doctrine in his *De fide orthodoxa* 86 (IV, 13): "God said 'This is my body' and 'This is my blood,' and 'do this in memory of me.' *And by his all-powerful command it is done until he comes.* For that is what he said, until he should come, and the overshadowing power of the Holy Spirit becomes, through the invocation [i.e., epiclesis], the rain to this new tillage."[68] This is the classic Eastern Orthodox teaching: the power of consecration comes from the words of Christ, the divine mandate that guarantees the eucharistic conversion for all time.[69]

(= *CPG* §4428). But in *In De coemet. et de cruce*, 3, Chrysostom is clearly speaking of the epiclesis: PG 49:397–398 (= *CPG* §4337).

[66] PG 49:380, 389–390 (= *CPG* §4336).

[67] See Nicholas CABASILAS, *Commentary*, chap. 29, SC 4bis:178–190; see the commentary of S. SALAVILLE, ibid., 314–315, and McKENNA, *Eucharist and Holy Spirit*, 59.

[68] Ed. B. KOTTER 2:194.71–76; see N. ARMITAGE, "The Eucharistic Theology of the Exact Exposition of the Orthodox Faith" (English trans. from *ibid.*, 293).

[69] But the epiclesis of the Holy Spirit is the decisive liturgical moment, for the Damascene continues: "the bread of the prothesis, the wine, and the water, are converted supernaturally into the body of Christ and the blood, through the invocation (epiclesis) and intervention of the Holy Spirit." Ed. B. KOTTER, 2:195; trans. ARMITAGE, 294.

But this is no different from the position of Ambrose (339–397), who obviously attributes the efficacy of Jesus' words not to the prayer of the priest,[70] but to the indefectible effectiveness of the Word of God, as is perfectly clear in his *De sacramentis*, IV, 4.14–417:

> 14. . . . to produce the venerable sacrament, the priest does not use his own words but the words of Christ. So it is the word of Christ which produces this sacrament. 15. Which word of Christ? The one by which all things were made. The Lord commanded and the heavens were made, the Lord commanded and the earth was made, the Lord commanded and the seas were made, the Lord commanded and all creatures were brought into being. You see, then, how effective the word of Christ is. If then there is such power in the word of the Lord Jesus that things which were not began to be, how much more effective must they be in changing what already exists into something else! . . .
>
> 17. Hear, then, how the word of Christ is accustomed to change all creatures and to change, when it will, the laws of nature.[71]

This is exactly what Chrysostom says on other occasions: in the liturgy the same Jesus accomplishes the same Eucharist, the same marvels, in the liturgy as at the Last Supper.[72] For instance, his *Homily 2 on II Timothy*, affirms:

> The gifts which God bestows are not such as to be the effects of the virtue of the priest. All is from grace. His [the priest] part is but to open his mouth, while God works all. He [the priest] only completes the sign *(symbolon)*. The offering is the same whoever offers it, Paul or Peter. It is

---

[70] As Nicholas CABASILAS accuses them in his commentary on the liturgy, chap. 29.10, *SC* 4bis:184–186.

[71] "14. . . . ut conficiatur uenerabile sacramentum, iam non suis sermonibus utitur sacerdos, sed utitur sermonibus Christi. Ergo sermo Christi hoc conficit sacramenturn. 15. Quis est sermo Christi? Nempe is quo facta sunt omnia. Iussit dominus facturn est caelum, iussit dominus facta est terra, iussit dominus facta sunt maria, iussit dominus omnis creatura generatus est. Vides ergo quam operatorius sermo sit Christi. Si ergo tanta uis est in sermone domini Iesu ut inciperent esse quae non erant, quanto magis operatorius est ut sint quae erant et in aliud commutentur. . . 17. Accipe ergo quemadmodum sermo Christi creaturam omnem mutare consueuerit et mutet quando uult instituta naturae. . . .": *SC* 25bis:110 = *CSEL* 73:52–53 (= *CPL* §154); English trans. adapted in part from E. MAZZA, *Mystagogy* (New York: Pueblo Publishing, 1989) 183; see AMBROSE, *De mysteriis*, IX, 52: "The sacrament you receive is produced by the word of Christ," *SC* 25bis:186 = *CSEL* 73:112 (= *CPL* §155).

[72] *In Mt hom.* 50 (51), 3 and *hom.* 82 (83), 5, PG 58:507, 744 (= *CPG* §4424).

the same one Christ gave to his disciples, and which priests now accomplish. The latter is in no way inferior to the former, because the same one who sanctified the one, sanctifies the other too. For just as the words which God spoke are the same as the ones the priest pronounces now, so is the offering the same, just like the baptism which he gave.[73]

In this same sense, therefore, *the Words of Institution are always consecratory, even when they are not recited, as in the Anaphora of Addai and Mari.* They are consecratory not because they are a formula the priest repeats in the Eucharistic Prayer, but because Jesus' pronouncing of them at the Last Supper remains efficaciously consecratory for every Eucharist until the end of time.

Conclusion

By way of conclusion, then, I believe one can say there *are* irreducible local differences in the *liturgical expression* of what I would take to be the fully reconcilable *teaching* of both East and West on the Eucharist: that the gifts of bread and wine are sanctified via a prayer, the anaphora, which applies to the present gifts of bread and wine what Jesus handed on. *How* the individual anaphoras make this application has varied widely depending on local tradition, particular history, and the doctrinal concerns of time and place. In my view, these differences *cannot* with any historical legitimacy be seen in dogmatic conflict with parallel but divergent expressions of the same basic realities in a different historico-ecclesial milieu.

That is the approach I have taken here with regard to Church, magisterium, and dogma, reasoning as follows:

1. The whole undivided Church of East and West held that the eucharistic gifts were consecrated in the Eucharistic Prayer.
2. The *theologia prima* in the Eucharistic Prayers of East and West expressed this differently.
3. The *theologia secunda* or theological reflection on these prayers in East and West also was different. The West stressed the *Verba Domini*. The East stressed the Spirit epiclesis, while not denying the efficacy of the Words of Institution.
4. Problems arose only in the Late Middle Ages, when the Latin West *unilaterally* shifted the perspective by dogmatizing its hylomorphic theology.

---

[73] PG 62:612 (= *CPG* §4437). On this point see Y. CONGAR, *Je crois en l'Esprit Saint* 3:303-304.

The above four points are not theory but demonstrable historical facts. From them, I would argue further:

1. Since this Western innovation narrows the earlier teaching of the undivided Church, the East rejected it—and in my opinion should have rejected it.

2. Since the post-Florentine Latin *Decreta* canonizing this view are highly questionable, I offered some elements for their reinterpretation.

3. Finally, I showed how Catholic teaching has for over a century been moving toward recovery of the view that what an earlier theology was pleased to call the "form" of a sacrament is the central prayer of the ritual, and not some single, isolated formula within that prayer. This prayer can be understood and interpreted only within its liturgical context. The Words of Institution are not some magical formula, but part of a prayer of the Church operative only within its worship context. In East and West this context was and is and will remain diverse within the parameters of our common faith that Jesus, through the ministers of his Church, nourishes us with the mystery of his Body and Blood.

4. None of this denies the teaching that the Words of Jesus are consecratory. For the Fathers, they are *always* consecratory because he once said them, not just because someone else repeats them. And so they are also consecratory in Addai and Mari, even though that ancient prayer does not have the priest repeat these words verbatim in direct discourse but adverts to them more obliquely.

Appendix

I. THE ROMAN CANON MISSAE (MID-FOURTH CENTURY)

1. Hanc igitur oblationem servitutis nostrae, sed et cunctae familiae tuae, quaesumus, Domine, ut placates accipias . . .

1. Therefore, Lord, we ask that you be pleased to accept this oblation of our ministry and also of your whole family . . .

2. Quam oblationem tu, Deus, in omnibus, quaesumus, benedictam, adscriptam, ratam, acceptabilemque facere digneris, ut nobis Corpus et Sanguis fiat dilectissimi Filii tui Domini nostri Jesu Christi.

2. Which oblation we ask you, God, deign to make in all things blessed, and acceptable, that it might become for us the Body and Blood of your beloved Son our Lord Jesus Christ.

3. Qui pridie quam pateretur . . . (= INSTITUTION NARRATIVE)

3. Who on the day before he suffered . . . (= INSTITUTION NARRATIVE)

4. Unde et memores . . . ejusdem Christi Filii tui Domini nostri tam beatae passionis, nec non et ab inferis resurrectionis, sed et in caelos gloriosae ascensionis, offerimus praeclarae majestati tuae, de tuis donis ac datis, hostiam puram, hostiam sanctam, hostiam immaculatam, Panem sanctum vitae aeternae, et Calicem salutis perpetuae.

4. Remembering, therefore . . . the blessed passion of this same Christ your Son our Lord, as well as his resurrection from the dead and glorious ascension into heaven, we offer to your glorious majesty, from your own given gifts, a pure offering, a holy offering, an immaculate offering, the holy Bread of eternal life and the Chalice of eternal salvation.

5. Supra quae propitio ac sereno vultu repicere digneris, et accepta habere, sicut accepta habere dignatus es munera pueri tui Abel . . .

5. Deign to look on them with a propitious and kindly regard, and accept them as you accepted the gifts of your child Abel . . .

6. Supplices te rogamus, omnipotens Deus, iube haec perferri per manus sancti angeli tui in sublime altare tuum in conspectu divinae majestatis tuae, ut quotquot ex hac altaris participatione sacrosanctum Filii tui corpus et sanguinem sumpserimus, omni benedictioni caelesti et gratia repleamur.

6. Humbly we implore you, almighty God, bid these offerings be carried by the hands of your holy angel to your altar on high in the presence of your divine majesty, so that those of us who, sharing in the sacrifice at this altar, shall have received the sacred body and blood of your Son, may be filled with every heavenly blessing and grace.

II. FROM THE POSTSANCTUS OF ADDAI AND MARI (THIRD CENTURY)[74]

1. Do you, O my Lord, in your manifold mercies make a good remembrance for all the upright and just fathers, the prophets and apostles and martyrs and confessors, 2. **in the commemoration of the Body and Blood of your Christ, which we offer to you on the pure and holy altar, as you have taught us in his life-giving Gospel** . . .

3. And we also, O my Lord, your servants who are gathered and stand before you, 4. **and have received by tradition the example which is from you, rejoicing and glorifying and exalting 5. and commemorating this mystery of the passion and death and resurrection of our Lord Jesus Christ.**

6. **And let your Holy Spirit come, O my Lord, and rest upon 7. this offering of your servants, 8. that it may be to us for the pardon of sins and for the forgiveness of shortcomings, and for the resurrection from the dead, and for new life in the kingdom of heaven.**

9. **And for your dispensation which is towards us we give you thanks and glorify you 10. in your Church redeemed by the precious Blood of your Christ,** 11. with open mouths and unveiled faces offering glory and honor and thanksgiving and adoration to your holy name, now and at all times, and for ever and ever. Amen!

---

[74] A. GELSTON, *The Eucharistic Prayer of Addai and Mari*, 121–123.

Index of Documents and Names